Cloud-Native DevOps

Building Scalable and Reliable Applications

Mohammed Ilyas Ahmed

Apress®

Cloud-Native DevOps: Building Scalable and Reliable Applications

Mohammed Ilyas Ahmed
Boston, MA, USA

ISBN-13 (pbk): 979-8-8688-0406-9 ISBN-13 (electronic): 979-8-8688-0407-6
https://doi.org/10.1007/979-8-8688-0407-6

Copyright © 2024 by Mohammed Ilyas Ahmed

This work is subject to copyright. All rights are reserved by the Publisher, whether the whole or part of the material is concerned, specifically, the rights of translation, reprinting, reuse of illustrations, recitation, broadcasting, reproduction on microfilms or in any other physical way, and transmission or information storage and retrieval, electronic adaptation, computer software, or by similar or dissimilar methodology now known or hereafter developed.

Trademarked names, logos, and images may appear in this book. Rather than use a trademark symbol with every occurrence of a trademarked name, logo, or image we use the names, logos, and images only in an editorial fashion and to the benefit of the trademark owner, with no intention of infringement of the trademark.

The use in this publication of trade names, trademarks, service marks, and similar terms, even if they are not identified as such, is not to be taken as an expression of opinion as to whether or not they are subject to proprietary rights.

While the advice and information in this book are believed to be true and accurate at the date of publication, neither the authors nor the editors nor the publisher can accept any legal responsibility for any errors or omissions that may be made. The publisher makes no warranty, express or implied, with respect to the material contained herein.

>Managing Director, Apress Media LLC: Welmoed Spahr
>Acquisitions Editor: Celestin Suresh John
>Development Editor: Laura Berendson
>Coordinating Editor: Gryffin Winkler

Cover designed by eStudioCalamar

Cover image by Enrique from Pixabay (www.pixabay.com)

Distributed to the book trade worldwide by Apress Media, LLC, 1 New York Plaza, New York, NY 10004, U.S.A. Phone 1-800-SPRINGER, fax (201) 348-4505, e-mail orders-ny@springer-sbm.com, or visit www.springeronline.com. Apress Media, LLC is a California LLC and the sole member (owner) is Springer Science + Business Media Finance Inc (SSBM Finance Inc). SSBM Finance Inc is a **Delaware** corporation.

For information on translations, please e-mail booktranslations@springernature.com; for reprint, paperback, or audio rights, please e-mail bookpermissions@springernature.com.

Apress titles may be purchased in bulk for academic, corporate, or promotional use. eBook versions and licenses are also available for most titles. For more information, reference our Print and eBook Bulk Sales web page at http://www.apress.com/bulk-sales.

Any source code or other supplementary material referenced by the author in this book is available to readers on GitHub (https://www.apress.com/gp/services/source-code). For more detailed information, please visit https://www.apress.com/gp/services/source-code.

If disposing of this product, please recycle the paper

To my beloved parents, Fareeda Tabassum and Mohammed Altaf Ahmed,

Your unwavering love, guidance, and sacrifices have shaped every step of my journey. Your endless support and belief in my abilities have been a constant source of strength. I am forever grateful for the values you have instilled in me and the lessons you have taught me.

Thank you for being my steadfast pillars of strength, for teaching me resilience, and for shaping the person I am today. This achievement is as much yours as it is mine.

With heartfelt gratitude and endless love,

—Mohammed Ilyas Ahmed

Table of Contents

About the Author xv

About the Technical Reviewer xvii

Chapter 1: Unveiling the Cloud-Native Paradigm 1

Pre-cloud Era 2

Evolution of Cloud Native 3

    Shift from Mainframe Computing to a Cloud-Native Approach 4

    Advantages of Cloud-Native Computing over Mainframe 5

    Disadvantages of Cloud-Native Computing over Mainframe 6

    The Twelve-Factor App 8

Introduction and Understanding of Cloud Native 14

    What Is CNCF? 15

    Core Pillars of Cloud Native 15

    Containerization 16

    Continuous Integration and Delivery 17

    Serverless Computing 17

    Advantages of Serverless Cloud Computing 18

    Popular Serverless Computing Platforms 18

    Disadvantages of Serverless Cloud Computing 19

    Cloud Concept 20

    Key Features of a Public Cloud 21

    Downside of Public Cloud 22

    Key Features of a Private Cloud 23

TABLE OF CONTENTS

    Downside of Private Cloud 24
    Key Features of Hybrid Cloud 26
    Downside of Hybrid Cloud 27
    Differences Between IaaS, PaaS, and SaaS 27
    Cloud Native Maturity Model (CNMM) 35
    Layers of Cloud-Native Landscape 37
        Provisioning Layer 38
        Runtime Layer 38
        Orchestration and Management Layer 40
        Application Definition and Development Layer 42
Summary 43

Chapter 2: Cloud-Native DevOps Architectural Overview 45

    Introduction to DevOps in Cloud-Native Environment 46
        What Is DevOps? 47
        Principles of DevOps 48
        7C's of DevOps Life Cycle 48
        Continuous Development 49
        Continuous Integration 49
        Continuous Testing 49
        Continuous Deployment 50
        Benefits of Infrastructure Automation 51
        Continuous Feedback 52
        Continuous Monitoring 53
        Continuous Operations 53
    Kubernetes Scalability 53
        What Is Kubernetes? 54
        Fundamental Architecture of Kubernetes Cluster 54

Master Node 55
Worker Node 56
Hardened Installation of Kubernetes...57
Perform the Following Steps on Master Node 58
  Perform the Following Steps on the Worker Node..62
  Kube-bench for Security of Kubernetes Cluster 62
  Steps to Set Kube-bench on Your Nodes 63
  Scaling of Kubernetes 64
  Recommended Practices for Kubernetes Scaling 64
  Manual Scaling 66
  What Is Autoscaling? 68
  Kubernetes Autoscaling..68
  Horizontal Pod Autoscaling (HPA) 68
  Description of Each Attribute Described in the Preceding YAML File 72
  Vertical Pod Autoscaling (VPA)...74
Comparison of Monolithic and Public Managed Kubernetes Cluster 76
Summary...79

Chapter 3: Security in Cloud-Native Applications with a Shift-Left Approach 81

Introduction to Shift-Left Security in Cloud Native 82
  Shift-Left Secure Right 84
  Risk from Third-Party Components 86
  Embracing Technologies to Shift Left...87
  Security Testing with Shift-Left Approach 94
  Benefits of Shift-Left Strategy..99
Infrastructure as Code (IaC) and Security 101
  Role of IaC in Cloud Native 101
  Security Strategy Using IaC for Organizations..103

vii

TABLE OF CONTENTS

    Tools for IaC Security 104

    IaC with Terraform 105

    Terraform Working 106

    Terraform Architecture 108

    IaC Tools 109

    Value Proposition of IaC Tools 112

    Best Practices for IaC 114

Securing API in Early Stages 116

    Common API Risk Factors 118

    What Is API Security Testing? 123

    Securing API Using Pynt 124

    Working of Pynt 124

    Pynt Setup 126

    Pynt Security Testing 127

Summary 133

Chapter 4: CI/CD Pipeline in Cloud-Native DevOps 135

Overview of CI/CD 136

    C1/CD Principles 137

    Principles of Continuous Integration 138

    Principles of Continuous Delivery 139

    CI/CD Pipeline Stages 141

    Source Stage 142

    Build Stage 144

    Test Stage 146

    Deploy Stage 148

    CI/CD Best Practices in Cloud Native 150

    Benefits of CI/CD in Cloud-Native DevOps 155

TABLE OF CONTENTS

Integration of Version Control 158
    Version Control Overview 158
    CI/CD Build Tool Implementation 160

Cloud-Agnostic in CI/CD Pipeline 161
    CI/CD Pipeline Using Jenkins 162

Security in CI/CD 167
    Threats in CI/CD 168
    Automated Tools for Securing CI/CD Pipeline 170
    Securing a CI/CD Pipeline: Recommended Approaches 173

Summary 177

Chapter 5: Open-Source Tools for Cloud-Native DevOps 179

Overview of Open-Source Tools in Cloud Native 180

Argo Streamlining Workflows 190
    Getting Started with Argo 191
    Concepts of Argo CD 192
    Implementation of Argo Workflows Using Custom
    Kubernetes Resources 193
    Implementation of CI/CD Through Argo Workflows 194
    Integration of Argo CD and Kubernetes 195

Kubeflow Pipelines 201
    Kubeflow Overview 202
    Kubeflow Principles 206
    Kubeflow Pipelines 207
    Kubeflow in Cloud Native Applications 208

Future Trends in Cloud-Native DevOps Tools 211
    DataOps 212
    AIOps (Artificial Intelligence for IT Operations) 212
    Hyperautomation 212

ix

TABLE OF CONTENTS

Adoption of Cloud-Native Technologies 213
Infrastructure as Code (IaC) Management 213
Artificial Intelligence (AI) Evolution 213
Security and Compliance 214
Collaboration Between DevOps Teams 214
Fresh Dimension in Quantum Computing 214
Adapting to Change 215
Artificial Intelligence for IT Operations (AIOps) 215
ChatOps 215
GitOps 216
No Operations (NoOps) 216
Summary 216

Chapter 6: Scalability and Autoscaling Strategies 219

Scaling Principles in Cloud-Native Applications 220
    Utilizing Automation in Cloud-Native Architecture 221
    Several Key Areas Within Cloud-Native Architecture
    Are Ripe for Automation 223
Multi-cloud Strategies 231
    Reactive and Preemptive Scaling 233
    Reactive Scaling 234
    Preemptive Scaling 235
    Cloud Native for Edge Computing 236
Autoscaling Implementation in AWS 246
    Benefits of Autoscaling 249
    Steps to Create Autoscaling 251
Future Trends in Scalability and Autoscaling 261
    Machine Learning-Driven Autoscaling 261
    Serverless Architectures and Event-Driven Scaling 261

TABLE OF CONTENTS

    Edge Computing and Distributed Scaling 262

    Hybrid and Multi-cloud Scalability 262

    Cost-Efficient Autoscaling Strategies 263

  Summary 263

Chapter 7: Collaborative Development in the Cloud Native 265

  Enabling Collaboration Between Developers and Operations 266

    DevOps Culture 267

  Agile and Scrum Methodology in Cloud Native 271

    Benefits of Agile Methodology 275

    Roles in Scrum 277

    Artifacts in Scrum 279

  Optimizing Cloud-Based Data Flow 281

    Data Pipeline Architecture Factors 288

    Prioritize Compliance in the Initial Stage 290

    Best Practices in Data Pipeline Architecture 291

    Consider Future Growth When Planning for Performance
    and Scalability 292

  ETL Processes and Supply Chain Management 294

    Transition from on-prem to ETL 295

    Securing Cloud-Integrated Logistics Operations 298

    Capabilities of Cloud Computing in Supply Chain Management 300

  Summary 305

Chapter 8: IAM Security in Cloud-Native Environment 307

  IAM Fundamentals in Cloud-Native Environments 308

    Foundational Elements of Cloud-Native IAM Infrastructure 308

    Fundamental Pillars of IAM 314

    IAM Components 320

TABLE OF CONTENTS

    Least Privileges Principles 322

    Implementation of Least Privileges 323

  IAM Best Practices for Service Accounts and API Access 326

    Key Components of User Management in Cloud-Native Applications 326

    Implementation of User Management in Cloud Native 329

    Secure Handling of API Keys 332

    Least Privilege for Service Accounts 336

    Difficulties Associated with Service Accounts 336

    Best Practices for Managing Service Accounts 339

  IAM Governance and Policy Management in Cloud Native 342

    Governance 342

    Risk Management 343

    Compliance 344

    IAM Standards 345

    Building Concrete IAM 350

  Summary 353

Chapter 9: Threat Analysis for Cloud-Native Deployments 355

  Understanding Cloud-Native Security Challenges 356

    Type of Threats in Cloud Native 360

  Challenges in Cloud-Native Security 363

    3R's of Cloud-Native Security 366

    Security Controls in Cloud Native 369

  Threat Vectors in Microservices Architectures 374

    Threat Modeling with STRIDE 374

  Security Testing and Validation 377

    Red Teaming in Cloud Native 377

    Implementation Steps 379

TABLE OF CONTENTS

Best Practices in Cloud-Native Security 380
    Conduct Due Diligence 382
    Audit and Improve Configurations 382
Security Controls and Countermeasures 382
    Key Management in Cloud Native..385
Summary...387

Chapter 10: Future Trends in Cloud Native 389

Serverless Computing and Function as a Service (FaaS) 390
    Benefits of Serverless Computing 391
    Function as a Service (FaaS) 394
    Benefits of FaaS 395
    Best Practices for FaaS 397
Key Challenges in Serverless Computing 398
AI and Machine Learning Integration Intersection in Cloud Native 401
    Challenges and Considerations Implementing AI in Cloud Native 405
    Challenges in Security and Compliance 405
    Complexity in Deployment and Model Training.......................................406
    Obstacles in Data Integration 406
    Scalability Management..407
    Best Practices of Integrating AI/ML in Cloud Native 407
Evolution of Containerization Technologies Beyond Docker and Kubernetes.....410
The Rise of No-Code/Low-Code Platforms in DevOps Workflows....................419
    Benefits of No Code and Low Code 420
    Use of No Code and Low Code 423
Summary...425

Index..427

xiii

About the Author

Mohammed Ilyas Ahmed is an industry professional with extensive expertise in security within the DevSecOps domain, where he diligently works to help organizations bolster their security practices. With a fervent dedication to enhancing security posture, Mohammed's insights and guidance are invaluable to those navigating the complex landscape of DevSecOps. In addition to his involvement in industry events, Mohammed is an active speaker and judge, lending his expertise to technical sessions at prestigious conferences. His commitment to advancing knowledge is evident through his research contributions at Harvard University, where he contributes to journal publications, enriching the academic discourse surrounding security practices, and, as a distinguished member of the Harvard Business Review Advisory Council, underscores his commitment to advancing knowledge and fostering collaboration between academia and industry.

Mohammed Ilyas Ahmed's influence extends even further as a Member of the Global Advisory Board at VigiTrust Limited, based in Dublin, Ireland. This additional role highlights his international reach and his involvement in shaping global strategies for cybersecurity and data protection.

ABOUT THE AUTHOR

Mohammed's dedication to excellence is further highlighted by his numerous certifications, which serve as a testament to his proficiency and depth of knowledge in the security domain. However, beyond his professional pursuits, Mohammed is a multi-faceted individual with a diverse range of interests, adding richness to his character and perspective.

From thought to action: Grow through what you go through.

About the Technical Reviewer

Shivakumar R. Goniwada is a renowned author, an inventor, and a technology leader with more than 25 years of experience in architecting cutting-edge cloud-native, data analytics, and event-driven systems. He currently holds a position as Chief Enterprise Architect at Accenture, where he leads a team of highly skilled technology enterprise and cloud architects. Throughout his career, Shivakumar has successfully led numerous complex projects across various industries and geographical locations. His expertise has earned him ten software patents in areas such as cloud computing, polyglot architecture, software engineering, and IoT. He is a sought-after speaker at global conferences and has made significant contributions to the field through his publications. Shivakumar holds a degree in technology architecture and certifications in Google Professional, AWS, and data science. He also completed an Executive MBA at the prestigious MIT Sloan School of Management. His notable books include *Cloud-Native Architecture and Design*, *Introduction to Datafication*, and *Introduction to One Digital Identity*, all published by Apress.

CHAPTER 1

Unveiling the Cloud-Native Paradigm

"Unveiling Cloud-Native: Embracing the future with digital brilliance!"

Welcome, fearless explorer. As we embark on our journey into the Cloud-Native DevOps realm, remember our motto: "Go Native, Go Cloud!" It's not just a saying; it's a guiding principle for those who dream of taking applications to new heights, much like your caffeine levels during those late-night coding sessions.

Cloud-Native DevOps isn't just the support crew; it's the star of the tech stage, delivering a performance with the precision of a finely tuned machine. Get ready for an adventure that's not just about adaptation but a fast-paced journey into digital excellence, seamlessly creating, deploying, and scaling applications like a top-tier show on opening night.

In the ever-evolving digital landscape, businesses are leveraging cloud-native technologies to develop and deploy applications at unprecedented speeds. It's like having a powerful toolkit for creating, deploying, and scaling applications efficiently.

Containers are our versatile tools, designed to handle every shift and change in the cloud environment. Microservices are the efficient building blocks, fine-tuning our applications with perfect precision. And automation? It's the backbone of our operations, ensuring our code performs brilliantly from the start. Whether you're an experienced tech professional or new to the field, this chapter promises an insightful and engaging journey through orchestration, microservices, and the fast-paced process of continuous integration and continuous delivery (CI/CD). So, prepare your code, because in the Cloud-Native DevOps arena, the only thing more impressive than our applications is the pace of innovation. Get ready to code your way to success in the dynamic world of digital innovation!

In this chapter, we will be encompassing the following foundational topics:

- Pre-cloud Era
- Evolution of Cloud Native
- Introduction and Understanding of Cloud Native

Pre-cloud Era

Before we dive into the cloud native, ever thought about how computing functioned before the cloud? Let's turn the clock back. Organizations relied on traditional infrastructure, in other words, on-prem IT infrastructure, where they used to have physical servers installed on their own building called data centers.

A number of intricate factors must be taken into account when establishing and managing a conventional data center. It is necessary to safeguard the physical space, either by acquiring new locations or by securing existing data centers. The often-overlooked electric power requirements force large-scale server array planning, make sure power conduits are adequate, and include backup generators for operational resilience. Physical security, which includes key/badged access points, surveillance tools, and security personnel, is crucial in enterprise deployments. There are obstacles associated with network connectivity, such as the need for redundant connections and possible infrastructure expansion by Internet service providers, contingent upon governmental approvals.

Because of the heat produced by equipment, cooling solutions are essential; some data centers have passive cooling systems. Last but not least, from ordering to testing, the procurement, setup, and utilization of physical hardware including network, computer, and storage components demand a substantial number of resources. The complete data center infrastructure must be designed, ordered, installed, and run simultaneously, requiring a sizable workforce.

Businesses now enjoy greater convenience because they don't have to worry about buying and maintaining servers. They can choose to save money by renting resources from cloud providers instead. With this approach, they can readily adapt their resources to meet their demands at any given time, and geographical barriers no longer limit access to data and applications.

Evolution of Cloud Native

In the swiftly changing realm of technology, the rise of cloud-native architecture has transformed the approach to developing, deploying, and managing applications. Leveraging the capabilities of cloud computing services and principles, cloud-native architecture stands as a pivotal driver for augmenting the scalability, reliability, and agility of contemporary applications. Embedded in the fundamental tenets of resilience and adaptability, this architectural paradigm serves as the foundation for pioneering technological advancements in the digital domain. Orchestration tools like Kubernetes further streamlined the deployment

CHAPTER 1 UNVEILING THE CLOUD-NATIVE PARADIGM

and management of containerized applications, marking a pivotal moment in the cloud-native landscape. As the landscape continues to evolve, organizations are poised to harness the full potential of cloud-native architectures to meet the ever-changing demands of the digital era.

Shift from Mainframe Computing to a Cloud-Native Approach

The transition from mainframe computing to a cloud-native approach is a significant trend in the IT industry, driven by the need for greater agility, scalability, and cost-efficiency. Mainframes have long been the backbone of enterprise computing, providing reliable and secure processing for mission-critical applications. However, their rigid architecture and high cost of ownership have made them less appealing in an increasingly dynamic and cost-conscious IT landscape (Figure 1-1).

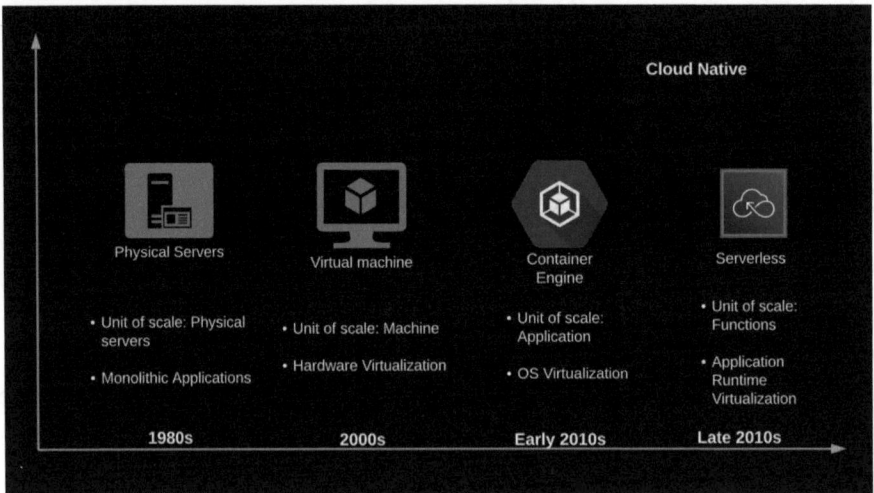

Figure 1-1. From mainframe computing to a cloud-native approach

In contrast, cloud-native computing offers a more flexible and scalable approach to software development and deployment. Cloud-native applications are designed to be lightweight, resilient, and easily deployed to cloud platforms. This makes them well-suited for the modern business environment, where organizations need to quickly adapt to changing market conditions and customer demands.

As monolithic applications became increasingly challenging to manage due to their complexity, the need for greater scalability, flexibility, and rapid deployment became apparent. In response, cloud computing emerged as a transformative force. The transition to cloud-based infrastructure opened up a plethora of opportunities for businesses to leverage scalable and cost-effective computing resources, thereby fostering innovation and facilitating the creation of responsive, on-demand applications. Additionally, in this evolving landscape, even monolithic applications are now being containerized, further enhancing their manageability and adaptability within cloud-native environments.

Advantages of Cloud-Native Computing over Mainframe

Scalability: Cloud-native applications can automatically scale up or down in response to workload changes, eliminating the need for organizations to over-provision or under-provision infrastructure resources.

Cost-Efficiency: Cloud-native applications often boast a lower total cost of ownership compared to mainframe applications. The pay-as-you-go model, where organizations pay for the resources they use, contributes to this cost-efficiency.

Agility: Cloud-native applications can be developed and deployed much faster than traditional mainframe applications because of the modular nature of cloud-native applications, with smaller components that can be independently developed and tested.

Innovation: Cloud-native computing fosters a more agile and innovative environment for software development. Cloud platforms offer access to a diverse range of tools and services, enabling the quick and easy development and deployment of new applications.

Disadvantages of Cloud-Native Computing over Mainframe

On the other hand, there are some disadvantages in transitioning from mainframe to cloud native. Migration of data can be a complex and time-consuming process. Applications on the mainframe need to be modernized before the migration as this is to restructure the code and substitute outdated components. Even though there are difficulties, the advantages of cloud-native computing are attractive, leading numerous organizations to invest in moving their mainframe applications to the cloud.

Higher Costs: Although cloud-native setups offer scalability, they can also be more expensive than mainframe systems, particularly for certain tasks. Mainframes may demand a hefty initial investment but can be more economical for consistent, large-scale workloads.

Increased Complexity: Cloud-native setups involve intricate distributed systems, microservice architectures, and containerization tools like Docker and Kubernetes. Managing and coordinating these elements can be more intricate than overseeing a single mainframe system.

Security Challenges: Cloud-native computing introduces additional security risks compared to mainframe environments. With data spread across various servers and services, there are more potential security vulnerabilities to address. Ensuring data security during transmission and storage becomes more complex.

Vendor Lock-In: Embracing cloud-native technologies often means relying on specific cloud provider services and APIs. This can lead to vendor lock-in, making it challenging to switch providers or migrate applications to different platforms in the future.

Performance Concerns: Although cloud computing offers scalability, the performance of cloud-native applications may sometimes lag behind mainframe systems, especially for tasks requiring high throughput or low latency processing. While advancements in cloud technologies may reduce this performance gap, it remains a consideration.

Data Sovereignty and Compliance Issues: Storing data in the cloud may raise concerns regarding data sovereignty and compliance with regulations, particularly in industries with stringent data protection requirements. Organizations must carefully manage where their data is stored and ensure compliance with relevant regulations.

The Twelve-Factor App

In today's digital landscape, software is commonly provided as a service, encompassing web apps or software-as-a-service. The Twelve-Factor App represents a systematic approach to constructing software-as-a-service applications. By employing declarative formats for automated setup, it streamlines the onboarding process for new developers, reducing both the time and costs associated with project integration. The establishment of a clear agreement with the underlying operating system ensures optimal adaptability across diverse execution environments. Minimizing disparities between development and production enables continuous deployment, fostering heightened agility in the software development life cycle. Additionally, the methodology showcases the ability to seamlessly scale up operations without necessitating significant modifications to tools, architecture, or development practices.

CHAPTER 1 UNVEILING THE CLOUD-NATIVE PARADIGM

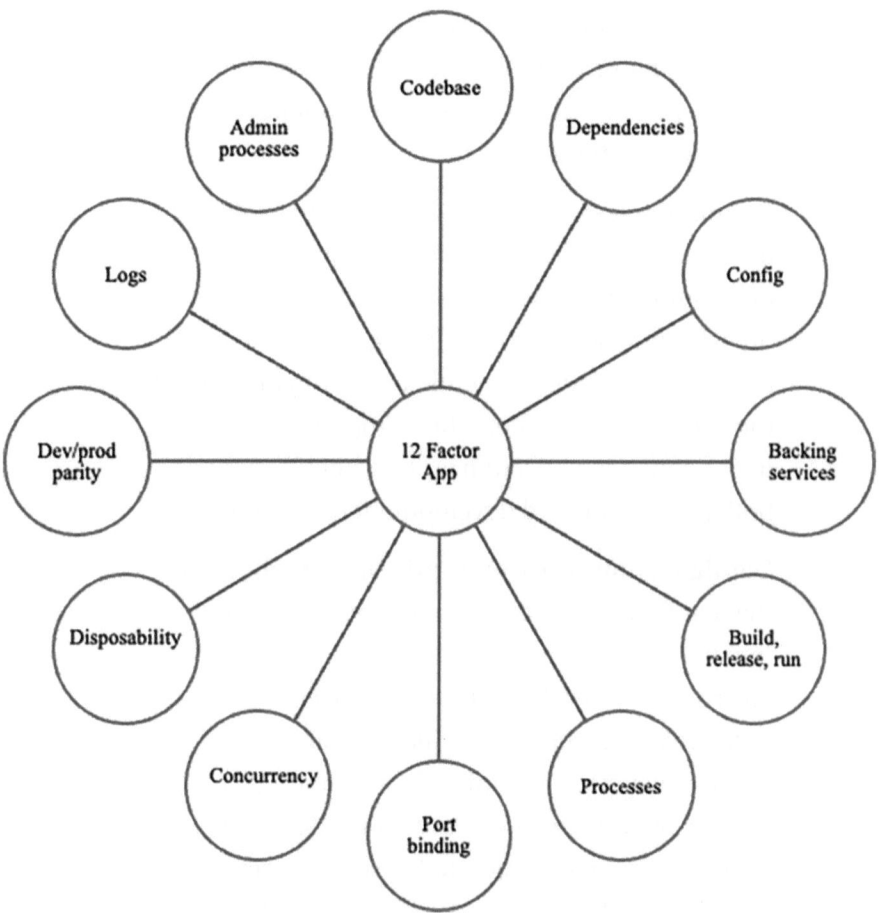

Figure 1-2. *Twelve-Factor*

Codebase: A codebase is the entirety of an application's source code, typically stored in a centralized or decentralized version control system. Each application should have a unique codebase; multiple codebases indicate a distributed system, where each component is an independent application that adheres to the Twelve-Factor App methodology. Sharing code between multiple applications violates the Twelve-Factor principle. Instead, shared code should be extracted into libraries and included through dependency management tools.

Dependencies: It comprehensively and explicitly declares all dependencies using a dependency declaration manifest. Additionally, it employs a dependency isolation tool during execution to prevent any implicit dependencies from infiltrating the surrounding system. This comprehensive dependency specification is consistently applied to both production and development environments.

Configuration: The Config principle emphasizes that configuration details should be introduced into the runtime environment through either environment variables or settings specified in a standalone configuration file. Although, in specific instances, retaining default settings directly within the code is acceptable for potential overrides, it is recommended to separate settings like port numbers, dependency URLs, and state configurations such as DEBUG. These should be maintained independently and applied during deployment. Instances of external configuration files include a Java properties file or config/database.yml file.

Backing Services: This principal advocates for architects to consider external elements like databases, email servers, message brokers, and standalone services that can be provisioned and managed by system personnel as connected resources. Examples include messaging systems – RabbitMQ – and database – MySQL.

Build, Release, Run: The Build, Release, and Run principle divides the deployment process into three distinct and repeatable phases that can be executed independently at any point in time. The Build phase involves retrieving code from the source code management system, compiling it into artifacts, and storing the artifacts in an artifact repository like Docker Hub or a Maven repository. Following the Build phase, configuration settings are applied during the Release phase. Finally, in the Run phase, a runtime environment is provisioned using scripts and a tool like Ansible, and the application along with its dependencies is deployed into the newly provisioned environment.

Processes: The Twelve-Factor App methodology advocates for stateless processes, meaning each process operates independently without maintaining state or session information. This facilitates easier scaling and prevents unintended side effects, enabling seamless addition or removal of processes to adapt to changing workloads.

Port Binding: The Twelve-Factor App methodology emphasizes using port numbers, not domain names, for service identification. Domain names and IPs can be dynamically assigned, making them unreliable references. In contrast, port numbers provide a more consistent and manageable approach for network exposure. To avoid potential port collisions, port forwarding can be employed. The port number standardization, with established conventions like port 80 for HTTP, port 443 for HTTPS, port 22 for SSH, port 3306 for MySQL, and port 27017 for MongoDB.

Concurrency: This methodology recommends organizing processes by purpose and scaling them independently to handle varying demands. As depicted earlier, an application is exposed via web servers behind a load balancer, which in turn utilizes business logic from Business Service processes behind their own load balancer. When web server load increases, that group can be scaled up separately. Similarly, if the Business Service becomes a bottleneck, it can be scaled independently. Supporting concurrency enables scaling individual application components to meet specific demands, avoiding the need to scale the entire application at once.

Disposability: This methodology emphasizes graceful application startup and shutdown. Graceful startup ensures that all necessary preparations, such as database connections and network resource access, are complete before making the application available to users. Graceful shutdown involves properly closing database connections, terminating other network resources, and logging all shutdown activities.

Dev/Prod Parity: Containers effectively package all service dependencies, reducing environment-related issues. Nevertheless, certain scenarios, particularly those involving managed services unavailable on-premises in the development environment, can be more challenging.

Logs: Streaming log data to enable access by various interested consumers. The process of routing log data should be independent of log data processing. For instance, one consumer might focus exclusively on error data, while another might prioritize request/response data. Additionally, another consumer might archive all log data for event tracking. A notable advantage of this approach is that log data persists even if the application terminates.

Admin Processes: The Admin Processes principle emphasizes that administrative tasks are integral to the software development life cycle and should be treated accordingly. As illustrated earlier, an Orders service is deployed as a Docker container alongside an admin service named Data Seeder. The data sender service is responsible for populating the Orders service with initial data.

CHAPTER 1   UNVEILING THE CLOUD-NATIVE PARADIGM

Introduction and Understanding of Cloud Native

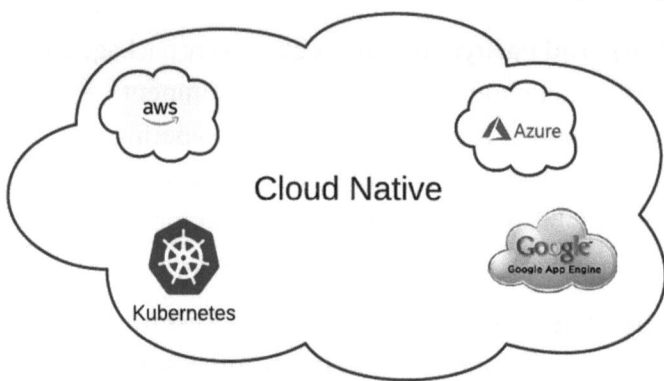

Figure 1-3. *Cloud-native fundamentals*

Cloud native has seized the spotlight in the industry and is presently creating ripples in the market. When you search for the term "What is Cloud Native?" on Google, you'll encounter numerous definitions that differ across articles. I prefer to define it as follows:

> Cloud-native is a methodology for developing and overseeing contemporary applications in the cloud. Modern enterprises aspire to construct applications capable of scaling, adapting, and swiftly updating to address dynamic customer demands. Achieving this involves employing tools seamlessly compatible with cloud systems. These technologies facilitate rapid adjustments to applications without causing service disruptions, providing businesses with a distinct competitive advantage.

What Is CNCF?

The Cloud Native Computing Foundation (CNCF), is an open-source nonprofit software organization that focuses on advancing the development of cloud-native technologies. The CNCF encourages cooperation and creativity within the cloud computing community by offering a vendor-neutral home for various open-source cloud-native computing initiatives. Prometheus, Kubernetes, Envoy, and other well-known projects are among those that fall under the CNCF's purview. The foundation is essential in pushing best practices and standardization in the quickly developing field of cloud-native computing.

Core Pillars of Cloud Native

Microservices are an architectural style that breaks down large applications into smaller, independent services. This approach promotes modularity and makes it easier to develop, deploy, and scale applications. Each microservice is responsible for a specific function and can be developed and deployed independently, without affecting the rest of the application. This allows a seamless and flexible way to handle automation in production without impacting other services.

Resilience in cloud native refers to the ability of an application to overcome failures without significant downtime as cloud-native applications are deployed in highly distributed environments. There are other characteristics as well that contribute to resilience.

- **Load balancing** distributes incoming traffic across multiple copies of a component, preventing any single copy from becoming overburdened. This strategy is crucial for ensuring an application's ability to handle high traffic volumes.

- **Redundancy** means maintaining multiple copies of essential components, like databases or microservices, and safeguards against failures by allowing another copy to seamlessly assume responsibility if one malfunctions. This strategy effectively guarantees the program's continued operation even in the event of hardware or software malfunctions.

- **Rate limiting** controls the amount of traffic that a component can receive. This helps prevent the component from becoming overloaded and crashing, which can protect the application from denial-of-service attacks.

- **Circuit breaking** is an automated mechanism that temporarily disables a component encountering frequent failures. This action prevents the component from triggering further disruptions and allows it to recover. This technique can effectively safeguard an application from complete crashes due to transient component issues.

Containerization

Cloud-native applications are constructed using containers, which are compact, transportable, and self-contained software units suitable for easy deployment on any infrastructure. These containers offer an alternative packaging approach compared to virtual machines (VMs) or direct deployment on physical servers. Each container encapsulates all the components required for an application to operate, including code, system libraries, and settings, in a standalone executable package. Unlike VMs, containers do not include a complete operating system, ensuring their lightweight nature. They can operate within a VM or on a physical server, providing increased flexibility and simplified deployment. By bundling an application's libraries and processes, containers not only enhance security and isolation but also contribute to cost reduction and scalability. The benefits extend to quicker deployment, enhanced portability, and improved overall application scalability and security.

Continuous Integration and Delivery

Cloud-native applications utilize container technology for deployment, offering a convenient method to package and release these applications. Containers not only facilitate straightforward packaging and deployment but also contribute to creating an isolated environment for cloud-native applications. This isolation enhances scalability and performance. The development and deployment of cloud-native applications often involve the implementation of a continuous integration and continuous delivery (CI/CD) pipeline. This pipeline is instrumental in enabling swift and frequent releases, underscoring the agility and efficiency of the development process.

Serverless Computing

Cloud computing execution model is the one in which the cloud provider dynamically allocates and manages servers on demand to run the code provided by the developer. This means that developers do not need to provision or manage servers themselves, which can save a significant amount of time and effort. Instead, they can focus on writing code and deploying it to the cloud provider's platform. The cloud provider will then take care of running the code and scaling it up or down as needed. Serverless computing is often used for applications that are event-driven, such as web applications, mobile backends, and data processing pipelines.

In these cases, code is only executed when there is an event, such as a user interacting with a web page, or a new data file being uploaded. This can save a significant amount of money, as developers only pay for the resources that they are using.

Advantages of Serverless Cloud Computing

Reduced Administrative Overhead: Developers do not need to provision or manage servers, which can free up their time to focus on writing code and deploying applications.

Cost Savings: Developers only pay for the resources that they are actually using, which can save money on infrastructure costs.

Scalability: Serverless applications can scale up or down automatically to meet demand.

High Availability: Serverless applications are typically highly available, as the cloud provider is responsible for managing the infrastructure.

Popular Serverless Computing Platforms

AWS Lambda: AWS Lambda is a serverless computing platform offered by Amazon Web Services (AWS). It allows developers to run code in response to events, such as changes to Amazon S3 or DynamoDB.

Azure Functions: Azure Functions is a serverless computing platform offered by Microsoft Azure. It allows developers to run code in response to a variety of events, such as HTTP requests, timers, and messages in Azure Queue Storage.

Google Cloud Functions: Google Cloud Functions is a serverless computing platform offered by Google Cloud Platform (GCP). It allows developers to run code in response to a variety of events, such as HTTP requests, Pub/Sub messages, and Cloud Storage changes. Serverless computing is a powerful tool that can help developers to build and deploy applications quickly and efficiently. By abstracting away infrastructure management, serverless computing can free up developers' time to focus on writing code and delivering value to their users.

Disadvantages of Serverless Cloud Computing

Possible Delays: Sometimes there can be delays when your function first starts up, slowing down your app.

Cost Uncertainty: Serverless can be cheap, but it's hard to predict costs. Your bill depends on how much your code runs, which can be unpredictable.

Dependence on Provider: If the cloud provider has problems, your functions might not work. You're at their mercy for reliability.

Trouble Monitoring and Fixing: It's harder to keep an eye on and fix problems with your code when it's in a serverless setup.

Limits on What You Can Use: Some features or tools you might want to use with serverless might not work because of the way it's set up.

New Security Risks: Using serverless means dealing with new security issues, like controlling who can access your code and data.

State Management Complexity: It's trickier to keep track of information between different times your code runs, which can make things more complicated.

Vendor Lock-In: You might get stuck using features that only work with one provider, making it hard to switch later.

Cloud Concept

There are multiple ways that cloud computing services can be delivered. The three most common cloud models are

- **Public cloud**
- **Private cloud**
- **Hybrid cloud**

A **public cloud** refers to a cloud computing service offered by third-party providers over the Internet. In a public cloud, computing resources such as virtual machines, storage, and applications are hosted and managed by a cloud service provider in their data centers. These resources are made available to the public or a large industry group and are accessible to users over the Internet on a pay-as-you-go or subscription basis.

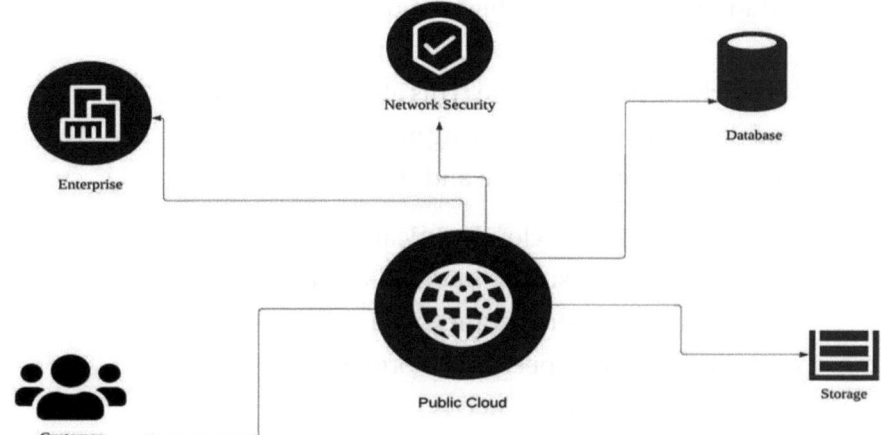

Figure 1-4. *Cloud-native essentials*

Key Features of a Public Cloud

Accessibility: Public cloud services are accessible to users from any location with an Internet connection. Users can access and manage their resources through web browsers or client applications.

Shared Resources: Resources in a public cloud are shared among multiple customers, allowing for economies of scale. This shared infrastructure enables cost savings and efficient resource utilization.

Scalability: Public clouds provide the flexibility to scale computing resources up or down based on demand. This scalability is particularly beneficial for businesses with variable workloads.

Managed Services: Public cloud providers handle the maintenance, security, and updates of the underlying infrastructure. This allows users to focus on developing and deploying applications rather than managing hardware and software.

Cost Model: Public clouds typically operate on a pay-as-you-go or subscription model. Users pay for the resources they consume, making it a cost-effective option, especially for organizations with fluctuating computing needs.

Well-known public cloud providers include Amazon Web Services (AWS), Microsoft Azure, Google Cloud Platform (GCP), and IBM Cloud. Organizations leverage public clouds for various purposes, including hosting websites, running applications, storing data, and accessing a wide range of cloud services without the need to invest in and maintain their own physical infrastructure.

Downside of Public Cloud

Outages and Service Disruptions: Public cloud services are vulnerable to outages and service interruptions, potentially impacting business operations and customer satisfaction. Businesses should have contingency plans in place to address such disruptions.

Limited Control over Infrastructure: Businesses have limited control over the underlying hardware and software infrastructure in a public cloud environment. This can make it challenging to troubleshoot performance issues or implement specific security measures.

Pay-as-you-go Model: This pricing model can lead to unanticipated expenses if usage patterns are not closely monitored and managed. Businesses should implement clear cost allocation policies and employ cost optimization strategies.

Network Egress Charges: Data transfer between the cloud and on-premises infrastructure can incur substantial charges, particularly for large data volumes or bandwidth-intensive applications. Businesses should consider using cloud providers with data centers located closer to their operations.

Private Cloud: This infrastructure is designed to serve just one company. The cloud infrastructure can be hosted by a third-party supplier or on-site by the company. Compared to public clouds, private clouds provide greater control and security, but they can also be more expensive to run.

Key Features of a Private Cloud

Improved Performance and Reliability: Private cloud provides dedicated resources for your applications, ensuring consistent performance and reliability. You are not sharing resources with other organizations, eliminating the potential for performance bottlenecks or disruptions caused by third-party activities.

Reduced Risk of Vendor Lock-in: Private cloud computing minimizes the risk of vendor lock-in, as businesses are not tied to a specific cloud provider's platform or services. This independence grants greater control over the infrastructure, allowing organizations to switch providers if necessary.

Enhanced Disaster Recovery and Business Continuity: A private cloud offers a secure and regulated setting for disaster recovery and business continuity strategies. It allows the duplication of data and applications within an organization's infrastructure, ensuring swift recovery in the face of disruptions.

Seamless Integration: Private cloud can be integrated with your existing IT infrastructure, allowing for seamless management and data exchange. You can maintain a hybrid cloud environment, leveraging the benefits of both private and public cloud solutions.

Downside of Private Cloud

Dependency: Maintaining and managing a private cloud necessitates a skilled IT team. Organizations lacking such expertise may encounter difficulties in day-to-day operations.

Bottlenecks for New Technologies: Private clouds may adopt new technologies at a slower pace compared to public clouds, potentially hindering organizations from leveraging the latest innovations.

Potential Obsolescence: Rapid technological progress can swiftly make private cloud infrastructure obsolete, necessitating regular hardware upgrades and software updates. This may result in supplementary costs and resource allocation.

Security Challenges: Ensuring the security of a private cloud environment demands a resilient security stance and ongoing surveillance. It is essential to deploy strong security measures and stay informed about the most recent vulnerabilities and threats.

A **hybrid cloud** integrates both public and private cloud components, offering businesses the flexibility to harness the advantages of each. This approach allows organizations to leverage a public cloud for less critical workloads and a private cloud for mission-critical tasks, optimizing their cloud infrastructure based on specific needs.

CHAPTER 1   UNVEILING THE CLOUD-NATIVE PARADIGM

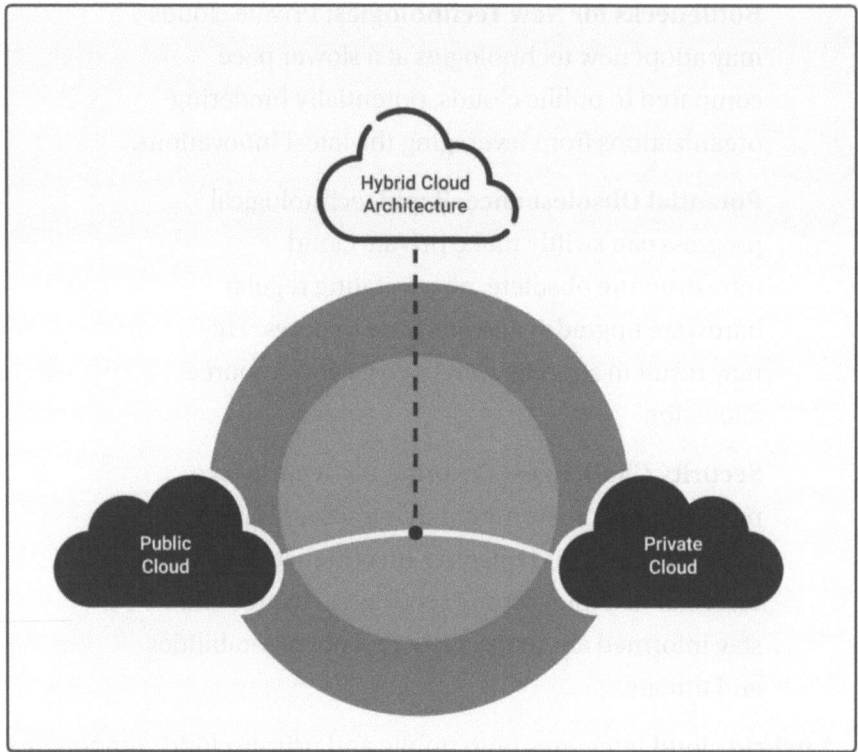

Figure 1-5. Types of cloud

Key Features of Hybrid Cloud

Scalability: Expanding infrastructure in exclusive reliance on private data centers requires the addition of new hardware and integration with existing systems, which can be a complex and disruptive process. In contrast, a hybrid cloud architecture allows for seamless scalability by acquiring more cloud storage space as needed.

  Cost-Efficiency: Establishing and maintaining one's data center is a costly endeavor, as is managing connectivity across multiple data centers. Transitioning to a hybrid cloud model offloads this challenging task to providers like Amazon AWS, reducing costs for the organization.

Flexibility: Complete migration from legacy infrastructure to a fully cloud-based setup is both demanding and disruptive for a company. Opting for a hybrid cloud infrastructure provides a more flexible approach, enabling companies to retain legacy software while benefiting from the flexibility of cloud computing. This flexibility is particularly advantageous for organizations transitioning to a remote workforce.

Downside of Hybrid Cloud

Challenges in Implementation: The implementation and maintenance of this system require a considerable amount of time. It involves intricate server specifications, robust local infrastructure, and heightened network capabilities.

Security Concerns: While the integration of both public and private cloud components mitigates some security risks found in public clouds, there remains a potential for security threats when engaging with third-party vendors.

Financial Implication: This cloud model stands out as the most expensive option, primarily due to the substantial investment, ongoing maintenance, and specialized expertise required for both on-premises hardware and private cloud components.

Differences Between IaaS, PaaS, and SaaS

Each solution involves specific resource types and is characterized by unique methods.

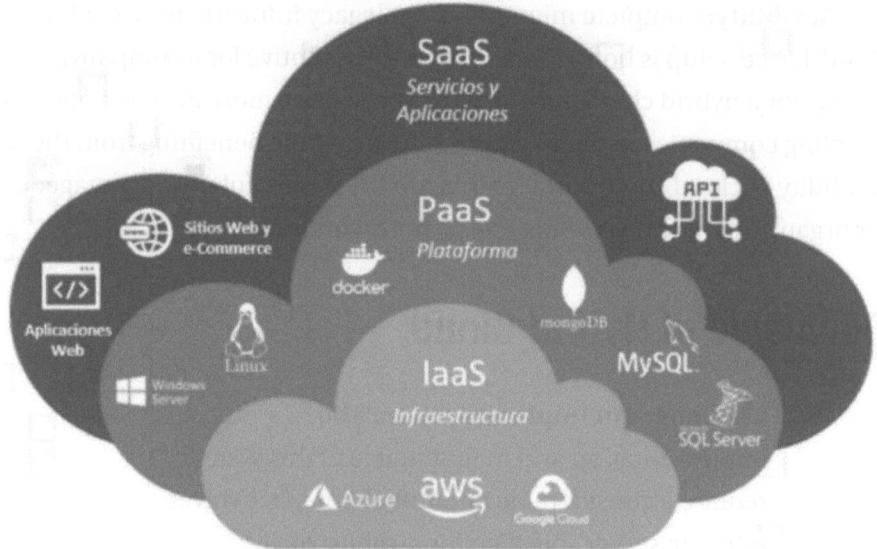

Figure 1-6. Cloud service models

Infrastructure-as-a-Service (IaaS)

This is an array of unprocessed IT resources that the cloud service provider provides to the customer. They can be applied to resource-intensive tasks or for virtualizing an infrastructure.

Advantages of IaaS

1. **Reduced Cost:** IaaS eliminates the need to invest in and maintain physical hardware, reducing upfront capital expenditures. Organizations can rent the resources they need on a pay-as-you-go basis, avoiding the large upfront costs of purchasing and maintaining hardware.

2. **Scalability:** IaaS resources can be easily scaled up or down on demand, allowing organizations to adapt to changing workloads and business needs. This flexibility enables organizations to respond quickly to surges in traffic or spikes in demand without having to worry about overprovisioning or underprovisioning resources.

3. **Pay-as-you-go Model:** IaaS providers typically charge based on usage, enabling organizations to pay for only the resources they consume. This pay-as-you-go model can lead to significant cost savings, especially for organizations with unpredictable or fluctuating workloads.

4. **Increased Agility:** IaaS facilitates faster deployment and provisioning of infrastructure, allowing organizations to respond quickly to market demands and opportunities. With IaaS, organizations can spin up new virtual machines or storage volumes in a matter of minutes, enabling them to bring new products or services to market more quickly.

Disadvantages of IaaS

1. **Vendor Lock-In:** Relying on a specific IaaS provider can lead to vendor lock-in, making it difficult or costly to switch to another provider. Organizations may become dependent on the provider's proprietary technologies or services, making it challenging to migrate to a different platform.

2. **Security Risks:** IaaS environments introduce new security challenges, and organizations need to implement robust security measures to protect their data and applications. Organizations must carefully manage access permissions, encrypt sensitive data, and stay up-to-date on the latest security vulnerabilities and threats.

3. **Limited Infrastructure Control:** With IaaS, organizations have less direct control over the underlying infrastructure compared to on-premises solutions. Organizations may have limited control over hardware configurations, network routing, and other infrastructure aspects, which may impact their ability to customize their IT environment.

4. **Potential Costs:** IaaS pricing models can be complex, and organizations may face unexpected charges if they exceed usage quotas or incur additional costs for specific services. Organizations should carefully review pricing tiers and service agreements to avoid unexpected charges.

Platform-as-a-Service (PaaS)

This is a platform that a supplier makes available to clients online. Teams, particularly developers, can use it to create software and apps on a platform without having to worry about maintaining it. Certain apps offer greater freedom than those hosted on a local infrastructure because they support a large range of programming languages.

Advantages of PaaS

1. **Reduced Time:** PaaS platforms provide a pre-built development environment, including databases, middleware, and other tools, eliminating the need for organizations to set up and maintain their own infrastructure. This can significantly reduce the time it takes to develop and deploy applications.

2. **Scalability:** PaaS platforms allow applications to scale up or down automatically based on demand. This eliminates the need for organizations to manually provision and manage infrastructure resources, ensuring that applications can handle fluctuating workloads without performance issues.

3. **Reduced Maintenance:** PaaS providers handle the maintenance and updates of the underlying infrastructure, including patching operating systems, updating middleware, and applying security patches. This frees up developers to focus on writing code and innovating rather than managing infrastructure.

4. **Cost-Effectiveness:** PaaS can be a cost-effective solution for organizations, as they only pay for the resources they use. This eliminates the upfront costs of purchasing and maintaining hardware and software, and it also reduces ongoing maintenance expenses.

Disadvantages of PaaS

1. **Vendor Lock-In:** Relying on a specific PaaS provider can lead to vendor lock-in, making it difficult or costly to switch to another platform. This is because applications may be built on proprietary technologies or APIs that are not compatible with other PaaS environments.

2. **Low Customization:** PaaS platforms often have limited customization options, as they provide a standardized environment for developing and deploying applications. This may restrict organizations that need to tailor their infrastructure to specific requirements or integrate with legacy systems.

3. **Security Concerns:** While PaaS providers handle some aspects of security, organizations still need to implement additional security measures to protect their data and applications. This may involve configuring access controls, encrypting sensitive data, and staying up-to-date on security vulnerabilities.

4. **Potential for Performance Issues:** In some cases, PaaS platforms may experience performance bottlenecks, especially if applications are not properly optimized or scaled. Organizations need to carefully monitor their applications and adjust resource allocation as needed to ensure optimal performance.

Software-as-a-Service (SaaS)

This is an array of unprocessed IT resources that the cloud service provider provides to the customer. They can be applied to resource-intensive tasks or for virtualizing an infrastructure.

Advantages of SaaS

1. **Reduced Costs:** SaaS eliminates the need to invest in and maintain physical hardware and software licenses, reducing upfront capital expenditures. Organizations can rent the software they need on a subscription basis, avoiding the large upfront costs of purchasing and maintaining software licenses.

2. **Scalability:** SaaS applications can be easily scaled up or down on demand, allowing organizations to adapt to changing workloads and business needs. This flexibility enables organizations to respond quickly to surges in demand or decreases in usage without having to worry about overprovisioning or underprovisioning software licenses.

3. **Easy Maintenance:** SaaS providers handle the maintenance and updates of the software, including applying security patches and releasing new features. This frees up IT teams to focus on other tasks and ensures that organizations are always using the latest version of the software.

4. **Accessibility:** SaaS applications can be accessed from anywhere with an Internet connection, providing users with flexibility and mobility.

This allows employees to work from home, travel seamlessly, or collaborate with colleagues across different locations.

Disadvantages of SaaS

1. **Vendor Lock-In:** Relying on a specific SaaS provider can lead to vendor lock-in, making it difficult or costly to switch to another provider. Organizations may become dependent on the provider's proprietary features or integrations, making it challenging to migrate to a different platform.

2. **Limited Customization:** SaaS applications often have limited customization options, as they are designed to provide a standardized user experience. This may restrict organizations that need to tailor their software to specific requirements or integrate with legacy systems.

3. **Data Privacy Concerns:** Storing data in a cloud-based SaaS application raises data privacy concerns, and organizations need to ensure compliance with relevant regulations. Organizations must implement appropriate data governance practices, data encryption mechanisms, and access controls to protect sensitive data and comply with privacy laws.

4. **Internet Connectivity:** SaaS applications require reliable Internet connectivity for access and use. Disruptions in network access can impact application availability and productivity, especially for organizations that rely heavily on SaaS tools for critical business operations.

Cloud Native Maturity Model (CNMM)

The Cloud Native Maturity Model (CNMM) is a framework that helps organizations assess their level of maturity in adopting and utilizing cloud-native technologies. It is designed to guide organizations through continuous improvement, enabling them to leverage the full benefits of cloud-native computing.

> **Business Outcomes:** Concentrating on aligning cloud-native initiatives with business goals and gauging their influence on key performance indicators (KPIs).
>
> **People:** Prioritizing the cultivation of a cloud-native culture, fostering the necessary skills, and empowering teams to embrace cloud-native practices.
>
> **Policy:** Underscoring the establishment of transparent cloud-native policies, governance frameworks, and risk management practices for ensuring security, compliance, and control.
>
> **Processes:** Highlighting the adoption of cloud-native development, deployment, and operational practices, encompassing infrastructure as code (IaC), continuous integration and continuous delivery (CI/CD), and automated testing.
>
> **Technology:** Concentrating on the selection and deployment of suitable cloud-native technologies, including containers, Kubernetes, serverless computing, and cloud-based infrastructure.

The CNMM outlines five maturity levels that provide a valuable tool for organizations to assess their current cloud-native maturity, identify areas for improvement, and develop a roadmap for continuous advancement. By adopting cloud-native practices, organizations can achieve greater agility, scalability, cost-efficiency, and innovation.

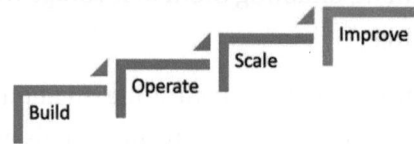

Figure 1-7. Cloud-native maturity model

Level 1: Build: At this stage, organizations possess a foundational understanding of cloud-native concepts and are in the initial phases of experimenting with cloud-based infrastructure.

Level 2: Operate: Organizations operating at this level have established a solid cloud-native foundation. They are capable of operating cloud-based applications in a production environment.

Level 3: Scale: Organizations reaching this level have developed the capability to scale their cloud-native applications efficiently and effectively, accommodating increased demands.

Level 4: Improve: At this stage, organizations are actively engaged in continuous improvement of their cloud-native practices. This involves optimizing resource utilization and enhancing security and compliance measures.

CHAPTER 1   UNVEILING THE CLOUD-NATIVE PARADIGM

Level 5: Optimize: Organizations at this pinnacle level of maturity have achieved a high degree of proficiency in cloud-native practices. They fully leverage the benefits of cloud-native computing to optimize efficiency, innovation, and overall business outcomes.

Layers of Cloud-Native Landscape

The provisioning layer forms the bedrock of cloud-native architecture, encompassing the tools that establish and secure the foundation upon which cloud-native applications reside. This layer governs the automated creation, management, and configuration of infrastructure, alongside the scanning, signing, and storage of container images. It additionally extends to security, providing tools for policy enforcement, integrating authentication and authorization into applications and platforms, and managing the distribution of secrets.

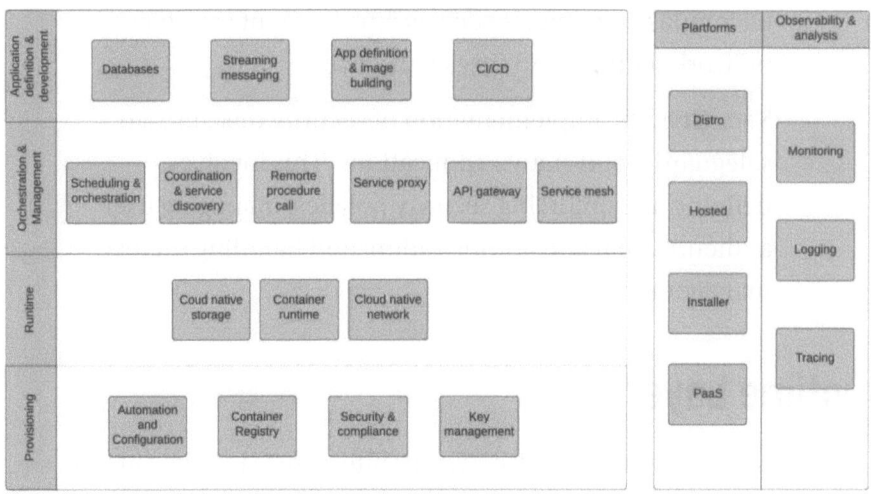

Figure 1-8. *Cloud-native runtime layer*

37

Provisioning Layer

The foundational element of cloud-native architecture is the provisioning layer, serving as the basis for constructing cloud-native applications. This layer involves the utilization of tools and procedures for the creation, administration, and configuration of the infrastructure supporting these applications.

- **Infrastructure Provisioning:** The establishment and oversight of fundamental hardware and software resources like servers, storage, and networking equipment.
- **Container Image Management:** The processes of constructing, scanning, signing, and storing container images – compact, self-contained packages that encapsulate an application's code, dependencies, and runtime environment.
- **Configuration Management:** The setup and administration of configuration for cloud-native applications, encompassing aspects such as environment variables, network settings, and service discovery.
- **Security:** The implementation of security measures to safeguard cloud-native applications. This involves defining and enforcing security policies, managing user authentication and authorization, and handling secrets management.

Runtime Layer

The runtime layer within cloud-native architecture is tasked with the execution and administration of cloud-native applications. It involves the utilization of tools and processes for deploying, expanding, overseeing, and safeguarding applications.

- **Container Runtime:** This component oversees the execution of container images and their life cycles. It furnishes the necessary environment for containers to operate, encompassing the kernel, libraries, and system services. Notable examples of container runtimes include Docker and Containers.

- **Service Mesh:** Serving as an infrastructure layer for managing microservices communication, the service mesh undertakes functions such as traffic routing, implementing retries and timeouts, and enforcing security policies. Noteworthy service mesh examples include Istio, Linkerd, and Consul Connect.

- **Container Orchestrator:** Responsible for handling container deployment, scaling, and networking, the container orchestrator automates tasks such as deploying containers across multiple hosts, managing container health and replication, and balancing container workloads. Examples of container orchestrators include Kubernetes, Docker Swarm, and Apache Mesos.

- **Logging and Monitoring:** Tools for logging and monitoring collect and analyze logs and metrics from cloud-native applications. This data is pivotal for monitoring application health and performance, troubleshooting issues, and identifying areas for enhancement. Logging and monitoring tools encompass Prometheus, Grafana, and the ELK Stack.

- **Configuration Management:** Configuration management tools are employed to oversee application and infrastructure configurations. They automate the deployment and update of configuration files, ensuring that applications operate with the correct settings. Notable configuration management tools include Ansible, Chef, and Puppet.

The runtime layer assumes a critical role in the triumph of cloud-native applications by furnishing a stable, scalable, and secure environment for their execution. Through the automation and streamlining of tasks related to deploying, overseeing, and monitoring applications, the runtime layer aids organizations in reducing operational expenses, enhancing application performance, and delivering a more consistent user experience.

Orchestration and Management Layer

The layer responsible for orchestrating and managing cloud-native architecture involves the utilization of tools and processes to automate the deployment, oversight, and monitoring of cloud-native applications. This layer is integral in guaranteeing the scalability, dependability, and security of cloud-native applications within a distributed environment.

- **Application Configuration Management:** Configuration management tools like Ansible and Chef handle the provisioning and management of application configurations across multiple instances. They automate the process of applying consistent configurations, ensuring that applications operate with the correct settings and parameters.

- **Container Orchestration:** Tools for container orchestration, such as Kubernetes, manage the life cycle of containerized applications. They automate tasks such as deploying, scaling, conducting health checks, and allocating resources for containers, ensuring efficient resource utilization and seamless application functionality.

- **Monitoring and Observability:** Monitoring tools such as Prometheus and Grafana collect and analyze metrics from both cloud-native applications and infrastructure. They furnish real-time insights into application performance, resource utilization, and potential issues, enabling proactive troubleshooting and optimization.

- **Service Discovery and Routing:** Tools for service discovery, such as Consul and etcd, enable applications to dynamically locate and communicate with each other. These tools maintain a registry of services and offer mechanisms for service discovery and routing, facilitating communication in microservices-based applications.

- **Logging and Tracing:** Logging tools like Fluentd and Elasticsearch gather and store logs from cloud-native applications, while tracing tools like Jaeger and Zipkin provide distributed tracing. This enables developers to track requests across multiple services and troubleshoot complex interactions.

- **API Gateways:** API gateways like Kong and Zuul serve as a centralized entry point for managing and controlling access to microservices-based applications. They provide features like authentication, authorization, rate limiting, and load balancing, thereby enhancing the security and performance of APIs.

Application Definition and Development Layer

The Layer for Application Definition and Development in cloud-native architecture involves employing tools and methodologies that empower developers to construct, deploy, and oversee cloud-native applications. This layer is dedicated to crafting applications designed for scalability, resilience, and easy management within a cloud environment.

- **Microservices Architecture:** Cloud-native applications typically adopt a microservices architecture, characterized by small, independent, and deployable units of code. This approach encourages modularity, loose coupling, and independent development and deployment, enhancing the scalability and manageability of applications.

- **Continuous Integration and Continuous Delivery (CI/CD):** CI/CD pipelines automate the processes of building, testing, and deploying applications. This automation facilitates rapid development cycles, quick feedback loops, and the swift deployment of new features.

- **Containerization:** Containers offer a lightweight, self-contained environment for running applications. They encapsulate the application's code, dependencies, and runtime environment, ensuring portability and ease of deployment across diverse environments.

- **Security and Compliance:** Security is an integral aspect of cloud-native development. Developers should integrate security controls, implement vulnerability management practices, and employ access control mechanisms to safeguard applications and data.

- **Declarative Infrastructure:** Tools for declarative infrastructure, such as Terraform and CloudFormation, articulate the desired state of infrastructure, with the tool automatically provisioning and managing the underlying resources. This approach promotes consistency, and repeatability and reduces manual configuration errors.

- **API-Driven Development:** Cloud-native applications frequently expose functionality through APIs, enabling communication with other services and applications. This API-driven approach encourages interoperability and facilitates composable architectures.

Summary

As we finish exploring Cloud-Native DevOps, we see it's not just about adjusting to change; it's about embracing new ideas and moving quickly in the digital world. Throughout this chapter, we've been on an exciting journey, comparing it to a fast race where Cloud-Native DevOps acts as our speedy vehicle navigating through technology.

We've learned about the evolution of cloud native and its main ideas, understanding how it's changed software development. We've compared businesses to wizards using their cloud tools to create applications super-fast.

Containers are like sleek racing cars, ready to handle the challenges of the digital world, while microservices are like skilled mechanics making sure everything runs smoothly. Automation speeds up our work like a checkered flag in a race.

CHAPTER 1   UNVEILING THE CLOUD-NATIVE PARADIGM

Whether you're experienced or just starting out, this chapter has given useful insights into Cloud-Native DevOps basics. With this knowledge, you're better prepared to use cloud tools and handle the changes in software development.

So, remember our motto: "Go Native, Go Cloud!" Embrace the speed, new ideas, and agility of Cloud-Native DevOps as you move forward in your digital journey toward success.

CHAPTER 2

Cloud-Native DevOps Architectural Overview

> *"Kubernetes, our digital maestro, conducts the orchestra of containers in our cloud symphony. It's like the Hans Zimmer of code, orchestrating a soundtrack of reliability and scale."*

In this chapter, we will be going beyond technical specifics it acts as a strategic guide as we compare the features of monolithic architectures with the managed cloud services, providing a complete understanding to aid your decision-making process. Look forward to key insights, covering fundamental scalability principles, and top security practices.

By the end of the chapter, you'll be equipped to craft cloud-native solutions that are not just robust and expandable but also tailored to the specific demands of your project. Buckle up for an immersive journey into the dynamic world of Cloud-Native DevOps architecture tailored for Google Cloud. You'll dive into the intricacies of Kubernetes, learning to scale it effectively and give your applications the flexibility to adapt to workload changes. The setup process will take center stage, with a focus on building security into your foundation and sharing insights on strengthening your Kubernetes setup against security threats. As we delve into the Google Cloud environment, we'll cover the specifics of deploying Kubernetes within Google Cloud's framework, ensuring that container management works hand in hand with Google Cloud's robust and flexible infrastructure.

In this chapter, we will be encompassing the following topics:

- Introduction to DevOps in Cloud-Native Environment
- Kubernetes Scalability
- Hardened Installation of Kubernetes
- Comparison of Monolithic and Public Managed Kubernetes Cluster

Introduction to DevOps in Cloud-Native Environment

DevOps, which involves the automation of workflows between development and operations, stands out as a crucial element in effectively adopting a cloud-native strategy. As the aim of cloud native is to minimize time-to-market and enhance operational efficiency for businesses, DevOps plays a pivotal role in aligning people, tools, and systems, thereby significantly contributing to the overall success of the organization. This integration of cloud native and DevOps represents a logical progression toward productivity improving efficiently.

Moreover, within the realm of DevOps, there are two notable approaches: cloud-native DevOps and cloud-agnostic DevOps.

Cloud-native DevOps emphasizes leveraging cloud-native principles and technologies, such as microservices, containers, and serverless computing, to build, deploy, and manage applications. This approach promotes agility and scalability by utilizing cloud-native services and infrastructure, enabling rapid development, deployment, and scaling of applications.

On the other hand, cloud-agnostic DevOps focuses on maintaining flexibility and portability by abstracting away dependencies on specific cloud providers. In this approach, DevOps practices and tools are designed to work across multiple cloud environments, allowing organizations to avoid vendor lock-in and seamlessly migrate between different cloud platforms as needed.

The realm of software development undergoes continuous transformation, and the ascendancy of cloud computing has given prominence to DevOps and cloud-native frameworks as indispensable methodologies for constructing, releasing, and overseeing contemporary applications. The utilization of a cloud-native DevOps methodology enhances agility through ongoing deployment by scaling the application without any substantial changes.

Before we immerse ourselves in the intricacies of cloud native and DevOps, let's take a closer look at the fundamental concept of DevOps.

What Is DevOps?

The term DevOps has evolved into a comprehensive buzzword encompassing various trends in both software development and IT operations. This evolution is reasonable, considering that DevOps is still in a state of ongoing development, covering diverse domains

DevOps comprises a fusion of methodologies that bridges the gap between software development (Dev) and IT operations (Ops), aiming to reduce the software development life-cycle duration and ensure continuous delivery of high-quality outcomes. It represents a cultural transformation necessitating a shift in collaboration between development and operations teams.

CHAPTER 2   CLOUD-NATIVE DEVOPS ARCHITECTURAL OVERVIEW

Principles of DevOps

The DevOps life cycle is like a set of automated steps in making software, happening over and over again. It's shown as an infinity loop to highlight that it's continuous. This loop represents how people work together and make improvements at each stage of creating a software application. On the left side, it's about creating and testing the software, while on the right side, it's about putting the software into action and managing it. Different tools and technologies are used at each step to make things smoother.

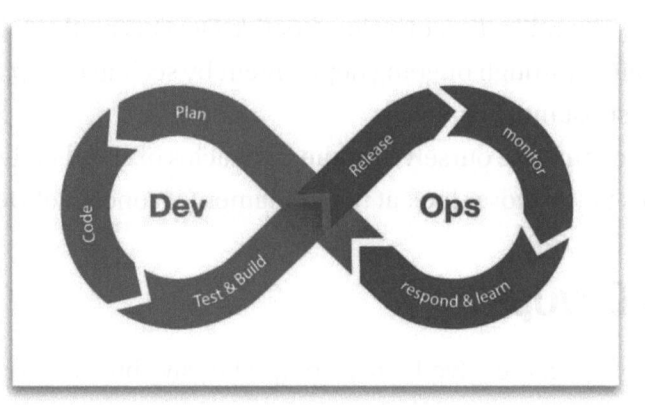

Figure 2-1. *DevOps SDLC process*

7C's of DevOps Life Cycle

As previously discussed, DevOps operates with a continuous flow, encompassing everything from planning to monitoring. Now, let's divide the complete life cycle into seven phases, emphasizing the central theme of continuity. Any stage within this life cycle can undergo multiple iterations across various projects until its completion.

Continuous Development

This crucial phase focuses on setting the vision for the software development cycle, emphasizing project planning and coding. It involves gathering project requirements, discussing them with stakeholders, and maintaining a product backlog based on customer feedback. Once the development team agrees on business needs, they begin coding for the specified requirements. This process is ongoing, requiring developers to code whenever project requirements change, or performance issues arise.

Walmart is the king of big box retailers in the American heartland adopted to streamline development, testing, and release processes. In a recent development, Walmart Labs implemented over 100,000 OpenStack cores to establish its private cloud, showcasing an ongoing commitment to advancing its Agile methodology. The tools used in this phase are GIT and JIRA.

Continuous Integration

The continuous integration phase stands out as a pivotal stage within the complete DevOps life cycle. The process involves detecting and identifying bugs through unit testing at each step, followed by modifying the source code accordingly. This establishes a continuous integration approach, with code being tested at every commit, and the necessary tests are planned during this phase. The tools used in this phase are Jenkin, CircleCI, and Bamboo, which are a few DevOps tools.

Continuous Testing

Teams have different ways of doing continuous testing. Some do it before they put everything together, while others do it afterward. In this phase, quality analysts use Docker containers to test the software and find any problems. If they find a bug or issue, they send the code back to the integration phase to fix it. Automation testing is important because it speeds up the process and saves time and effort. Tools like Selenium help with this. Continuous testing makes the test report better and saves money by reducing the costs of setting up and maintaining test environments. Some tools used in this phase include Selenium, TestSigma, and TestNG.

Backend testing is when we test the parts of a software application that users don't see. This includes things like the database, APIs, and code that run on the server. We do this to make sure the application can handle a lot of users and works correctly and safely.

Database testing is about checking if the database can handle a lot of work and if it does things right and fast. We also test to make sure it's safe from bad people trying to get in and change things.

Non-functional testing looks at how well a software system works in different situations, not just what it does. These tests check things like how fast it is, how reliable it is, and how easy it is to use. Doing non-functional testing helps us make sure the software meets what users need and what the business wants. It makes the software better and more trustworthy for users.

Continuous Deployment

In the DevOps life cycle, this phase is crucial as it involves deploying the final code onto production servers. Continuous deployment ensures that the code is smoothly and accurately deployed, incorporating configuration management to maintain consistency. Development teams release code to servers and schedule updates to ensure that configurations remain consistent across production environments. Containerization tools play a key role in maintaining consistency across different environments, facilitating the continuous delivery of new features to production. Some tools used in this phase include Chef, Puppet, and Ansible. Infrastructure automation refers to a set of processes and tools aimed at reducing the need for manual support in managing workloads across various environments, including public clouds, on-premises IT infrastructure, and hybrid setups. It involves using automation solutions to manage software, hardware, networks, operating systems, and storage, thereby delivering IT services with minimal human intervention.

Benefits of Infrastructure Automation

Improving Workflows: Automation makes IT tasks more repeatable and accurate. Operations teams can set up conditions for when infrastructure needs to be provisioned, and automation tools take care of the rest.

Provisioning: It helps organizations set up new networking and virtual machines (VMs) much faster, reducing the time from weeks to minutes. This is especially useful in today's complex IT environments with multiple cloud services. Automation tools make sure everything runs smoothly and products get deployed quickly.

Capacity Planning: Infrastructure automation helps organizations avoid wasting resources by making sure they have just the right amount of performance. Sometimes, organizations waste resources because they don't have proper standards in place for their projects. Automation helps reduce these inconsistencies by making processes more standardized and less complex. It also helps identify areas where resources are being wasted and fixes them.

Cost Management: Managing an IT budget can be tough, especially with cloud resources where costs can quickly get out of control. Automation tools like Torque help keep track of costs and prevent overspending.

Reducing Mistakes: Automating infrastructure tasks reduces the chances of mistakes that can happen when people do things manually. This means teams can focus more on important tasks instead of wasting time fixing errors.

Managing Business Risk: Security is a big concern for businesses. It's hard to keep everything secure and follow all the rules at the same time. Infrastructure automation tools help by providing a blueprint for setting up secure cloud environments quickly and easily.

Scalability: Many companies struggle to scale up their operations. Bottlenecks in setting up new environments can cause problems, as can using too many different tools. Infrastructure automation helps by simplifying workflows and reducing the time spent on troubleshooting.

Continuous Feedback

The application's source code underwent continuous assessment and improvement through regular feedback. In this stage, client behavior is consistently analyzed with each release, aiming to improve subsequent releases and deployments. Companies can acquire feedback through either a structured approach involving questionnaires and surveys or an unstructured method via social media platforms. This phase holds significance in enabling continuous delivery for the release of an enhanced program version. Tools used in this phase are Qentelli's TED and Pendo.

Continuous Monitoring

In this stage, we keep a close eye on how the application works, checking for any problems like running out of memory or not connecting to the server. This helps the IT team quickly find and understand issues with how the app is working. If they discover a big problem, they go through the whole process of building, testing, and releasing the app again to fix it. Also, any security problems can be found and fixed automatically in this stage. The tools used in this phase are Kibana, Nagios, Splunk, Sensu, and PagerDuty.

Continuous Operations

The last step in the DevOps cycle is crucial for reducing planned maintenance and scheduled downtime. Usually, developers must take the server offline to make updates, leading to increased downtime and potential financial losses for the organization. Continuous operation solves this by automating the app's startup and upgrades, avoiding downtime with container management platforms like Kubernetes and Docker. Tools used in this phase are Docker and Kubernetes

Kubernetes Scalability

Before we delve into the intricacies of scaling in Kubernetes, it's essential to grasp a comprehensive understanding of what Kubernetes entails and how it operates.

CHAPTER 2   CLOUD-NATIVE DEVOPS ARCHITECTURAL OVERVIEW

What Is Kubernetes?

Kubernetes is popularly known as K8s; since 2014, Kubernetes has experienced a significant surge in popularity. Many IT professionals are starting to use this tool more because it's safe and easy to learn. But like with any tool, it's important to understand how it works.

Let's talk about the basics of Kubernetes: what it is, why it's important, and take a closer look at its parts.

Kubernetes is a helpful system created by Google to manage applications that are put into containers. It was made to work in different places. At first, Google started this project (after another one called Google Borg), and in 2014, they shared it with everyone to use for managing applications in the cloud. Now, the Cloud Native Computing Foundation oversees the Kubernetes.

Fundamental Architecture of Kubernetes Cluster

Typically, the architecture of a Kubernetes cluster consists of two major nodes - The Master node and the Worker node.

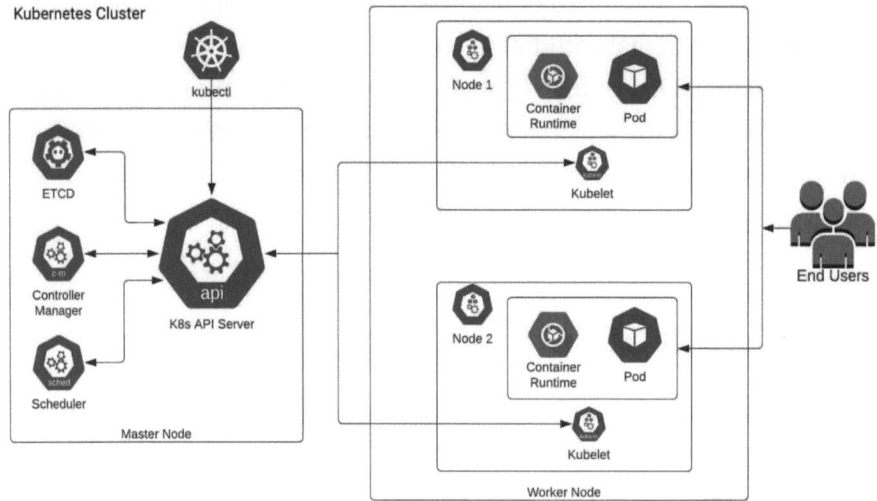

Figure 2-2. *Kubenetes cluster*

Master Node

The master node serves as the control plane overseeing and coordinating the operations of the entire Kubernetes cluster. It comprises several essential components:

- a. **API Server:** Acting as the forefront interface for the Kubernetes control plane, the API server exposes the Kubernetes API. It functions as the central communication hub for all cluster components, with clients such as the Kubernetes CLI (kubectl) interacting with it to manage the cluster.

- b. **etcd:** Functioning as a distributed and consistent key-value store, etcd stores the configuration data and system state for the entire cluster. It acts as the authoritative source for cluster information, playing a pivotal role in ensuring high availability and consistency.

- c. **Controller Manager:** The Controller Manager is tasked with executing controller processes that govern the cluster's state. These controllers operate as control loops, handling responsibilities such as node discovery, pod replication, and endpoint monitoring.

- d. **Scheduler:** In charge of placing pods onto suitable nodes within the cluster, the Scheduler considers factors such as resource requirements, node health, and affinity rules to make informed decisions for optimal pod placement.

Worker Node

Worker nodes serve as the operational environment where containers are deployed and executed. Each worker node hosts various components.

a. **Kubelet:** Functioning as an agent on each node, the Kubelet communicates with the master node, ensuring the proper execution of containers within a Pod. It also provides status updates about the node to the master.

b. **Container Runtime:** The container runtime is the software responsible for the actual execution of containers. Common runtimes, such as Docker and containerd, are specified in the kubelet configuration. This component handles tasks such as pulling container images and running the containers.

c. **Kube Proxy:** Responsible for managing network communication within the cluster, Kube Proxy maintains network rules on nodes. These rules facilitate communication to pods from network sessions both inside and outside the cluster.

d. **Pod:** A Pod represents the smallest deployable unit in Kubernetes. It signifies a collection of one or more containers running together on a node. Containers within a Pod share the same network namespace, enabling them to communicate with one another using the local host.

CHAPTER 2   CLOUD-NATIVE DEVOPS ARCHITECTURAL OVERVIEW

Hardened Installation of Kubernetes

Configuring Kubernetes requires different elements to establish a fully operational cluster. The installation can differ based on your environment, operating system, and the selected Kubernetes distribution. The following are general guidelines for configuring Kubernetes components with hardening with the following requirements:

- CentOS VM with root access
- 2 or more CPUs
- 2GB RAM (recommended 4GB+)
- Full network connectivity between all nodes in the cluster
- Product_uuid for every node
- Unique hostname and MAC address

Kube-Proxy Service: This service is responsible for allowing services within the cluster to communicate with each other.

Each worker node runs docker containers for different applications. The number of containers on each node can vary based on how the workload is distributed. Worker nodes are usually more powerful than master nodes because they have to handle running many containers. However, master nodes are essential for managing the workload distribution and overall state of the cluster.

CHAPTER 2   CLOUD-NATIVE DEVOPS ARCHITECTURAL OVERVIEW

Perform the Following Steps on Master Node

1. Make sure to update with latest security patches rolled out

   ```
   $ sudo yum update
   ```

2. Add repository to install docker package

   ```
   $ sudo dnf config-manager –add repo=https://download.docker.com/linux/centos/docker-ce.repo
   ```

3. Install container.io

   ```
   $ sudo dnf install https://download.docker.com/linux/centos/7/x86_64/stable/Packages/containerd.io-1.2.6-3.3.el7.x86_64.rpm
   ```

4. Install docker from the repository

   ```
   $ sudo dnf install docker-ce --nobest -y
   ```

5. Start the docker service

   ```
   $ sudo systemctl start docker
   ```

6. Enable automatic execution upon server reboot

   ```
   $ sudo systemctl enable docker
   ```

7. To check the docker version

   ```
   $ docker version or docker –version
   ```

8. To list the docker images

    ```
    $ docker images
    ```

9. Installing Kubernetes components by configuring the Kubernetes repository

    As Kubernetes repository packages are not available in RHEL repositories

    ```
    cat <<EOF > /etc/yum.repos.d/kubernetes.repo
    [kubernetes]
    name=Kubernetes
    baseurl=https://packages.cloud.google.com/yum/repos/kubernetes-el7-x86_64
    enabled=1
    gpgcheck=1
    repo_gpgcheck=1
    gpgkey=https://packages.cloud.google.com/yum/doc/yum-key.gpg https://packages.cloud.google.com/yum/doc/rpm-package-key.gpg
    EOF
    ```

10. Install the components of Kubernetes

    ```
    $ sudo yum install -y kubelet kubeadm kubectl
    ```

11. Start anf enable kubelet service

    ```
    $ sudo systemctl enable kubelet
    ```

    ```
    $ sudo systemctl start kubelet
    ```

12. Disable SELinux – This temporarily deactivates SELinux and set it to permissive mode. Kubernetes may encounter difficulties when SELinux is in enforcing mode, hence it is commonly advised to switch it to permissive or disable it.

    sudo setenforce 0

    sudo sed -i 's/^SELINUX=enforcing$/SELINUX=permissive/' /etc/selinux/config

13. Initialize Kubernetes Master with 'kubeadm init' Replace <Your_Pod_CIDR> with suitable CIDR range

    $ sudo kubeadm init --pod-network-cidr=<Your_Pod_CIDR>

Note The output gives you a command called "kubeadm join." Run this command on your worker nodes to connect them to the Kubernetes cluster. The "--token" part of the command is like a secret code that lets the worker nodes join the cluster.

---

14. kubectl configuration for the user by adjusting permissions

    mkdir -p $HOME/.kube
    sudo cp -i /etc/kubernetes/admin.conf $HOME/.kube/config
    sudo chown $(id -u):$(id -g) $HOME/.kube/config

CHAPTER 2   CLOUD-NATIVE DEVOPS ARCHITECTURAL OVERVIEW

15. Install calcio - Calico acts as a plug-in for the Kubernetes Container Network Interface (CNI) and supplies agents to Kubernetes for container and pod networking. It establishes a flat layer-3 network and assigns each pod a fully routable IP address.

    ```
    $ kubectl apply -f https://docs.projectcalico.org/manifests/calico.yaml
    ```

16. Secure kubeconfig file

    ```
    $ chmod 600 $HOME/.kube/config
    ```

17. Check if Master node is enabled and running

    ```
    $kubectl get nodes
    ```

In addition to the foundational steps for installing Kubernetes on master node, a comprehensive approach to security involves additional measures tailored for each node type. Secure configurations include isolating ETCD on a separate machine with TLS for communication and restricted access. The API server is fortified with certificate-based communication, disabled insecure ports, and limited client access. Kubelet, the node agent, is configured with TLS and restricted API access. Role-Based Access Control (RBAC) and network policies ensure resource and access control. Audit logging, container image security, and monitoring tools contribute to a robust security posture. Backup strategies and disaster recovery plans are emphasized. Security scanning and regular documentation, along with training programs, enhance the overall resilience of the master node.

Perform the Following Steps on the Worker Node

To configure Kubernetes on the worker node, replicate the steps outlined for the master node, spanning from 1 to 12. To connect worker nodes to the master node, you need a token. After initializing the Kubernetes master, the output provides a command along with a token. Copy and execute this command on worker node(s).

```
$ sudo kubeadm join <master-node-ip>:<master-node-port>
--token <token>
```

Look for a message confirming that the node is now part of the cluster. Additionally, there might be instructions in the output on how to set up kubectl on the worker node. On the master node, run the "kubectl get nodes" to verify that the worker node has joined the cluster.

Additionally, the focus extends to securing Kubelet communication, implementing firewall rules, and authorizing node access. Container runtime security, regular vulnerability scanning, and adherence to OS-specific hardening guidelines are emphasized. Node integrity monitoring and network policies are employed, and continuous updates and training efforts are recommended. Recognizing security as an ongoing process, staying informed about evolving practices, and promptly addressing emerging threats is pivotal for maintaining a robust Kubernetes cluster.

Kube-bench for Security of Kubernetes Cluster

When deploying Kubernetes-based applications in a production environment, it is crucial to pay careful attention to cluster security, as it is a significant aspect that requires careful management.

No need to lose sleep over creating a custom vulnerability-checking contraption; it's like trying to reinvent the wheel when there's a perfectly good set of wheels available! Picture this: worrying about vulnerabilities without using these tools is like trying to catch a fish with your bare hands

CHAPTER 2   CLOUD-NATIVE DEVOPS ARCHITECTURAL OVERVIEW

when there's a fully stocked fishing rod nearby. Let's make life easier and let those tools do the heavy lifting; they're like the superheroes of the cybersecurity world, ready to swoop in and save the day.

To safeguard our cluster from potential threats, it is essential to identify vulnerabilities within the cluster and address them appropriately. Adhering to a benchmark is a recommended practice for handling vulnerabilities, and for Kubernetes, the CSI benchmark serves as a valuable resource.

Kube-bench, the unsung hero in our Kubernetes security saga! Think of it as your trusty sidekick, tirelessly scanning your Kubernetes cluster for vulnerabilities and ensuring it's as secure as a vault.

It's like having a personal security guard for your cluster, but without the awkward small talk. Kube-bench goes through your cluster settings, checks for compliance with security benchmarks (like the CIS Kubernetes Benchmark), and gives you a report card that says, "Hey, your cluster is as secure as a corgi in a fortress."

Steps to Set Kube-bench on Your Nodes

1. **On the master node download and extract the files**

   ```
   $ wget https://github.com/aquasecurity/kube-bench/releases/download/v0.6.19/kube-bench_0.6.19_linux_amd64.tar.gz
   $ tar -xvf kube-bench_0.6.19_linux_amd64.tar.gz
   ```

2. **To perform the test, run the following command on the master node**

   ```
   $ ./kube-bench --config-dir `pwd`/cfg --config `pwd`/cfg/config.yaml master
   ```

3. **To perform the test, run the following command on the worker node(s)**

   ```
   $ ./kube-bench --config-dir `pwd`/cfg --config `pwd`/cfg/config.yaml node
   ```

Scaling of Kubernetes

Consider a scenario where an application becomes unresponsive because it lacks the necessary resources to handle the current workload. While one solution could involve manually adding resources whenever this issue arises, this approach is often impractical due to time constraints. This is where auto-scaling becomes invaluable. Scaling is broadly divided into two categories – horizontal and vertical scaling. Horizontal scaling involves the addition of extra replicas or machines to share the workload among them. In contrast, vertical scaling works by adjusting the size of the existing infrastructure, such as increasing the server's CPU or memory.

Recommended Practices for Kubernetes Scaling

1. **Define Resource Requirements:** Define the resource requests and limits for your containers. Kubernetes relies on resource requests to schedule pods on nodes, and resource limits are essential to prevent pods from using too many resources. It is important to consistently check resource utilization to guarantee that the configuration of requests and limits is optimized for efficient scaling.

CHAPTER 2 CLOUD-NATIVE DEVOPS ARCHITECTURAL OVERVIEW

2. **Cluster Design and Capacity Planning:**
   Automate scaling using the Horizontal Pod Autoscaler (HPA) and Vertical Pod Autoscaler (VPA) based on CPU, memory, or custom metrics. Establish suitable target utilization levels and thresholds to initiate scaling actions. Adjust the autoscaling configurations regularly by application requirements and performance patterns. Keep a close eye on monitoring to ensure optimal scaling.

3. **Scalability:** Design your applications with scalability as a priority from the outset. Ensure they are stateless and loosely coupled, enabling horizontal scaling through the addition or removal of instances. Microservices can be created by breaking down monolithic applications, allowing for independent scaling of various components. Effectively manage and scale your application components using Kubernetes features such as Deployments, ReplicaSets, and StatefulSets.

4. **Autoscaling:** Automate scaling using the Horizontal Pod Autoscaler (HPA) and Vertical Pod Autoscaler (VPA), which respond to CPU, memory, or custom metrics. Establish suitable target utilization levels and thresholds to initiate scaling actions. Consistently monitor and adjust autoscaling configurations based on application requirements and performance patterns.

5. **Observability and Monitoring:** Establish strong monitoring and observability procedures to gather metrics, logs, and events from both your Kubernetes cluster and applications. Employ monitoring tools such as Prometheus, Grafana, or proprietary solutions to gain a comprehensive understanding of resource utilization, application performance, and scaling patterns. Configure alerts and notifications to promptly detect and address issues related to scaling.

6. **Cost and Efficiency Management:** Consistently track resource usage and modify resource allocations to enhance efficiency and reduce expenses. Utilize functionalities such as Kubernetes cluster autoscaling to adaptively alter the number of nodes according to workload requirements.

7. **Scaling Challenges:** Comprehend the limitations and restrictions of your applications during the scaling process. Use relevant controllers such as StatefulSets to meet the needs of stateful applications. Integrate mechanisms to manage data consistency, session persistence, and distributed caching for applications undergoing scaling.

Manual Scaling

In the context of Kubernetes, manual scaling involves the manual adjustment of the replica count (pods) for a designated deployment or replica set. This stands in contrast to automatic scaling, where Kubernetes dynamically alters the replica count based on predefined metrics and policies.

To manually adjust the scale of deployment in Kubernetes on a CentOS system, the "kubectl" command-line tool can be utilized. The following steps outline the process:

1. Install kubectl

   ```
   $ sudo yum install -y kubectl
   ```

   Following the installation, it is necessary to set up kubectl to establish a connection with your Kubernetes cluster. If you haven't completed this step, you can refer to the instructions tailored to your specific cluster environment.

2. Listing the current deployments in the cluster

   ```
   $ kubectl get deployments
   ```

3. Deployment scaling

   ```
   $ kubectl scale --replica=COUNT deployment/name-of-your-deploymnet
   ```

The Kubectl scale serves as a command-line utility within Kubernetes, enabling you to adjust the number of replicas (instances) associated with a particular resource, be it pods, deployments, replication controllers, or stateful sets.

This tool is integral for dynamically modifying your application or workload's capacity, responding to fluctuating demands seamlessly, and eliminating the need for manual creation or deletion of resources.

--replicas=COUNT Indicates the intended number of replicas for scaling, where you replace COUNT with the desired quantity.

-f FILENAME or TYPE NAME You can designate the resource for scaling either by utilizing a YAML or JSON file (-f FILENAME) defining the resource or by directly specifying the resource type (TYPE) and its name (NAME).

> **Note** Remember that while manual scaling offers a direct means of altering replica numbers, for automated scaling driven by metrics, Kubernetes offers the Horizontal Pod Autoscaler (HPA) that autonomously modifies the replica count by assessing observed metrics such as CPU utilization or other customized metrics.

What Is Autoscaling?

Autoscaling represents a type of scaling in which software autonomously determines whether to augment or diminish the load. In essence, it introduces resources when your application experiences heightened activity and withdraws them when they are no longer required. Given the dynamic nature of fluctuating loads throughout the day, manual scaling can prove cumbersome and inefficient.

Kubernetes Autoscaling

Autoscaling capabilities, such as the Horizontal Pod Autoscaling (HPA) and Vertical Pod Autoscaling (VPA), enhance scalability by dynamically adjusting resources based on defined metrics.

Horizontal Pod Autoscaling (HPA)

Horizontal scaling in Kubernetes means adjusting the number of identical pods running together. This helps spread out the workload, using resources better and making the application more available. With horizontal scaling, you can add or remove pods based on certain measures, like how busy the system is. It's handy when tasks can be split

CHAPTER 2 CLOUD-NATIVE DEVOPS ARCHITECTURAL OVERVIEW

among many instances, like in simple apps or services. This kind of scaling improves the availability of your application and lets it handle more users or tasks by adding more pods.

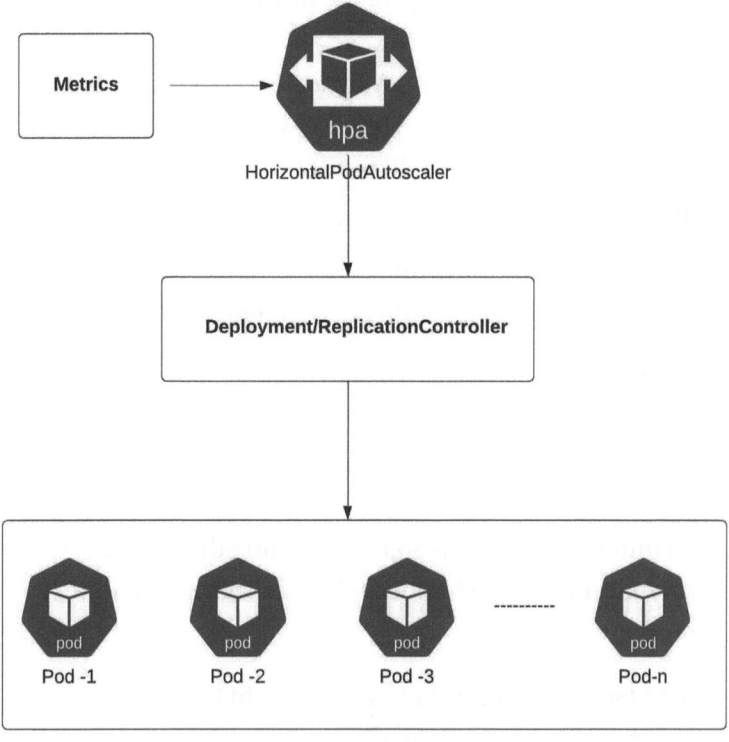

Figure 2-3. *Working of horizontal pod autoscaler*

Let's say, for example, that you set a maximum memory usage of 85% in the Horizontal Pod Autoscaler (HPA), the HPA controller will introduce a new pod when the average usage across all pods in the replicaSet reaches 85% or exceeds it. It's crucial to note that accurate configuration of resource requests and limits for the pod plays a significant role in this process.

If metrics are not set, the HPA controller assumes 100% for the intended measurement during scale-down and 0% during scale-up. Metrics for pods are delayed until 300 seconds after the pod initiates. This timeframe is adjustable by modifying the **horizontal-pod-autoscaler-cpu-initialization-period flag.**

Steps to deploy Horizontal Pod Autoscaler (HPA) and Metric Server using Helm in Kubernetes cluster. Here we will be using a CentOS 8 box to deploy. Also, make sure to install one of the cluster management tools (Docker/Minikube/kind)

1. Before you deploy the metric server make sure you have installed the following dependencies

    a. Git client

    b. Helm

    c. Kubectl for interaction with Kubernetes

2. To initiate the process start integrating the metric server repository with the Helm package collection as follows:

    ```
    $ helm repo add metrics-server https://kubernetes-sigs.github.io/metrics-server
    ```

3. To refresh the pool update the helm repo

    ```
    $ helm repo update metrics-server
    ```

4. Install the metric-server using helm

    ```
    $ helm install metrics-server metrics-server/metrics-server
    ```

5. To check the status of all the Kubernetes resources deployed to the metrocs-server

   ```
   $ kubectl get all -n metric-server
   ```

6. Create deployment file – **my-testapp.yaml**

   ```yaml
   apiVersion: apps/v1
   kind: Deployment
   metadata:
     name: my-testapp
   spec:
     replicas: 2
     selector:
       matchLabels:
         app: my-testapp
     template:
       metadata:
         labels:
           app: my-testapp
       spec:
         containers:
           - name: test-container
             image: test-image
             resources:
               limits:
                 cpu: "50m"
               requests:
                 cpu: "20m"
   ```

7. Deploy the development file

   ```
   $ kubectl apply -f my-testapp.yaml
   ```

8. Create Horizontal Pod Autoscaler

```
apiVersion: autoscaling/v2beta2
kind: HorizontalPodAutoscaler
metadata:
  name: test-hpa
spec:
  scaleTargetRef:
    apiVersion: apps/v1
    kind: Deployment
    name: my-app
  minReplicas: 1 # Minimum pods to maintain
  maxReplicas: 5 # Maximum pods to scale
  metrics:
  - type: Resource
    resource:
      name: cpu
      target:
        type: Utilization
        averageUtilization: 80 #Scale up if CPU
        threshold exceeds 80%
```

Description of Each Attribute Described in the Preceding YAML File

spec.scaleTargetRef: This field indicates the specific Kubernetes entity that the Horizontal Pod Autoscaler (HPA) is set to monitor and scale. In this context, it is configured to observe the deployment named "my-app," overseeing its performance and adjusting the number of pods as needed.

CHAPTER 2   CLOUD-NATIVE DEVOPS ARCHITECTURAL OVERVIEW

spec.minReplicas: This parameter establishes the minimum threshold for the number of replicas within the deployment. In this instance, the Horizontal Pod Autoscaler (HPA) ensures that the deployment is never scaled down to fewer than 1 pod.

Spec.maxReplicas: This attribute sets the maximum allowable number of replicas within the deployment. In this scenario, the Horizontal Pod Autoscaler (HPA) prevents the deployment from scaling beyond 5 pods.

metrics.type: This parameter designates the metric type employed by the Horizontal Pod Autoscaler (HPA) to determine the desired replica count. In this example, the HPA utilizes the Resource type, indicating that it scales the deployment according to the average CPU utilization.

metrics.resource.name: This field identifies the specific resource monitored by the HPA.

metrics.resource.averageUtilization: This attribute establishes the threshold for the metric. In this case, the HPA initiates scaling if the average CPU utilization surpasses 80%.

1. Deploy the HPA file

   ```
   $ kubectl apply -f test-hpa.yaml
   ```

2. Monitor HPA

   ```
   $ kubectl get hpa
   ```

Vertical Pod Autoscaling (VPA)

Besides the Horizontal Pod Autoscaler (HPA), there exists a Vertical Pod Autoscaler (VPA), alternatively referred to as the Vertical Pod Autoscaler. Vertical scaling involves modifying the allocated resources for a pod such as CPU and memory. This enables you to expand or reduce the capacity of a single pod without altering the number of instances.

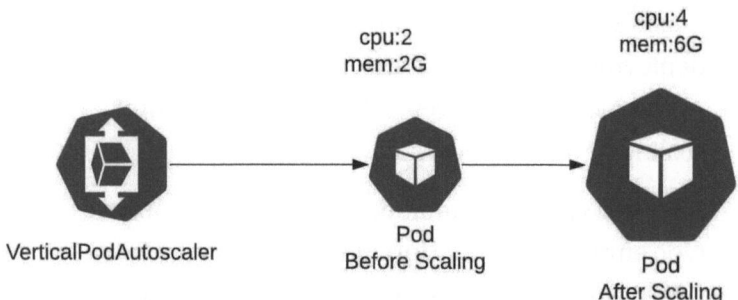

Figure 2-4. *Working of vertical pod autoscaler*

Vertical scaling becomes handy when an application needs more computer power or memory to handle extra work or demanding tasks. It's a good fit for applications that don't get much benefit from having many copies running at once. For example, big applications or databases that need more resources on one computer. Vertical scaling can make applications work better and not waste resources by giving just the right amount of power to each part as it needs it.

Steps to deploy Vertical Pod Autoscaler (VPA). Here we will be using a CentOS 8 box to deploy. Also, make sure to install one of the cluster management tools (Docker/Minikube/kind).

1. To deploy VPA first clone the source code of VPA

   ```
   $ git clone https://github.com/kubernetes/autoscaler.git
   $ cd /autoscaler/vertical-pod-autoscaler/hack
   $ ./vpa-up.sh
   ```

CHAPTER 2 CLOUD-NATIVE DEVOPS ARCHITECTURAL OVERVIEW

2. To print the yaml contents with resources

   ```
   $ ./vpa-process-yamls.sh print
   ```

3. Create deployment file – **my-testapp.yaml**

   ```yaml
   apiVersion: apps/v1
   kind: Deployment
   metadata:
     name: my-testapp
   spec:
     replicas: 2
     selector:
       matchLabels:
         app: my-testapp
     template:
       metadata:
         labels:
           app: my-testapp
       spec:
         containers:
           - name: test-container
             image: test-image
             resources:
               limits:
                 cpu: "50m"
               requests:
                 cpu: "20m"
   ```

4. Deploy the development file

   ```
   $ kubectl apply -f my-testapp.yaml
   ```

5. Monitor VPA

   ```
   $ kubectl get vpa
   ```

Comparison of Monolithic and Public Managed Kubernetes Cluster

Monolithic Cloud: It suggests a setup where a single, all-in-one Kubernetes system operates in the cloud, handling and organizing large, integrated applications or workloads. However, this approach may not align with the current best practices in building cloud-native applications, where it's common to favor smaller, more flexible microservices and distributed systems for better scalability and adaptability.

1. **Responsibility:** Users, in a self-managed context, bear the responsibility for overseeing the entire Kubernetes cluster, covering tasks such as upgrades, security patches, and scalability. This demands a higher level of expertise and hands-on management.

2. **Resource Allocation:** In self-managed environments, users enjoy direct control over resource allocation, networking, and other decisions related to the infrastructure.

3. **Infrastructure:** Within a self-managed framework, users retain the flexibility to deploy the Kubernetes cluster on their chosen infrastructure, be it on-premises, in a private cloud, or on a public cloud provider.

4. **Utilization:** Self-managed solutions are fitting for organizations with specific infrastructure requirements, custom configurations, or stringent security and compliance needs. They are particularly favored by those seeking complete control over the cluster.

5. **Maintenance:** Self-managed setups require users to plan and execute upgrades for both the control plane and worker nodes. Tasks like node replacements fall under their purview.

6. **Customization:** In a self-managed setting, users possess full control over the Kubernetes infrastructure, encompassing both master and worker nodes. This allows for extensive customization and flexibility in configuring the cluster.

7. **Cost:** While potentially cost-effective in terms of infrastructure, self-managed configurations may demand more effort and resources for ongoing maintenance.

Public Managed Cloud: "Public Kubernetes Cloud" means using Kubernetes on the Internet with a public cloud service. In this arrangement, the Kubernetes system is placed on the cloud, which anyone can access online. People can use the features and tools given by a public cloud provider, like AWS, Azure, or Google Cloud, to run, handle, and expand their containerized apps using Kubernetes. These cloud platforms make it easy to set up and control Kubernetes clusters, letting users concentrate on their apps without worrying too much about the technical details of the infrastructure.

1. **Automation:** Public managed services provided by cloud providers abstract much of the underlying infrastructure and automate tasks associated with the Kubernetes control plane, simplifying operational responsibilities for users.

2. **Cost:** While public managed services may have a more predictable cost structure and reduced operational burden, users may be subject to pricing models specific to the managed service.

3. **Infrastructure:** Users opting for public managed services are constrained to the infrastructure provided by the cloud provider. The managed service is closely integrated with the features and services of the cloud platform.

4. **Maintenance:** Cloud providers take charge of control plane upgrades and maintenance tasks in public managed environments. Users typically receive advance notification of any disruptions.

5. **Responsibility:** In public managed scenarios, the cloud provider assumes responsibility for managing the Kubernetes control plane, including aspects like upgrades, scaling, and maintenance. Users primarily focus on managing and deploying their applications.

6. **Resource Allocation:** Resource allocation in public managed setups is often abstracted, with users interacting at a higher level of service. The cloud provider takes charge of the underlying infrastructure details.

7. **Utilization:** Public managed services are well-suited for organizations seeking a more hands-off approach to infrastructure management. They prove convenient for those prioritizing ease of use, automation, and rapid deployment of applications.

Summary

In this chapter, we've gone beyond technical details to help you make strategic decisions about your project. We compared old-fashioned monolithic architectures with modern managed cloud services, giving you insights into how they work and what's best for your needs. We also talked about important things like how to make sure your project can grow and stay safe from cyber threats.

By the end of the chapter, you've learned how to create cloud-native solutions that are strong, flexible, and perfect for your project. We took you on a journey through the world of Cloud-Native DevOps, focusing on Google Cloud. You've learned about scaling Kubernetes, a tool that helps manage your applications, and how to set it up securely to keep your project safe.

We also talked about deploying Kubernetes within Google Cloud, making sure everything works smoothly together.

Throughout the chapter, we covered topics like what DevOps means in a Cloud Native Environment, how to make Kubernetes scale to fit your needs, setting up Kubernetes securely, and comparing old-fashioned and modern cloud setups. Now, armed with this knowledge, you're ready to make informed decisions about your project and succeed in the world of Cloud-Native DevOps.

CHAPTER 3

Security in Cloud-Native Applications with a Shift-Left Approach

"Securing Cloud-Native: Shifting left to stay ahead of the curve!"

In this chapter, we delve into the complex world of security within cloud-native applications, guided by the proactive philosophy of the "shift-left" approach. As cloud-native applications become increasingly integral to modern software development, the shift-left approach, which emphasizes embedding security measures early in the development process, allows us to preemptively address vulnerabilities and mitigate the risks of security breaches. This chapter serves as your comprehensive guide, covering a wide range of topics essential to securing cloud-native applications effectively.

By the end of the chapter, you'll understand the critical need for comprehensive and proactive security measures in the world of modern, cloud-based applications. These applications are complex and face a range of ever-evolving cyber threats, making robust security practices

CHAPTER 3   SECURITY IN CLOUD-NATIVE APPLICATIONS WITH A SHIFT-LEFT APPROACH

not just beneficial, but essential. The concept of "shift-left" is central to this approach. It means integrating security early and throughout the application development process, rather than treating it as an afterthought. By adopting this approach, organizations can greatly improve their ability to protect their cloud-native applications. This not only makes the applications stronger against potential cyberattacks but also ensures they comply with relevant regulations and standards. You will also learn how to effectively implement these security measures in your organization. This includes using specific tools and strategies designed for the unique challenges of cloud-native environments.

In this chapter, we will be encompassing the following topics:

- Introduction to Shift-Left Security in Cloud Native
- Infrastructure as Code (IaC) and Security
- Securing API in Early Stages

Introduction to Shift-Left Security in Cloud Native

Imagine if "shift-left security" was a superhero in the world of software development. In the traditional software development universe, security is like the hero who always arrives in the final act, after the villains (aka security vulnerabilities) have already caused chaos. This latecomer hero often finds themselves battling costly and complicated problems, wishing they had a time machine to go back and prevent the chaos in the first place.

Enter shift-left security, the proactive superhero who believes in the mantra, "The early bird catches the worm, and the early coder catches the bug." This hero starts their mission at the dawn of the project, embedding themselves into the very DNA of the software development life cycle.

They're in every plot twist and turn, from the initial storyboard to the final credits, ensuring that no villainous vulnerability sneaks past their watchful eye.

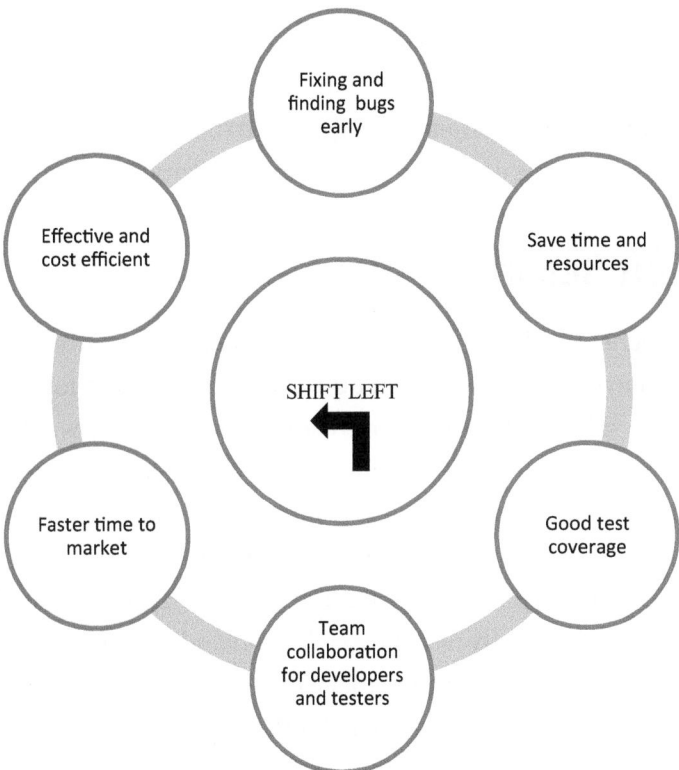

Figure 3-1. Shift-left secure model

In this world, development, operations, and security teams unite like a superhero squad, collaborating continuously. They're like a band, with security as the lead singer, development on guitar, and operations on drums, each playing their part in harmony from the first note. This approach not only enhances the overall security of the application but also turns the development process into a well-oiled machine, humming along with security as its constant rhythm.

CHAPTER 3   SECURITY IN CLOUD-NATIVE APPLICATIONS WITH A SHIFT-LEFT APPROACH

In the dynamic and ever-changing landscape of cloud-native applications, shift-left security is the agile hero we need. They're not just putting out fires; they're preventing them from igniting in the first place. So, when you think of shift-left security, picture a cape-wearing, bug-zapping superhero who's always one step ahead, ensuring that every code commit, and deployment is as safe as houses. After all, in the fast-paced world of software development, being early to the party doesn't just mean better snacks; it means a safer, more secure application.

Shift-Left Secure Right

"Securing Right" involves realizing that just focusing on early security practices, known as "Shift Left," isn't the complete solution for keeping your software safe. When you release your software, it enters a dynamic environment where changes and unexpected security issues are common. This means that the security work you start early on needs to be continued and adapted even after your product is live in the market.

The process is ongoing. After your product is released, you need to keep a close eye on it for security weaknesses. This includes checking not just your own software but also any components you've used. To do this effectively, you extract Software Bills of Materials (SBOMs) from your product. These SBOMs are like detailed lists of all the components in your software. You then regularly compare these lists against the latest security threat information to identify new risks. The final crucial step in this process is to assess which of these identified risks are the most dangerous and need to be addressed first, ensuring that you're always tackling the most critical issues.

In your organization, you have different teams with different roles and perspectives on security. Your development teams are the creators. They build and refine the software that is essential for your business to provide services and stay competitive. They typically prioritize their work based on urgency; unless a task is marked as high-priority, it might not get immediate attention.

CHAPTER 3 SECURITY IN CLOUD-NATIVE APPLICATIONS WITH A SHIFT-LEFT APPROACH

Your DevOps teams are like the efficient engineers of the software world. They're responsible for taking the software from its development stage to being fully operational. They emphasize speed, efficiency, and reliability. They're also big fans of automation; if they find themselves doing the same task repeatedly, they'll likely automate that process to save time and reduce errors.

Then there are your operations teams, including SecOps, who are in charge once the software is live. SecOps are the security experts, constantly on the lookout for potential threats and vulnerabilities. They have to stay alert and adaptable because new challenges and security alerts come up regularly.

The challenge lies in finding strategies and tools that bring these diverse teams together, harmonizing their different approaches and expectations. The aim is to simplify the complex array of potential issues that arise once the software is in production. This involves condensing these issues into a focused set of problems that the development teams can effectively address. The tools you choose should be compatible with cloud-native applications and serve as a bridge between operations and development teams, fostering a collaborative environment focused on enhancing overall security. By achieving this, you not only improve your security posture but also facilitate better teamwork and efficiency across different departments.

Risk from Third-Party Components

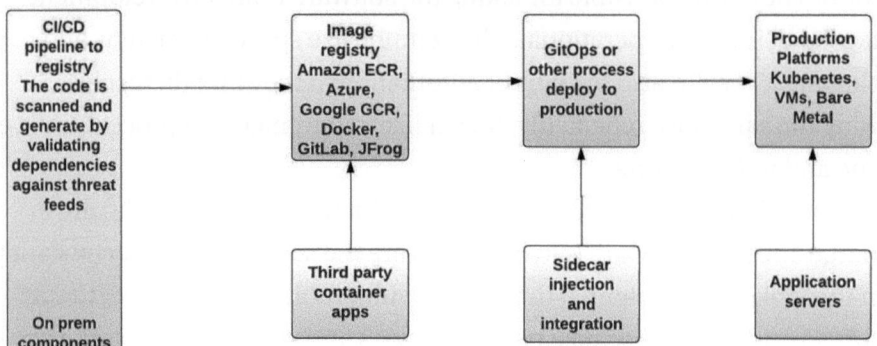

Figure 3-2. *Third-party component matrix model*

Integration of Third-Party Components: The first stage shows the integration of third-party components into a production environment. This can be in the form of libraries, frameworks, modules, or other software elements.

Potential Vulnerabilities in Third-Party Components: The next stage highlights that these components may contain vulnerabilities. These could be due to outdated code, lack of updates, inherent security flaws, or other weaknesses.

Exposure to External Networks: The diagram then shows how these components, now part of a production system, are exposed to external networks, making them accessible to potential attackers.

Exploitation of Vulnerabilities: This critical stage demonstrates how attackers can discover and exploit the vulnerabilities in these third-party components. This exploitation could lead to unauthorized access, data breaches, or other malicious activities.

Impact on the Production System: The final stage shows the consequences of such exploits, which can range from data theft, system compromise to complete production shutdown.

Embracing Technologies to Shift Left

There are different tools available that help bring security into the early stages of software development. Each tool has its strengths and can work together to make your code, software, and the parts and pieces it depends on more secure. DevOps teams understood that they needed to focus on security earlier in the process to prevent creating too many security issues for their security and operations teams to handle. This led to the creation of DevSecOps, which combines development, security, and operations. DevSecOps uses different tools and technologies to quickly and automatically check security as part of the continuous integration and continuous delivery (CI/CD) pipeline.

1. Static Application System Testing (SAST)
2. Dynamic Application Security Testing (DAST)
3. Interactive Application Security Testing (IAST)
4. Software Composition Analysis (SCA)
5. Runtime Application Self-protection (RASP)
6. IaC Scanning
7. Infrastructure Scanning
8. Compliance Check

1. Static Application System Testing (SAST)

This is all about mixing security right into the process of making and running software, think of SAST as a kind of early alert system. It looks over the code before the code even starts working, like checking a building's plan for any mistakes before you start building.

In DevSecOps, the aim is to make sure security is a core part of making software from start to finish, not just something you add at the end. SAST helps do this by spotting possible security problems early on when the code is being written. This means security gets taken care of as part of the normal process of making the software.

By using SAST, teams who work in DevSecOps can make sure security is included right from the start in what they create. This lowers the chance of finding big security problems later on, which can take a lot of time and money to sort out. Plus, it fits well with the DevSecOps way of constantly integrating and delivering security, leading to a safer and more smooth process of developing software.

Example: Before deploying a new version of their banking application, a development team uses SAST tools to analyze the codebase. The tool flags potential security vulnerabilities such as SQL injection or cross-site scripting flaws in the code. By addressing these issues early in the development process, the team ensures that the application is more resilient to attacks when it goes live.

2. Dynamic Application Security Testing (DAST)

DAST (Dynamic Application Security Testing) is different from SAST because it checks the software when it's being used, like testing a car for safety while it's driving. In DevSecOps, the idea is to make security a part of the whole process of creating and running software. DAST is special because it tests the software when it's live and active. This is important because some problems only show up when the software is in use, not when you're just looking at the code.

DAST works well alongside SAST. If SAST is like checking the blueprint of a building, DAST is like inspecting the building while people are using it. It helps DevSecOps teams find any security issues that might have been missed earlier or that only appear when the software is actually working. Additionally, DAST helps identify issues like insufficient logging and monitoring, enabling the team to enhance the application's ability to detect and respond to security incidents, as recommended in the OWASP Top 10.

By using DAST, DevSecOps teams can make sure they're continuously checking for and fixing security problems in a more real-life setting. This ongoing testing is a big part of DevSecOps, which is all about keeping security in mind at every step of making and managing software.

Example: After launching a new ecommerce website, the operations team conducts DAST by simulating various attack scenarios. They use automated tools to probe the website for vulnerabilities such as improper error handling or insecure server configurations. By regularly running DAST tests, the team can detect and mitigate security threats in real-time, safeguarding customer data and transactions.

3. Interactive Application Security Testing (IAST)

Interactive Application Security Testing (IAST) is a mix of both the SAST and DAST methods. Think of IAST as a security guard who not only checks the plans and the finished building but also keeps an eye on things as the building is being constructed.

For DevSecOps, which is all about including security at every step of making and running software, IAST is super helpful. It gives instant updates on security issues while the software is being tested. This means it can find problems that might only show up in certain situations or when different parts of the application are working together.

IAST is special in DevSecOps because it gives quick feedback about security problems. This lets teams fix these issues as part of their normal process of developing and testing. It fits right in with the DevSecOps idea of always keeping security in mind. By using IAST, DevSecOps teams can better make sure their applications are safe. They can keep checking and improving security all through the software's life, leading to safer software and a smoother development process.

Example: During the development of a mobile banking app, the development team implements IAST tools that continuously monitor the application's behavior while it undergoes testing. If the application attempts to access sensitive user data without proper authorization, the IAST tool immediately alerts the developers. By integrating IAST into their testing workflow, the team can quickly identify and remediate security issues before releasing the app to customers.

4. Software Composition Analysis (SCA)

Software Composition Analysis (SCA) is all about making sure security is part of the whole process of creating and running software. SCA looks closely at the parts of the software that come from outside sources, like open-source or third-party components, which are common in software development today.

The main job of SCA in DevSecOps is to check these outside parts for any security issues, problems with licenses, or the need for updates. Since modern software often uses these outside pieces, SCA makes sure they don't bring in any security risks. In a DevSecOps setting, where the aim is to keep security in mind all through the process of integrating and deploying software continuously, SCA helps do this automatically. This is really important because it lets teams keep up the speed of DevOps while also staying safe.

By using SCA, DevSecOps teams can take care of security issues related to these outside software pieces before they become a problem. This helps stop security problems before they start and makes sure the software meets security and licensing rules.

In short, SCA supports the goal of DevSecOps to always include security, helping teams to create safer software while still using helpful external software components.

Example: A software development team is building a new web application using various open-source libraries and third-party components. Before finalizing the release, they utilize SCA tools to scan the dependencies for known vulnerabilities and license compliance issues. By conducting SCA scans, the team ensures that the application's dependencies are secure and compliant with legal requirements, reducing the risk of exploitation and licensing conflicts.

5. Runtime Application Self-protection (RASP)

Runtime Application Self-Protection (RASP) is all about mixing security into the process of making and looking after software. RASP is like a smart security system that is built into the software when it's running. It's always checking for and stopping security threats in real-time, similar to a security guard who is on the lookout during a big event, ready to act if there's any trouble.

For DevSecOps teams, RASP is great because it doesn't just find problems; it also stops them right then and there, on its own. This helps the teams keep making and updating software quickly, which is a big part of DevOps, while making sure that security is always switched on and working.

With RASP, DevSecOps teams can give their software a strong layer of security that works well with other security tools they use. It's especially good because it keeps the software safe even after it's out there for people to use, which is exactly what the DevSecOps approach wants to achieve: keeping security going strong at all times.

Example: A financial institution implements RASP technology within its online banking system. When a user attempts to execute a potentially malicious transaction, the RASP solution dynamically intercepts the request and applies security controls in real-time. By deploying RASP, the institution strengthens its defense against attacks such as account takeover and fraud, enhancing the overall security posture of its digital banking services.

6. IaC Scanning

Infrastructure as Code (IaC) scanning is an important part of DevSecOps, which is all about making sure security is part of building and managing software. IaC scanning checks the code that sets up the technical infrastructure of a project, like the digital version of a building's blueprint. It looks for any mistakes or security gaps before the system is used.

In DevSecOps, IaC scanning is super helpful because it finds and fixes security issues before the system is even up and running. It fits perfectly with the fast-paced cycle of constantly improving and updating software, where checking for security is part of the routine.

By using IaC scanning, DevSecOps teams can make sure that the foundations of their software are solid and secure right from the start. This helps them build and look after their systems more safely and saves time by catching any problems early on, keeping with the idea of thinking about security at every step of creating and running software.

Example: A cloud infrastructure team adopts IaC scanning practices to review the configuration scripts used to deploy virtual servers and networking components. By analyzing the IaC templates, the team identifies misconfigurations and security weaknesses before provisioning the infrastructure. Through regular IaC scanning, they ensure that the cloud environment is securely configured, minimizing the risk of data breaches and unauthorized access.

7. Infrastructure Scanning

Infrastructure scanning in the DevSecOps approach is all about regularly checking the technical setup that software runs on, much like you'd regularly check a car to make sure it's safe to drive. In the world of DevSecOps, where adding security into every step of software development and maintenance is key, these scans are like routine check-ups for the digital "buildings" that hold your software.

Automated tools are used to look over the servers, networks, and other parts involved in running the application, making sure everything is secure and there are no weak spots that could let hackers in. Imagine it as having a safety inspector who doesn't just visit once but keeps coming back to ensure that everything remains safe over time.

In the DevSecOps mindset, these regular infrastructure scans are essential because they're all about being ahead of the game. They're not just done and forgotten; they're part of an ongoing process that keeps security tight while the software is being made, and even after it's out there for people to use. By making infrastructure scanning a regular part of their routine, DevSecOps teams can find and fix problems early on. This continuous approach to security helps keep the software safe and fits right in with the DevSecOps way of keeping a constant eye on security throughout the entire life cycle of software.

Example: An ecommerce company conducts regular infrastructure scans across its server farms and network infrastructure. Automated tools examine system configurations and network traffic patterns to detect anomalies or vulnerabilities. By performing infrastructure scans proactively, the company mitigates security risks and maintains the availability and integrity of its online storefront, ensuring a secure shopping experience for customers.

8. Compliance Check

Compliance checks in DevSecOps are like ongoing health inspections for software to ensure it meets legal and industry rules at all stages of its life. In DevSecOps, where the goal is to include security from the start to finish of software creation and use, ensuring compliance is a key part of this.

Imagine compliance checks as a series of checkpoints that software must clear during its development to confirm it's in line with specific laws and standards. It's not just about looking at these requirements once; it's about making sure the software always follows the rules.

In the DevSecOps approach, these checks happen regularly. Automated tools help verify that the software respects security protocols, protects user information, and meets other necessary guidelines continuously. This is done to avoid any legal troubles and to make sure the software is safe and reliable for users. By doing these compliance checks often, DevSecOps teams can quickly find and fix any parts of the software that might not be up to standard. This forward-thinking strategy helps dodge potential legal problems, safeguards user data, and keeps the trust in the software high, all while making sure it's ready for use by as many people as possible.

Example: A healthcare software provider integrates automated compliance checks into its DevSecOps pipeline to ensure adherence to HIPAA regulations. Throughout the development life cycle, automated tests validate that the software encrypts patient data, maintains audit trails, and implements access controls as required by law. By continuously verifying compliance, the provider avoids regulatory penalties and builds trust with healthcare organizations relying on their software solutions.

Security Testing with Shift-Left Approach

Integrating security early and consistently, "Shift Left" Security Testing adopts a smarter approach to crafting secure software, benefiting not only the development team but the entire organization. This method aligns with the broader "Shift Left" movement in software development, which emphasizes addressing potential challenges, such as security vulnerabilities, at an early stage. This early intervention strategy ensures that security is not an afterthought but a fundamental aspect of the development process, leading to a more robust and secure product.

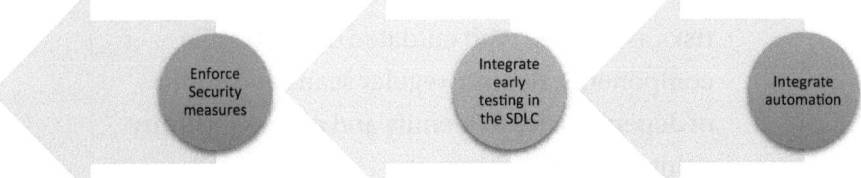

Figure 3-3. Advancing security testing to the left

- **Enforce Security Measures**

    Integrating security policies is a crucial initial step in implementing shift-left testing strategies. Such policies serve to establish automatic and consistent boundaries before the commencement of work, offering essential information that enhances development processes, notably in terms of security.

    1. **Code Review Policy:** Require code reviews for all changes to the codebase, focusing not only on functionality but also on security considerations. Enforce the use of secure coding standards and guidelines during code reviews.

    2. **Security Training and Awareness Policy:** Require developers to undergo regular security training to stay updated on common security risks, best practices, and emerging threats. Establish policies for promoting security

awareness among development teams, emphasizing the importance of security throughout the software development life cycle.

3. **Dependency Management Policy:** Enforce policies for managing and updating third-party dependencies and libraries to mitigate security risks associated with outdated or vulnerable components. Require regular scans and audits of dependencies to identify and address security vulnerabilities.

4. **Incident Response and Remediation Policy:** Define policies and procedures for responding to security incidents and vulnerabilities identified during the development process. Establish escalation paths and timelines for addressing and remediating security issues in a timely manner.

It's important to include a consensus on coding standards (`https://owasp.org/www-project-secure-coding-practices-quick-reference-guide/`) within your security policy framework. These standards specify the programming languages and configurations to be used by your team under various circumstances. Uniformity in understanding among all developers is key. This uniformity not only accelerates code review processes but also ensures a higher caliber of code quality. Adhering to these policies should lead to a reduction in bugs, as following best practices enables developers to steer clear of poor or insecure coding practices.

- **Integrate Early Testing in SDLC**

  As developers become more proficient in secure coding techniques, it's advisable to reassess your Software Development Life Cycle (SDLC). By examining your current methodologies, you can pinpoint incremental steps to integrate testing earlier in the process. This evaluation also aids in determining which tools might be most effective for your specific codebase.

  One approach to consider is adopting an Agile SDLC model. This model focuses on developing small increments of code. In this framework, each sprint encompasses both development and testing phases, ensuring that every minor feature is thoroughly tested.

  1. **Iterative Development:** Agile SDLC is characterized by iterative development cycles, known as sprints or iterations, typically lasting one to four weeks. Each iteration results in a potentially shippable product increment, allowing for continuous feedback and improvement.

  2. **Cross-Functional Teams:** Agile teams are cross-functional, consisting of members with diverse skills and expertise, including developers, testers, designers, and product owners. This structure promotes collaboration and shared ownership of the product.

3. **Customer Collaboration:** Agile places a strong emphasis on customer collaboration throughout the development process. Stakeholders, including end-users and product owners, provide feedback and prioritize features, ensuring that the product meets their needs and expectations.

4. **Adaptive Planning:** Agile SDLC embraces change and adapts to evolving requirements and priorities. Planning is done incrementally, with detailed plans created for the upcoming iteration while allowing for flexibility to accommodate changes in scope or priorities.

5. **Value Delivery:** Agile prioritizes delivering value to customers early and frequently. Features are prioritized based on their business value, and the development team strives to deliver working software with each iteration, allowing stakeholders to realize benefits sooner.

For some organizations, a sudden and complete transition to shift-left testing may not be feasible. In such cases, development teams can aim to create unit tests for each new feature they develop, gradually incorporating more robust testing practices into their workflow.

- **Integrate Automation**

    Embracing security automation tools is a key aspect of shift-left testing, which emphasizes more frequent security checks during the development process. Security automation employs software to automatically detect, investigate, and resolve external threats to applications and systems. This approach not only expedites the development life cycle but also contributes to a quicker time-to-market. Tools that are widely adopted for automation are Jenkins, GitLab CI/CD, Selenium, CircleCI, Ansible, and Kubernetes (K8s).

Incorporating security automation can significantly streamline the development process, reducing the time it takes to launch products.

One practical implementation of this is the application of security gating on pull requests, a method that integrates seamlessly with automated security in the early development stages. Pull requests, crucial in Git-based development workflows, facilitate collaboration by allowing developers to commit and merge changes into code repositories. Automated tools can scrutinize these pull requests for both security and licensing issues before the merging of the code, enhancing the overall security posture of the development process.

Benefits of Shift-Left Strategy

Enhanced Security: Moving security to the earlier stages of the Software Development Life Cycle (SDLC) allows for increased and repeated testing. This approach leads to stronger security and greater confidence in your code, software, and applications. By shifting security left, you ensure that the software and applications you release are secure and of high quality.

Error Reduction: Identifying bugs early in the Software Development Life Cycle (SDLC) simplifies their resolution. By conducting testing at earlier stages, issues can be addressed and rectified before they escalate, mitigating the risk of larger problems arising. This proactive approach ensures that vulnerabilities are tackled prior to the final stages of production, where resolving flaws is more demanding in terms of time and resources. Consequently, adopting a shift-left model allows for a more efficient and timely delivery of products. Enterprises that have embraced this approach have reported a significant 45% increase in quality. (`www.apisec.ai/blog/shift-left-security`)

Enhanced Product Quality: The sooner you identify and fix problems, the less risk they pose, and the less potential damage they cause. As a result, the quality of your final product is higher. More rigorous and earlier testing leads to a more dependable and stable product for users.

Increased Speed: By identifying and resolving issues earlier in the SDLC, flaws and vulnerabilities are fixed before they can cause harm. This not only protects your code, software, and applications but also enhances productivity by speeding up the production process and reducing the time it takes to bring your software and applications to market.

Infrastructure as Code (IaC) and Security

It's a big deal in the DevOps world. Instead of setting up and managing data centers with actual hardware or by clicking around in software, IaC uses text files or scripts that computers can read. In simpler terms, IaC means you handle all your tech stuff – like servers, networks, and databases – using code, just like you would with computer programs.

In the old days, setting up tech stuff was hands-on and tricky, and people often made mistakes. But with IaC, everything is automatic, smoother, and more dependable. Using IaC means all the parts of your tech setup are written in code. This makes it possible to set up and change your tech infrastructure quickly, accurately, and safely whenever you need to.

Role of IaC in Cloud Native

IaC, or Infrastructure as Code, is not just for automating infrastructure processes; it's also a strong tool for keeping cloud environments safe. Here's how IaC can really help in securing the cloud:

1. **Making Compliance and Auditing Easier:** IaC helps a lot with following rules and checking everything's okay. Businesses often have to stick to different security and privacy laws. With IaC, the whole setup of the technology is written in code and kept track of. This makes it easy to see any changes and keep a record of everything, which helps a lot in making sure everything is compliant. It's also clear and easy to understand for auditors who need to make sure the systems are safe. This saves time, reduces the chance of missing something, and makes sure every part of the technology is checked properly.

2. **Keeping Everything Consistent:** IaC is key for making sure everything in the technology setup is the same. This uniformity is important for safety. Before IaC, tech setups could change over time because of manual updates, leading to security risks. With IaC, this issue is pretty much gone. By defining the tech setup in code, every part is the same, which cuts down on differences. If there's a security problem in one place, fixing it in the IaC code fixes it everywhere.

3. **Automating Security Rules:** Instead of manually putting security rules in place, which can lead to mistakes, IaC lets you put these rules right into the tech setup. This makes sure they're always followed the same way everywhere, cutting down on human errors.

4. **Supporting Immutable Infrastructure:** IaC helps create a setup where servers aren't changed once they're up and running. If changes are needed, new servers are made using a standard template, and the old ones are shut down. This keeps things more secure by limiting the ways attackers can get in. Because everything stays the same, any odd changes or access can be spotted and dealt with quickly. It also stops unauthorized changes because each new deployment is fresh and doesn't keep any risky settings from before.

5. **Speeding Up Response to Incidents:** If there's a security problem, IaC lets you act fast. Infected servers can be taken down and replaced quickly using IaC. This quick action reduces downtime and damage, helping businesses get back on track fast.

CHAPTER 3   SECURITY IN CLOUD-NATIVE APPLICATIONS WITH A SHIFT-LEFT APPROACH

> By making it easier to fix security issues quickly,
> IaC strengthens the cloud against cyberattacks,
> giving businesses more confidence in their digital
> operations.

Security Strategy Using IaC for Organizations

Implementing DevSecOps principles is key to integrating IaC into an organization's security strategy. DevSecOps merges security practices with DevOps, ensuring security measures are part of the coding process from the start, not added later by applying IaC within a DevSecOps framework, infrastructure becomes a part of the coding process. This enables seamless integration and deployment, allowing any changes to be efficiently tested and implemented, keeping the infrastructure secure and current.

Embracing a security-first approach is crucial when using IaC. This involves prioritizing security from the onset of infrastructure development, not as an afterthought. With IaC, you can embed security measures and policies into your infrastructure's code, ensuring new deployments automatically adhere to your security standards, minimizing human error, and strengthening your cloud security.

Addressing environmental drift is another important aspect. This drift, often caused by manual changes, can create inconsistencies in your infrastructure. IaC tackles this by serving as the definitive blueprint for your setup, ensuring uniformity. Regular checks against this blueprint can quickly spot and rectify any deviations.

Simplifying your infrastructure is also beneficial. Complexity can be a security hazard; the simpler your setup, the easier it is to manage and secure. IaC aids in reducing complexity by defining infrastructure in code, streamlining management, and reducing security risks. In summary, properly integrating IaC into your security strategy can significantly reduce human error risks and uphold high compliance standards, making it an essential tool for managing and securing cloud infrastructures.

CHAPTER 3 SECURITY IN CLOUD-NATIVE APPLICATIONS WITH A SHIFT-LEFT APPROACH

Tools for IaC Security

1. **Public Key Infrastructure (PKI)**

   It is a system that includes digital certificates, certificate authorities (CAs), and registration authorities. These elements work together to confirm and authenticate identities on the Internet, making communications secure and establishing trust between parties. A common use of PKI is in the Transport Layer Security (TLS) protocol. TLS encrypts conversations between web browsers and servers, and email clients and servers, also building trust for information exchange. TLS relies on the Rivest, Shamir, and Adleman (RSA) algorithm, a form of public-key cryptography. RSA creates digital signatures to confirm sender identities and maintain data integrity.

   For managing Infrastructure as Code (IaC), the Certificates-as-Code feature of HashiCorp Vault is widely used. It allows the creation and management of TLS certificates and keys within Vault. You can generate, store, revoke, and audit certificates and keys for applications through Vault.

2. **Vault**

   Vault is an open-source tool for handling secrets and sensitive data. It's used to store passwords, keys, and manage TLS certificates. It builds on HashiCorp for service and network management, and HashiCorp Nomad, for application and resource management. Vault is known for managing secrets, data, TLS certificates, and keys. Its Certificates-as-Code feature enables managing TLS certificates and keys efficiently.

3. **AWS Certificate Manager (ACM)**

    It is a cloud-based service for creating and managing TLS certificates and keys, particularly for AWS applications. It's a convenient tool for handling TLS needs in the cloud, offering creation, storage, revocation, and auditing functionalities.

    IaC security tools are essential for managing and securing infrastructure effectively. They automate deployment and configuration and enhance security. Popular IaC security tools include Puppet for server configuration, Chef for automating application deployment, and Ansible for both deployment automation and server management. When using these tools, it's important to stay updated with the latest versions, understand how the tool works, ensure your infrastructure is secure with up-to-date patches and configurations, and have a solid security incident response plan.

IaC with Terraform

Terraform, an Infrastructure as Code (IaC) tool, is primarily used by DevOps teams, automates various infrastructure tasks, such as cloud resource provisioning. This open-source tool is cloud neutral, developed in Go language by HashiCorp. With Terraform, you can define your entire infrastructure through code, handling servers from different providers like AWS or Azure simultaneously. Think of Terraform as a unifying language that enables you to manage your entire IT infrastructure.

Terraform's primary use is in provisioning public cloud infrastructure on major platforms like AWS and Azure. It works through a provider system, which are plugins that adapt existing APIs and languages (like

Azure Bicep) into Terraform's syntax. Another key function of Terraform is supporting multi-cloud deployments. Unlike some other IaC tools, Terraform operates across various cloud providers at once. This allows engineers to use the same syntax across different environments without needing to learn multiple tools. Also, terraform is a valuable tool for managing infrastructure in private cloud environments as well since it allows you to define and deploy infrastructure resources using code, automating provisioning and management tasks. By treating infrastructure as code, Terraform ensures consistency, reproducibility, and scalability across environments. It integrates seamlessly with various private cloud providers, enabling efficient infrastructure management and orchestration.

Additionally, Terraform is used for deploying, managing, and orchestrating resources with custom cloud providers. This means wrapping any existing API into Terraform's declarative syntax, even outside major cloud services like AWS. Providers can also be tailored for specific internal requirements, converting existing tools or APIs into Terraform-compatible formats. In essence, Terraform is a versatile tool for managing your IT infrastructure, whether it's in a single cloud, across multiple clouds, or in customized environments, all through the lens of IaC.

Terraform Working

Terraform works by allowing users to define their desired infrastructure configuration in configuration files using HashiCorp Configuration Language (HCL). These configuration files specify the infrastructure resources, settings, and dependencies required for deployment.

Terraform interacts with various cloud providers, infrastructure platforms, and services through provider plugins. These plugins translate Terraform configuration into API calls and manage the life cycle of resources. Terraform supports a wide range of providers, including AWS, Azure, Google Cloud Platform (GCP), Kubernetes, and more.

The fundamental Terraform workflow comprises three main stages:

- **Definition:** In this stage, you specify the resources needed for your infrastructure, which can span various cloud providers and services. For instance, you might craft a configuration to deploy an application on virtual machines within a Virtual Private Cloud (VPC) network, incorporating security groups and a load balancer.

- **Planning:** Terraform generates an execution plan outlining the actions it will take, such as creating, updating, or deleting infrastructure components, based on your defined configuration and the current state of the infrastructure.

- **Execution:** Once approved, Terraform executes the planned operations in the correct sequence, adhering to any specified resource dependencies. For example, if modifications are made to the properties of a VPC and the number of virtual machines within that VPC is altered, Terraform will first re-create the VPC before adjusting the virtual machine scaling.

Terraform Architecture

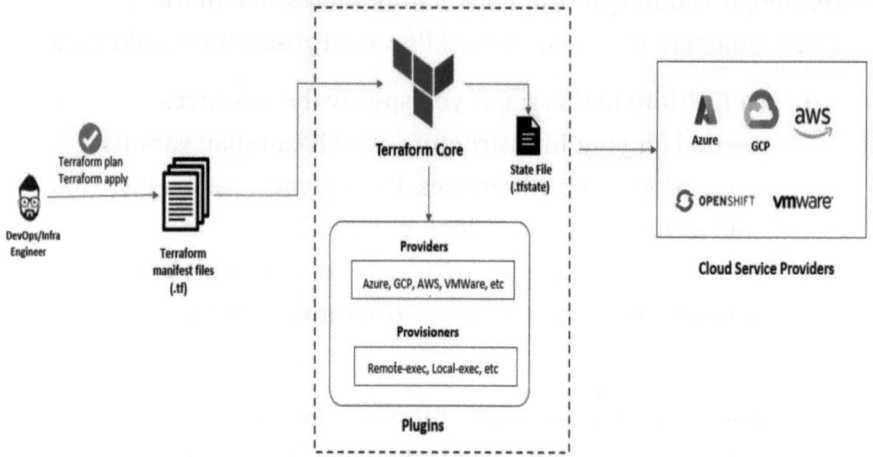

Figure 3-4. *Terraform architecture*

Terraform Core (Terraform CLI): Terraform's main part is built using the Go programming language. This creates the Terraform command line tool, or CLI, which is how users interact with Terraform. This tool is open source and available on Terraform's GitHub page.

Terraform Providers: Providers in Terraform are like special modules that help it talk to various services, including cloud platforms, databases, and DNS services.

Each provider is designed to let Terraform manage specific resources in a service and turn Terraform's setup instructions into actions that the service understands. There are many providers for different services, including big cloud services like AWS, Azure, and Google Cloud, and others created by the community. With these providers, Terraform users can consistently manage their setups, no matter what service they're using.

Terraform State File: The state file is an important part of how Terraform works. It's a file that saves details about what Terraform is managing and the current condition of those resources. Terraform uses

CHAPTER 3 SECURITY IN CLOUD-NATIVE APPLICATIONS WITH A SHIFT-LEFT APPROACH

this file to figure out what changes need to be made when new instructions are given. It helps make sure that Terraform doesn't redo the same task over and over again.

This file can be stored on your computer or somewhere else, like Azure Storage Account, Amazon S3, or HashiCorp. It's important to keep this file safe and back it up regularly, as it has important information about your setup.

IaC Tools

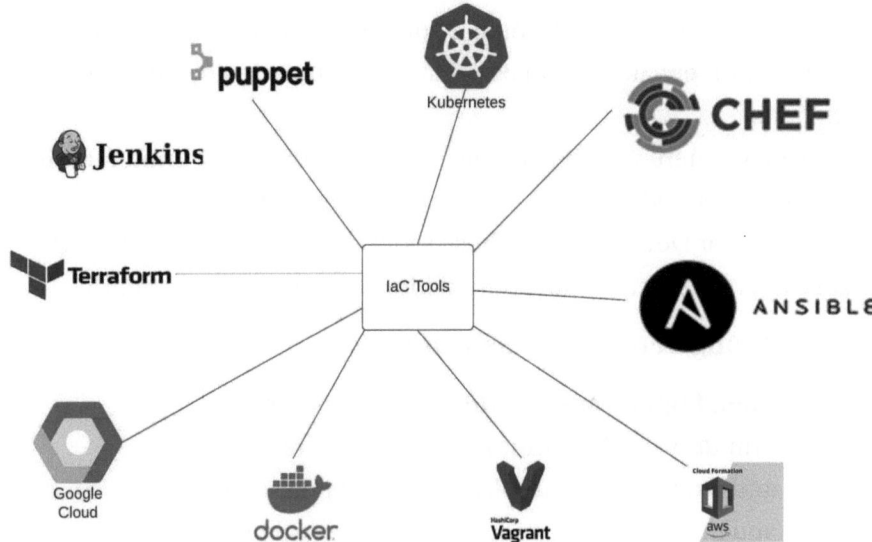

Figure 3-5. *Infrastructure as code tools*

Infrastructure as Code (IaC) tools are crucial in modern software development for managing and setting up technology systems. These tools have transformed traditional approaches, moving from manual configurations and physical hardware to using code-based, machine-readable definitions for infrastructure.

Essentially, IaC treats infrastructure like software: it's managed and provisioned through code instead of manual methods. This means the entire setup of an application's infrastructure, including networks, servers, databases, and other services, is defined and maintained in source code files. These files are subject to version control, enabling auditing and review like application code.

The automation provided by IaC tools streamlines the process of establishing, altering, and maintaining versions of infrastructure. This not only boosts efficiency but also significantly cuts down on errors that are common in traditional manual setups. By automating environment configurations, IaC reduces human error, leading to a more reliable, consistent, and repeatable process in infrastructure deployment and maintenance.

Nowadays, there's a broad range of tools accessible for implementing Infrastructure as Code, and the most suitable one varies for each Infrastructure or DevOps team. These tools, diverse in their usage and capabilities, can generally be grouped into several distinct categories

1. **Configuration Management Tools**

    Chef, Puppet, and Ansible: These tools are primarily used to automate the configuration and management of software on existing servers and infrastructure. They ensure that systems are configured consistently and maintained in a desired state.

    Chef uses "recipes" and "cookbooks" to define how systems should be configured.

    Puppet employs "manifests" and "modules" to enforce system configurations.

Ansible is known for its simplicity and uses "playbooks" to automate tasks across multiple systems.

2. **Container Orchestration Tools**

    Kubernetes and Docker Swarm: These are used for managing containerized applications across a cluster of machines.

    Kubernetes offers advanced features for container orchestration, including autoscaling, load balancing, and self-healing.

    Docker Swarm provides native clustering functionality for Docker containers and is known for its ease of use and integration with the Docker ecosystem.

3. **Server Tools**

    Docker and Vagrant: These tools are used for creating reproducible and consistent server environments.

    Docker packages software into containers, ensuring that it runs the same regardless of where the container is deployed.

    Vagrant provides a simple way to manage and provision virtual machines with a consistent environment, defined in a single configuration file.

    The concept of immutable infrastructure promoted by these tools means once a server or container is deployed, it is not modified. If changes are needed, a new server or container is built from a base image.

4. **Provisioning Tools**

   Tools like Terraform, Azure Resource Manager (ARM), Google Cloud Deployment Manager, and AWS CloudFormation are designed to automate the provisioning of infrastructure in their respective cloud environments.

   Terraform stands out for its ability to manage multiple cloud services and its declarative configuration language.

   ARM, Google Cloud Deployment Manager, and AWS CloudFormation are specific to their respective cloud platforms and provide native tooling for infrastructure automation within those ecosystems. IaC tools play a crucial role in automating and managing various aspects of IT infrastructure, from configuration and server templating to container orchestration and cloud-specific provisioning. By utilizing these tools, organizations can achieve more efficient, consistent, and reliable infrastructure deployment and management.

Value Proposition of IaC Tools

1. **Consistency Across Environments**

   Single Source of Truth: IaC maintains all infrastructure configurations in code, serving as the definitive source of truth. This approach ensures that the infrastructure setup is consistent across different environments, be it development, testing, or production.

Reliable and Predictable Infrastructure: With IaC, you can replicate your infrastructure setup accurately at any time. This reliability is crucial in situations like disaster recovery, where rapid restoration of services is necessary, or during the scaling process where identical environments are needed.

2. **Time Savings Through Automation**

   Automating Repetitive Tasks: IaC tools automate the process of provisioning and managing infrastructure, which traditionally involves repetitive manual tasks. Automation leads to a significant reduction in the time and effort required for these tasks.

   Focus on Strategic Initiatives: By reducing the time spent on manual setup and maintenance, developers and operations teams can redirect their efforts toward more strategic activities. This includes enhancing the application's functionality, optimizing performance, or innovating new features.

3. **Promoting DevOps Culture**

   Facilitating Collaboration: IaC bridges the gap between development (Dev) and operations (Ops) teams. Both teams can understand, modify, and manage the infrastructure setup through code, which promotes a better understanding and collaboration.

Shared Understanding and Responsibility: With IaC, infrastructure configuration becomes part of the codebase, which both developers and operations teams interact with. This shared environment fosters responsibility and understanding across teams, leading to more efficient problem-solving and decision-making.

Harmonious Working Environment: Adopting IaC encourages a culture where teams work together toward common goals, sharing responsibilities and collaborating effectively. This harmonious environment is conducive to faster innovation and improved overall productivity.

Best Practices for IaC

1. **Continuous Integration and Delivery (CI/CD):** Integrate infrastructure code into CI/CD pipelines to automate testing, validation, and deployment processes, enabling rapid and reliable delivery of infrastructure changes.

2. **Version Control:** Store infrastructure code in a version control system (e.g., Git) to track changes, facilitate collaboration, and enable rollback to previous versions if needed.

3. **Monitoring and Logging:** Implement monitoring and logging solutions to track infrastructure changes, monitor resource usage, and troubleshoot issues effectively, ensuring visibility and accountability.

4. **Modularization:** Break down infrastructure code into modular components to promote reusability, maintainability, and easier management of complex configurations.

5. **Testing:** Implement automated testing for infrastructure code to validate configurations, detect errors, and ensure desired outcomes before deployment. This includes unit tests, integration tests, and end-to-end tests.

6. **Dependency Management:** Manage dependencies carefully, including versioning of external modules and libraries, to prevent compatibility issues and ensure reproducibility of infrastructure deployments.

7. **Documentation:** Document infrastructure code comprehensively, including comments, README files, and inline documentation, to enhance understanding, facilitate onboarding, and ensure maintainability.

8. **Security and Compliance:** Embed security and compliance measures into infrastructure code, such as encryption, access controls, and compliance checks, to ensure that security requirements are met consistently.

9. **Collaboration and Communication:** Foster collaboration and communication among development, operations, and security teams to align on infrastructure requirements, share knowledge, and address challenges effectively.

10. **Immutable Infrastructure:** Treat infrastructure as immutable, where changes result in replacing existing resources rather than modifying them in place. This ensures consistency and reduces the risk of configuration drift.

11. **Infrastructure as Documentation:** Use infrastructure code as the single source of truth for documenting the desired state of the infrastructure, making it easier to understand and replicate environments.

12. **Infrastructure as Data:** Utilize data-driven approaches to define infrastructure configurations, leveraging variables, templates, and parameterization to make configurations more dynamic and adaptable.

Securing API in Early Stages

Let's begin with the basics. What exactly are APIs? In the world of today's mobile, SaaS, and web applications, APIs are incredibly important. You'll find them in apps meant for customers, partners, and even internal use. APIs give away parts of the app's core functions and sensitive information, which often includes personal details that need to be kept private. This makes them a big target for cybercriminals. Having secure APIs is important because it allows for quick innovation and easy connection between systems. Keeping APIs secure is a must for any organization that wants to keep the data flowing through APIs safe. Key steps to securing an API include confirming user identities, controlling access, encrypting data, and keeping an eye on API activity. These security steps are critical for stopping unwanted access and attacks, such as SQL injections. A secure API setup is crucial for maintaining the trust and reliability of any online service or platform.

Integrating security into the start of making apps and APIs is super important. It helps you find and fix weak spots early on, which means you're less likely to have problems when people start using the software. The goal is to make security a regular part of making the app, not something you try to add at the end. This makes sure that keeping things safe is a basic part of the app and API infrastructure from the foundational element.

To integrate security into the start of making apps and APIs, follow these steps:

- **Threat Modeling:** Begin by identifying potential threats and vulnerabilities in your application or API. Consider the various attack vectors and potential weak points.

- **Security Requirements:** Define specific security requirements for your project. These should include authentication, authorization, data encryption, input validation, and other relevant measures.

- **Secure Design:** Incorporate security principles into the design phase of your development process. This includes implementing secure coding practices, using secure frameworks and libraries, and following industry best practices.

- **Code Reviews:** Conduct regular code reviews with a focus on security. This helps identify and address security issues early in the development life cycle.

- **Automated Testing:** Implement automated security testing tools to scan your codebase for vulnerabilities continuously. This includes static analysis tools, dynamic analysis tools, and vulnerability scanners.

- **Security Training:** Provide security training for developers, designers, and other team members involved in the project. This ensures everyone understands their role in maintaining security throughout the development process.

- **Secure Deployment:** Ensure that security measures are maintained during the deployment phase. This includes securely configuring servers, implementing secure communication protocols, and applying necessary security patches.

- **Continuous Monitoring:** Monitor the application and API for security incidents and anomalies continuously. Implement logging and monitoring solutions to detect and respond to security threats promptly.

Common API Risk Factors

1. **Object-Level Authorization Issues**

    This vulnerability occurs when an API doesn't properly check whether a user has the right to access or modify a particular piece of data. Attackers might manipulate the identifier in a request (like changing the ID number of an account they want to access) to bypass these checks. This could lead to data breaches where unauthorized users gain access to other people's data. This can be overcome by implementing proper authentication and authorization mechanisms within the API by ensuring each request to access or modify data is thoroughly validated against the user's permissions. This involves verifying not only the user's identity but also their entitlements to specific resources. Engineers also conduct rigorous testing to identify and mitigate any vulnerabilities that could allow attackers to manipulate identifiers or bypass authorization checks. Additionally, they continuously monitor and update the authorization mechanisms to adapt to evolving security threats and ensure robust protection against unauthorized access and data breaches.

Mitigation Strategies: Implement robust authentication and authorization checks for each API call, ensuring only entitled users can access or modify data. Engineers need to strengthen the authentication and authorization mechanisms of the API. This involves implementing comprehensive checks for each API call to verify the user's identity and permissions before allowing access to sensitive data. By enforcing strict authentication protocols and authorization rules, engineers can prevent unauthorized users from accessing or modifying data they are not entitled to.

2. **Function-Level Authorization Issues**

    Sometimes, the access control policies are so complex that they fail to strictly adhere to the "least privilege" principle, where users are given the minimum access necessary for their role. This flaw might let attackers perform critical operations or access sensitive parts of the system reserved for administrators or specific roles.

Mitigation Strategies: To mitigate Function-Level Authorization Issues, engineers should simplify access controls to ensure that users are granted only the minimum privileges necessary to perform their roles. This involves conducting regular audits to review and adjust user permissions based on the principle of least privilege, where users are granted the lowest level of access required to carry out their tasks effectively. By simplifying access controls and adhering to the principle of least privilege, engineers can reduce the risk of unauthorized access to sensitive functions and data.

3. **Excessive Data Exposure**

    APIs may inadvertently provide more data in their responses than is necessary for the client's request. This could include sensitive information that, while not displayed to the user, could be intercepted and misused by an attacker.

    Mitigation Strategies: To address Excessive Data Exposure, engineers should implement strict data filtering mechanisms on the server side to ensure that only the necessary data is included in API responses. This involves carefully defining and filtering the data returned by the API to exclude any sensitive information that is not required for the specific request. By implementing strict data filtering measures, engineers can minimize the risk of exposing sensitive information to unauthorized users and mitigate the potential impact of data breaches.

4. **Improper Asset Management**

   In the rush to release, teams may forget to properly document or secure all API endpoints, which can leave some APIs unprotected. Also, unclear documentation can lead to improper usage of APIs, potentially opening up security gaps.

   Mitigation Strategies: To mitigate Improper Asset Management issues, engineers should maintain an updated inventory of all API endpoints and ensure comprehensive documentation is available for each endpoint. This involves documenting the purpose, functionality, and security requirements of each API endpoint to ensure that they are properly secured and maintained. Additionally, engineers should regularly review and decommission unused or outdated APIs to reduce the attack surface and minimize the risk of unauthorized access to sensitive resources.

5. **Insufficient Resource Management and Rate Limiting**

   Without proper limitations on the number or size of requests, APIs can be vulnerable to attacks that aim to overwhelm the system, such as DoS attacks, or to brute-force attacks that repeatedly attempt to guess user credentials.

   Mitigation Strategies: To address Insufficient Resource Management and Rate Limiting issues, engineers should implement rate limiting and size checks on API requests to prevent abuse and mitigate the risk of denial-of-service (DoS) attacks.

CHAPTER 3   SECURITY IN CLOUD-NATIVE APPLICATIONS WITH A SHIFT-LEFT APPROACH

This involves setting limits on the number and size of requests allowed per user or client to ensure that the API infrastructure is not overwhelmed by excessive traffic. Additionally, engineers should monitor traffic patterns and implement automated mechanisms to identify and mitigate attacks quickly, such as temporarily blocking or throttling malicious users or IP addresses.

6. **Injection Flaws**

   APIs must rigorously validate all incoming data to prevent injection attacks, where attackers insert malicious commands into data inputs to manipulate the backend systems.

   Mitigation Strategies: To mitigate Injection Flaws, engineers should implement strict input validation mechanisms to sanitize and validate all user input before processing it. This involves validating input data against predefined rules and rejecting any input that does not meet the specified criteria. Additionally, engineers should use parameterized queries to interact with databases and avoid direct execution of client-side data to prevent injection attacks. By implementing strict input validation measures, engineers can minimize the risk of injection attacks and protect the integrity and security of the API.

7. **Mass Assignment Issues**

   Some frameworks allow developers to automatically bind input data from clients to data models. If not carefully controlled, attackers can exploit this feature to update fields that should be immutable, like user permissions or credentials.

Mitigation Strategies: To address Mass Assignment Issues, engineers should carefully define which properties in the data models can be bound to user inputs explicitly and review all data binding operations for potential vulnerabilities. This involves explicitly specifying the properties that can be modified through user input and restricting access to sensitive fields that should not be updated directly. Additionally, engineers should implement strict validation checks to ensure that only authorized users can modify sensitive data and prevent unauthorized changes to critical system settings. By defining explicit data binding rules and conducting thorough reviews of data binding operations, engineers can minimize the risk of mass assignment vulnerabilities and protect the integrity of the application.

What Is API Security Testing?

API security is about keeping your API safe from bad guys who want to break into it and making sure you build your APIs to be tough against attacks. It's not just a bonus part of your API; it's a whole different thing you need to think about. Making your API secure is more about how you think about security, not just adding it as an extra.

When you're ready to check if your API is secure, you start by laying out all the details about your API. Testers need to know what kind of information the API sends and receives. They use different tools like OpenAPI, Postman, or HAR files to get a clear picture of what's going on with the API.

Securing API Using Pynt

Pynt offers a security testing service for APIs that helps developers and testers ensure their APIs are secure by finding and addressing security issues at any stage of development. This tool is key for building APIs that are reliable and secure from the ground up.

According to the 2023 Postman State of the Art survey, performance and security are what people care about most when they're using an API, just like they did the year before. These two aspects are always at the top of their list.

Pynt is great for making sure your APIs are up to par with security standards. It spots the security gaps in your APIs to strengthen them. Pynt, catching and fixing issues early on is easier, helping to maintain secure and safe APIs. In today's digital age, where online security is crucial, choosing Pynt is a smart move for keeping your APIs solid and reliable.

Working of Pynt

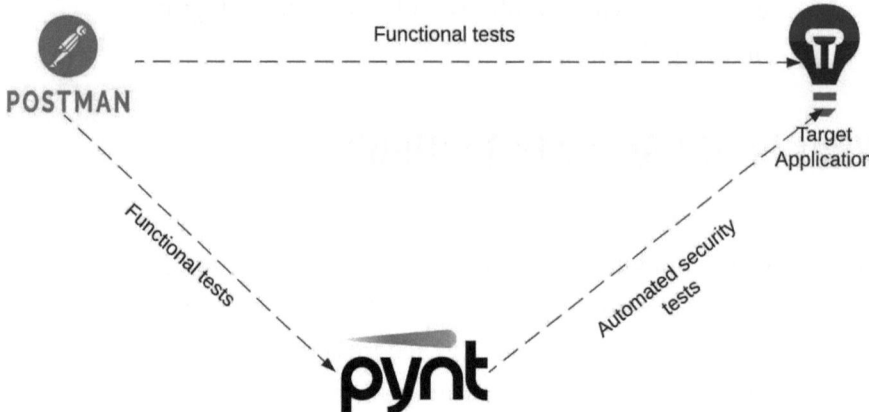

Figure 3-6. *API security using Pynt*

Automated Test Preparation: Pynt streamlines the process of setting up security tests for your APIs. It smartly utilizes your existing setups from platforms like Postman, automating the preparation stage without extra effort on your part.

Seamless Tool Compatibility: Integrating Pynt into your existing workflow is hassle-free. It's designed to work effortlessly with the API testing tools you're already familiar with, such as Postman or Newman, meaning there's no need to switch tools or learn new software.

Intelligent Security Testing: What makes Pynt stand out is its ability to comprehend the purpose and function of your existing tests. It leverages this understanding to craft security tests that are directly relevant to the scenarios covered by your functional tests, ensuring that the security aspect aligns with your API's operational context.

Fast and Precise Feedback: Efficiency is a key feature of Pynt. It delivers the outcomes of your security tests rapidly, ensuring that you don't have to wait long to get the insights you need. This quick turnaround time for results means you can act on the findings promptly, enhancing the security posture of your APIs with minimal delay.

Expanding on this, Pynt's ability to automate and integrate seamlessly makes it a valuable asset in modern API development environments, where speed and accuracy are critical. It ensures that security testing is not a bottleneck but rather a streamlined part of the development process.

CHAPTER 3   SECURITY IN CLOUD-NATIVE APPLICATIONS WITH A SHIFT-LEFT APPROACH

By providing smart, context-aware security testing that aligns with your functional requirements, Pynt helps maintain a high-security standard without slowing down the development cycle, making it an ideal choice for teams looking to balance agility with robust security practices.

Pynt Setup

Before starting with the Pynt solution, it's important to make sure you have the following prerequisites in place:

- **Install Postman on Your Computer:** First, download and install the Postman application. You can find it on Postman's download page (www.postman.com/downloads). Remember, Pynt needs to work with Docker and requires access to your local host, so the web version of Postman won't work for this.

- **Set Up Docker:** Ensure that Docker is installed and active on your machine. If you haven't installed Docker yet, you can download it from the Docker installation guide (https://docs.docker.com/engine/install/)

- **Prepare Your API Test Collection in Postman:** Check that your collection of functional API tests is ready and accessible in your Postman workspace. Run all the APIs and test cases using Postman's collection runner to ensure they are functioning correctly.

- **Configure Environment Variables:** If your API tests depend on specific environment variables, double-check that these are set up correctly in Postman.

CHAPTER 3   SECURITY IN CLOUD-NATIVE APPLICATIONS WITH A SHIFT-LEFT APPROACH

- **Check API Accessibility:** Before you start using Pynt for testing, make sure that the API or service you plan to test is operational and accessible. This is important to ensure that Pynt can interact with it effectively for security testing.

Pynt Security Testing

1. At this point, you should already have the Postman application installed on your computer. Please go ahead and open the application.

2. Now, you need to import the Pynt Collection to use for a dry run. To do this, visit the following link: Pynt Collection on Postman. Once there, create a fork of the collection. For guidance on how to do this, you can refer to the following screenshot.

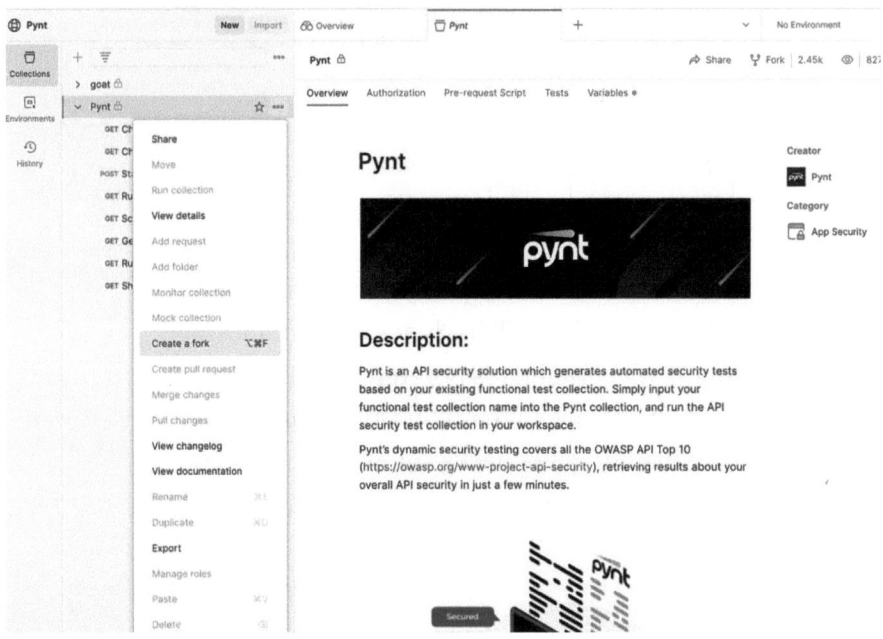

CHAPTER 3   SECURITY IN CLOUD-NATIVE APPLICATIONS WITH A SHIFT-LEFT APPROACH

3. To verify that the Postman app is up and running and Docker is operational, you should run the Pynt Collection. To do this, click on the three dots (…) located on the Pynt Collection in Postman. From the dropdown menu that appears, select the "Run Collection" option. This action is illustrated in the following screenshot.

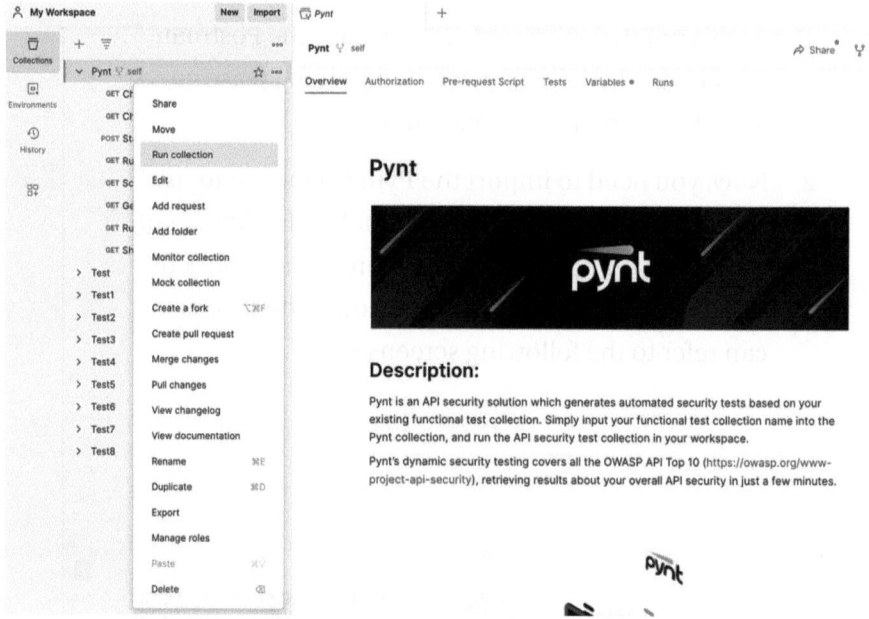

4. If you haven't started Docker yet and you try to run the Pynt CLI, you'll likely see an error message saying "Pynt container is not running." This is because the Pynt CLI relies on Docker to run the Pynt container in the background. To understand this better, you can refer to the following screenshot.

CHAPTER 3   SECURITY IN CLOUD-NATIVE APPLICATIONS WITH A SHIFT-LEFT APPROACH

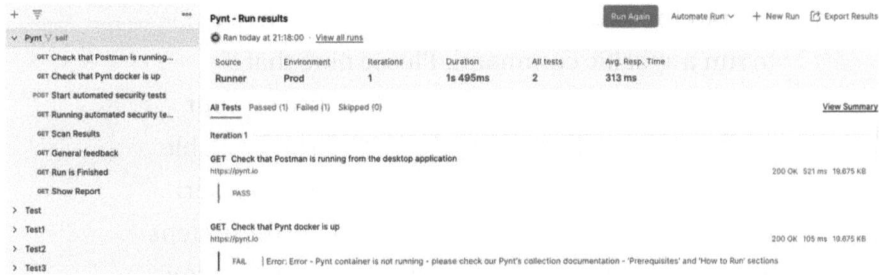

5. First, ensure that Docker is installed on your machine. Installing Docker is quite straightforward. If you need guidance, refer to the link provided in the Prerequisite section.

6. Open the Docker Desktop application and wait until Docker is fully operational. Once Docker Desktop is up and running, you will see the following screen, indicating that it's ready for use.

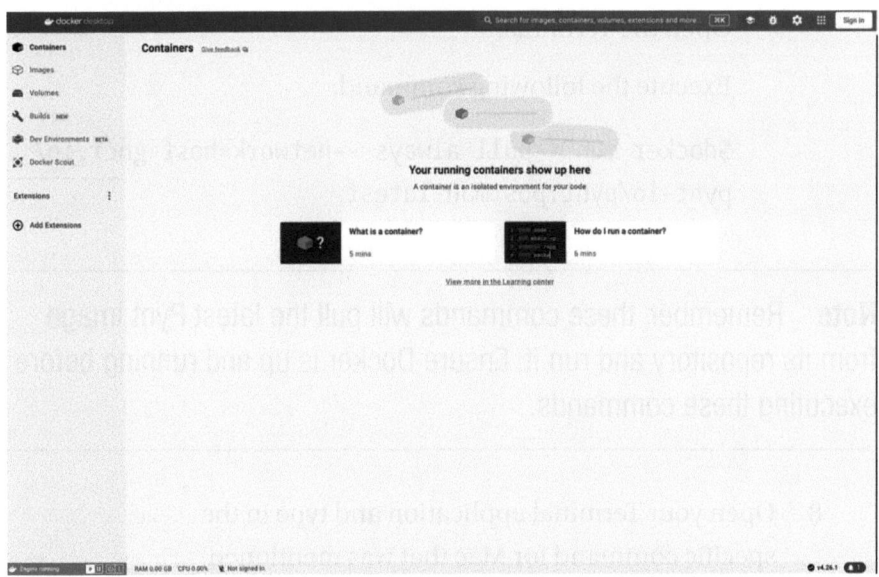

129

7. To start the Pynt Docker container, you'll need to run a specific command. Please note that if the default port number is already in use on your system, you might need to change it to an available one. Here's the command to run the Pynt Docker: To run the Pynt Docker container, follow these steps based on your operating system and Docker setup:

    – **For Docker Desktop on Windows, Mac, or Linux:**

    Open Command Prompt (cmd) on Windows, or Terminal on Mac/Linux.

    Execute the following command:

    ```
    $ docker run -p 5001:5001 --pull always ghcr.io/pynt-io/pynt:postman-latest
    ```

    – **For Docker Engine on Linux:**

    Open the Terminal.

    Execute the following command:

    ```
    $docker run --pull always --network=host ghcr.io/pynt-io/pynt:postman-latest
    ```

Note Remember, these commands will pull the latest Pynt image from its repository and run it. Ensure Docker is up and running before executing these commands.

---

8. Open your Terminal application and type in the specific command for Mac that was mentioned earlier. After running this command in the Terminal, you should see a success message indicating that

the operation has been completed successfully. You can refer to the example shown in the following screenshot.

9. Now that the Pynt Docker container is up and running, you can proceed to execute step 4 again. This step involves running the Pynt collection. Ensure that everything is functioning correctly. If all components are operational, including the Pynt Docker container and the Pynt CLI, you should successfully receive output from the execution of the Pynt collection. This output will indicate that your API security tests are being processed as expected.

10. We need to create a fork of the "goat" project to enhance our understanding. Subsequently, we will set up variables as outlined in the following text. If you're unfamiliar with the process of forking, you can easily learn how by visiting this link: Postman Workspace for Pynt.

CHAPTER 3   SECURITY IN CLOUD-NATIVE APPLICATIONS WITH A SHIFT-LEFT APPROACH

11. Go to the "Variables" section in the "Pynt" collection and enter the needed details in the "CURRENT VALUE" column.

    a. **API-KEY:** Put in your Postman API key here. If you already have one, just type it in. If not, go to this link to make a new one. Remember, you can only copy the API key when you first create it. You don't need to change this unless your API key expires.

    b. **port:** This is the left-side port number you used in the Docker command. The default is 5001.

    c. **YOUR-COLLECTION:** Enter the name or UID of your functional test collection. If you have two collections with the same name, use the UID. This is for Pynt to identify the collection for automated security tests. If you need an example app to test, Pynt offers a "goat" app you can use. Just fork it from Pynt's public workspace then save.

12. Start the "Pynt" collection to obtain the security findings. For instructions on how to run the collection, see step 3. Once you initiate the execution, you'll be able to view the security results for the OWASP-10 categories.

13. Wait for the entire collection to finish executing. Once the execution is complete, you will receive a notification indicating run finished.

14. To view a summary of the results, click on "View Summary." For a detailed report, navigate to the "Pynt" collection and expand it. There, find the final request titled "Show Report" and select "Send." After

sending the request, you can see the full report by choosing the "Visualize" tab located in the lower part of the interface.

Summary

In this chapter, we discussed the importance of security in cloud-native applications and explored the proactive "shift-left" approach to ensure robust protection. As cloud-native applications become increasingly vital in modern software development, it's essential to embed security measures early in the development process.

We emphasized the significance of preemptively addressing vulnerabilities and mitigating the risks of security breaches through the "shift-left" approach. By integrating security throughout the application development life cycle, organizations can effectively protect their cloud-native applications against evolving cyber threats.

Throughout the chapter, we covered various topics essential for securing cloud-native applications comprehensively. We highlighted the critical need for proactive security measures, given the complexity and ever-evolving nature of cyber threats faced by cloud-based applications.

The central concept of "shift-left" was emphasized, stressing the importance of integrating security early in the development process rather than treating it as an afterthought. This approach not only strengthens applications against potential cyberattacks but also ensures compliance with regulations and standards.

Furthermore, we provided insights into implementing these security measures effectively within organizations, including the utilization of specific tools and strategies tailored to the unique challenges of cloud-native environments.

CHAPTER 4

CI/CD Pipeline in Cloud-Native DevOps

"Laugh in the Face of Bugs: CI/CD Pipeline in Cloud-Native DevOps – Making software delivery a stand-up comedy act in the cloud!"

In this chapter, we will explore the simplification of software development through the utilization of Continuous Integration and Continuous Deployment (CI/CD) pipelines. These pipelines facilitate seamless collaboration among developers and expedite the delivery of software.

Imagine CI as the Avengers assembling to put together a software puzzle. They're like Iron Man spotting errors with his tech-savvy suit and Captain America fixing them with his shield – all before things get out of hand. Now, meet Continuous Deployment, the Flash of the coding world, zooming around and automatically delivering the final product faster than you can say "supercalifragilisticexpialidocious."

We will commence by comprehending the essence of CI/CD and its significance. Visualize Continuous Integration as a collective effort to assemble puzzle pieces, identifying and rectifying errors early in the development process. On the other hand, Continuous Deployment automates the distribution of completed work to various destinations. The chapter emphasizes the application of CI/CD pipelines within cloud-based settings, ensuring compatibility with cloud technologies like Amazon Web Services or Microsoft Azure. Practical guidance will be provided on establishing these pipelines, automating testing procedures, and deploying software seamlessly. Additionally, we will delve into aspects of ensuring security, monitoring processes, and adeptly managing errors.

By the conclusion, you will have a comprehensive understanding of leveraging CI/CD pipelines in cloud environments for your software projects. The use of straight forward examples and narratives aims to facilitate a clear understanding, empowering you to enhance your approach to software development.

In this chapter, we will be encompassing the following topics:

- Overview of CI/CD
- Integration of Version Control
- Cloud-Agnostic in CI/CD Pipeline
- Security in CI/CD

Overview of CI/CD

To put it simply, the CI/CD pipeline is like a helpful system that automates how software is delivered. CI/CD stands for Continuous Integration/Continuous Delivery, and it's a way for development teams to deliver their code changes more often and with fewer errors. It uses automation to make things smoother.

Continuous Integration is about developers making small, regular changes to the code and combining them into a shared place. Think of it like a teamwork puzzle – everyone adds their piece regularly, and the system checks to make sure nothing is broken. This automation makes it easier for teams to share changes often, making collaboration better and the software higher quality. Continuous Delivery is like a process that checks for mistakes and puts the team's code changes in a waiting area for further testing.

The CI/CD process is important because it makes deploying software easier and more predictable. It brings order and trust to the software development process, making teams work together better and creating better applications at a lower cost.

DevOps emerged as a response to a crucial problem within the Agile development movement. The challenge was that while Agile developers were creating new applications and code updates more frequently, traditional operations teams faced difficulties in testing and deploying them. This issue counteracted the benefits of swift development. DevOps addresses this by extending Agile principles throughout the entire software development life cycle (SDLC), aiming to enhance the entire workflow through continuous improvement. Exceptional DevOps teams not only experience quicker code iterations and deployments but also achieve a shorter time to market for new concepts, a reduction in bugs, and a more stable infrastructure.

C1/CD Principles

Organizations grappling with improperly implemented continuous integration frequently encounter a cultural obstacle. Although engineers are adept at addressing technical issues, the effective embrace of CI/CD principles demands a substantial cultural shift, which is inherently difficult. Merely introducing a continuous integration tool may address technical aspects, but succeeding with CI/CD requires a transformation in work methods, collaboration, and a more extensive cultural change. Without a shift in the team's culture, the implementation of continuous integration and continuous delivery becomes notably challenging.

Principles of Continuous Integration

1. **Commit to the Mainline:** A crucial aspect of continuous integration is committing changes regularly. While automated builds can be set up to run on every commit, the cultural practice of infrequent commits or prolonged branching undermines the principles. Delayed commits or extended branches make it challenging to identify the source of integration issues if a build breaks.

2. **Maintain a Single-Source Repository:** In intricate applications, developers often create branches off the main trunk, introducing complexity and preventing a unified source of truth. Teams should commit or merge changes to the main trunk at least once a day, ensuring a continuous and unified codebase.

3. **Build Automation:** While many organizations claim to practice CI by scheduling builds, true continuous integration involves testing and validating each build. Automation of the build process is essential for effective CI.

4. **Make Builds Self-testing:** Validating builds involves not only detecting failures but also ensuring that the build product operates as expected. Incorporating fast functional and non-functional testing within the build process is crucial for effective CI.

5. **Build Quickly:** Swift build times are essential to encourage regular changes and prevent large change sets. Quick builds facilitate the isolation of changes, making it easier to identify and address issues promptly.

6. **Test in a Clone:** Validating software in its intended environment is vital for accurate results. Testing in a different environment may lead to misleading outcomes.

7. **Fix Broken Builds Immediately:** Detecting and rectifying problems promptly is critical in CI. Establishing a "stop-the-line" approach, where issues are addressed immediately, prevents downstream complications.

Despite the challenges organizations face in implementing true continuous integration, it's noteworthy how the software development community has embraced modern processes to enhance operational value. Overcoming cultural, emotional, and technical attachments to legacy technologies is a significant hurdle, and achieving a mindset shift is crucial for delivering successful continuous integration.

Principles of Continuous Delivery

1. **Ensure a Consistent and Dependable Process:** Utilize the same release process across all environments. When a feature or enhancement undergoes different processes for integration and QA, issues are prone to arise.

2. **Implement Automation Across the Board:** Automate builds, testing, releases, configuration changes, and other tasks. Manual processes are less repeatable, more susceptible to errors, and less efficient. Automation not only reduces the effort needed to run and monitor processes but also ensures consistent results.

3. **Enforce Version Control for Everything:** Maintain version control for code, configuration, scripts, databases, and documentation. A single, reliable source of truth provides a stable foundation for building processes.

4. **Tackle Challenges Early:** Address time-consuming or error-prone tasks at the outset. Dealing with difficult issues first makes the subsequent tasks likely to be easier to perfect.

5. **Embed Quality in Processes:** Establish short feedback loops to address bugs immediately after their creation. Early detection of issues during post-build tests allows developers to produce higher-quality code faster, reducing the number of problems discovered later in the process.

6. **Define "Done" as Released:** Establish short feedback loops to address bugs immediately after their creation. Looping issues back to developers post-build test enables quicker production of higher-quality code, leading to fewer problems in later, more costly stages of the process.

7. **Shared Responsibility for Everyone:** "It works on my station" is not a valid excuse. Responsibility extends to production. Although cultural change is challenging, having management support and an enthusiastic champion facilitates the process.

8. **Embrace Continuous Improvement:** Out of the initial eight principles of continuous delivery, this one holds the utmost importance for effective automation. Cultivating a culture that seeks continuous improvement is crucial, and automation often serves as the most accessible and effective means toward that goal.

9. **Don't Overlook the Database:** While Agile, source control, and DevOps practices are standard in software development, manual processes persist in database releases. Robust source control and DevOps solutions for databases exist today, offering secure and efficient automation that accelerates feedback loops between developers and DBAs, saving time and reducing costly rework.

CI/CD Pipeline Stages

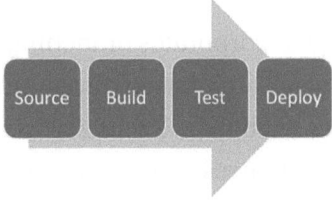

Figure 4-1. CI/CD stages

Source Stage

The source stage is a fundamental step in the CI/CD (Continuous Integration/Continuous Deployment) pipeline, commonly known as the version control stage. It acts as the cornerstone of the entire pipeline, with a primary focus on organizing and storing source code in a controlled and versioned manner.

- **Source Code Management**

    Developers create or modify code on their local machines, and the source code is then uploaded to a version control system like Git or Subversion. This ensures organized code management, allowing easy tracking of changes and providing a safety net for developers to retrieve or revert modifications.

- **Version Control**

    The source stage involves monitoring different versions of the code to facilitate collaboration among developers. Version control systems maintain a history of changes, enabling the review, comparison, and reverting to previous states when necessary.

- **Branching Strategies**

    The source stage incorporates branching strategies such as GitFlow or trunk-based development. These strategies enable developers to work on different features or fixes concurrently without the risk of overwriting each other's work. They support effective feature development, bug fixing, and experimental research without disrupting the primary codebase.

CHAPTER 4 CI/CD PIPELINE IN CLOUD-NATIVE DEVOPS

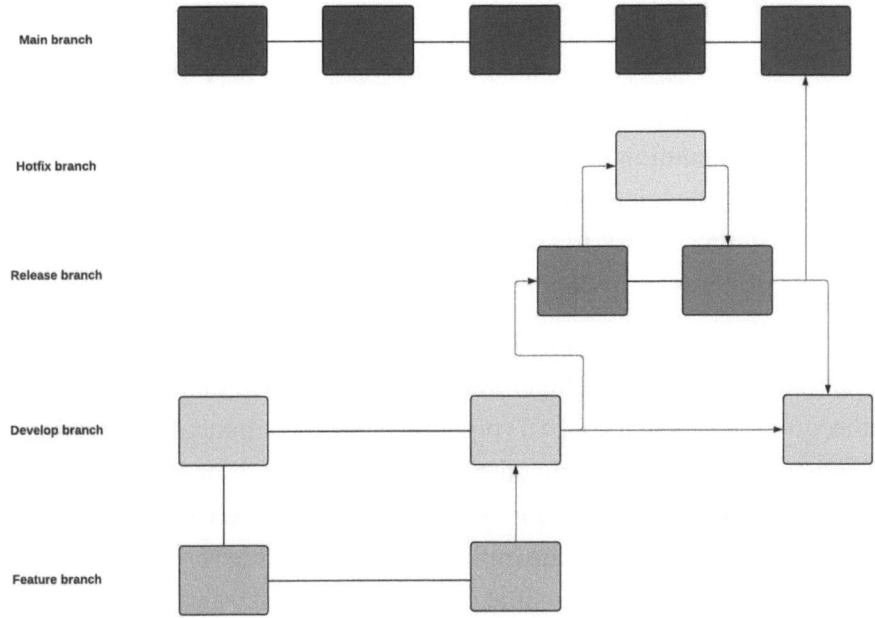

Figure 4-2. *Release branching strategies*

The release branching strategy is a way of organizing work when teams want to put new features into the final product all at once. Unlike another strategy where each feature is added directly to the main project, here, a special branch called "develop" is made to gather all the new features. This branch is where new features are added one by one.

When a feature is finished and checked, it's added to the "develop" branch. When enough features are in the "develop" branch for a new version, a new branch for that version is made.

After testing and fixing any problems in the version branch, it's added to the main project. Usually, the version branch is deleted after it's been added.

- **Pipeline Triggering**

    In the CI/CD context, the source stage is where the pipeline run is activated, typically triggered by a new commit or a pull request. This stage may also include initial quality checks, such as linting or syntax checks, to ensure that the committed code adheres to predefined standards and styles.

The source stage is pivotal in upholding code integrity, fostering collaboration among developers, and establishing a foundation for subsequent stages in the CI/CD pipeline. It ensures meticulous tracking of code modifications, offering the flexibility to retrieve or revert changes as needed. The implementation of branching strategies facilitates efficient parallel development, and the initiation of the pipeline run guarantees that the code undergoes essential processes for quality assurance and deployment in subsequent stages.

Common tools used in the source stage:

- Azure Repos
- GIT
- AWS CodeCommit

Build Stage

The build stage plays a crucial role in the CI/CD (Continuous Integration/Continuous Deployment) pipeline, acting as a pivotal phase where the source code, managed and versioned in the source stage, is transformed into a tangible product ready for execution in a specific environment. This stage is essential for converting the human-readable source code into a deployable artifact, laying the groundwork for the subsequent phases in the pipeline.

- **Code Compilation and Transformation**

  Depending on the application type, this phase involves compiling source code into machine-readable instructions. For example, in Java applications, source code is compiled into bytecode, while applications meant for Docker environments are transformed into Docker images using a Dockerfile.

- **Dependency Resolution and Management**

  The build stage handles dependencies by resolving and integrating external libraries necessary for the application's functionality. This ensures that the application is self-contained and includes all the required components for execution.

- **Language Translation**

  Language translation may be needed to ensure compatibility with the target environment. For instance, translating code from one programming language to another that is better suited for the deployment environment.

- **Asset Bundling**

  This involves bundling various assets, such as images, stylesheets, and scripts, into a format suitable for deployment. Bundling streamlines the deployment process and ensures that all necessary assets are included in the final artifact.

- **Preliminary Testing**

    Preliminary tests, often in the form of unit tests or static code analysis, are carried out to ensure the basic correctness and quality of the code. If these tests fail or issues are identified in the build process, the pipeline may be halted, and developers are notified.

The build stage acts as a critical checkpoint for the CI/CD pipeline. Its successful completion results in the generation of one or more deployable artifacts that can seamlessly progress to subsequent stages, such as testing and deployment. The automation of the build process enhances the efficiency, consistency, and reliability of software development, aligning with the "fail fast" principle by promptly detecting and addressing issues early in the development life cycle.

Common tools used in the build stage:

- Jenkins
- AWS Code Build
- Azure Pipelines
- Gradle

Test Stage

During the testing phase, the application undergoes a thorough automated testing process to ensure that it complies with both functional and non-functional requirements before being released to end-users. This stage encompasses various test types, each targeting different aspects of the application's performance and dependability.

- **Integration Tests**

  Integration tests guarantee the seamless collaboration of various parts within the application. They verify that different modules or features work together as intended, ensuring the proper functioning of the integrated system.

- **Functional Tests**

  Functional tests, often in the form of end-to-end tests or user interface tests, confirm that the application behaves as expected from an end-user's standpoint. This includes testing user interfaces, interactions, and overall functionality to ensure a positive user experience.

- **Performance Tests**

  Performance tests gauge the application's ability to handle anticipated loads, respond swiftly, and remain stable under stress. This type of testing helps identify and address any performance bottlenecks, ensuring efficient performance in real-world scenarios.

- **Security Tests**

  Security tests are conducted to uncover potential vulnerabilities or security risks within the application. This involves checking for weaknesses that could be exploited by malicious entities. Detecting and resolving security issues at this stage contributes to delivering a more secure final product.

The testing phase plays a crucial role in the CI/CD pipeline as it serves as the ultimate checkpoint before deploying the application to production. Through the automation of these tests, developers can consistently and efficiently ensure the reliability, functionality, and security of the application, resulting in a higher-quality software release. If any issues arise during this stage, the CI/CD pipeline can pause, enabling developers to address and rectify problems before the application is made available to end-users.

Common tools used in the test stage:

- Puppeteer
- Jest
- Selenium
- PHPUnit

Deploy Stage

The Deploy stage represents the final phase in the CI/CD (Continuous Integration/Continuous Deployment) pipeline, where the application is launched into the production environment, becoming accessible to end-users. This stage encompasses the seamless transfer of the built and tested software to the server or cloud platform where it will be operational.

- **Deployment Process**

    The deployment process varies depending on the application's nature and the production environment. It may involve actions such as deploying a Docker container to a Kubernetes cluster, updating a web application on a cloud service like AWS or Google Cloud, or simply uploading files to a server.

- **Automation**

    The Deploy stage is anticipated to be entirely automated, reducing the need for manual intervention. Automation promotes consistency and minimizes the risk of human error throughout the deployment process.

- **Post-deployment Tests**

    Following deployment, post-deployment tests or smoke tests are often conducted to ensure that the application operates as expected in the production environment. These tests validate the stability of the deployed software and its adherence to specified requirements.

- **Production Monitoring**

    Once the application is live, continuous monitoring becomes essential to promptly identify and address any issues. Monitoring tools track performance metrics, identify potential bottlenecks, and ensure the ongoing health and stability of the application.

- **Rollback Mechanism**

    In case unexpected problems are identified after deployment, a rollback mechanism allows developers to swiftly return to a previous version. This ensures a quick response to issues without causing prolonged downtime for end-users.

The Deploy stage marks the conclusion of the CI/CD pipeline. By automating the deployment process and incorporating testing and monitoring measures, the Deploy stage aims to guarantee a seamless and dependable transition of the application from development to production. This contributes to the overall efficiency, consistency, and reliability of the software development and release process.

Common tools used in the Deploy stage:

- Chef
- AWS Elastic
- Ansible
- AWS Code Deploy

CI/CD Best Practices in Cloud Native

1. **Unified Source Repository**

    Imagine a scenario where a software development team is working on a project with multiple modules and components. Without a unified source repository, each team member might store their code and related files in different locations or even use disparate version control systems. This can lead to confusion, difficulty in tracking changes, and challenges in collaborating effectively. By centralizing all code, configuration files, and documentation in a single version control system like Git, team members can easily access, review, and contribute to the project. For example, GitHub provides a centralized platform where developers can collaborate on code, track changes, and manage project documentation in a unified repository.

2. **Automation Across the Board**

   Consider a continuous integration/continuous delivery (CI/CD) pipeline for a web application. Automating various steps in the pipeline, such as building, testing, deployment, and monitoring, can greatly enhance efficiency and reduce the likelihood of errors. For instance, whenever a developer pushes code changes to the repository, an automated build process is triggered, which compiles the code, runs automated tests, and generates deployable artifacts. These artifacts are then automatically deployed to a staging environment for further testing and validation. By automating these processes, teams can achieve faster delivery cycles and ensure consistent, high-quality releases.

3. **Consistent Build Processes**

   In a software development project involving multiple developers working on different features, maintaining consistency in the build process is crucial. For example, imagine a team of developers working on a mobile app using React Native. Each developer may have their development environment set up with different versions of Node.js, npm packages, and build tools. By establishing a consistent build process that mirrors the CI/CD pipeline, developers can ensure that their local development environments closely match the production environment. This reduces the risk of compatibility issues and ensures a smoother transition from development to deployment.

4. **Parallelization Implementation**

   Suppose a software development team is running a suite of automated tests as part of their CI/CD pipeline. By parallelizing these tests, they can significantly reduce the overall execution time and accelerate the feedback loop. For example, instead of running all tests sequentially, the team can split them into multiple batches and execute them concurrently on different servers or containers. This allows them to leverage the available computing resources more efficiently and speed up the testing process. As a result, developers receive timely feedback on their code changes, enabling them to iterate quickly and deliver updates faster.

5. **Utilize Build Artifacts**

   Consider a scenario where a team is developing a cloud-based microservices architecture using Docker containers. After each successful build, the application artifacts, such as Docker images, are stored in a centralized repository like Docker Hub or Amazon ECR. These artifacts contain everything needed to deploy the application, including the code, dependencies, and runtime environment. By storing build artifacts in a centralized repository, teams can easily deploy their applications to different environments, such as development, staging, and production, with minimal effort. Additionally, in case of any issues or rollbacks, teams can revert to previous versions of the artifacts stored in the repository.

CHAPTER 4   CI/CD PIPELINE IN CLOUD-NATIVE DEVOPS

6. **Comprehensive Testing Integration**

    Imagine a software development project where a team is building an ecommerce platform. As part of their CI/CD pipeline, they include a variety of automated tests to ensure the quality and reliability of the application. This includes unit tests to verify the functionality of individual components, integration tests to test the interaction between different modules, and end-to-end tests to validate the entire application workflow. By integrating these diverse tests into their pipeline, the team can identify and fix bugs early in the development process, leading to a more stable and robust application.

7. **Effective Management of Environment Configurations**

    Suppose a team is deploying a web application to multiple environments, including development, staging, and production. To ensure consistency across these environments, they use Infrastructure as Code (IaC) tools like Terraform or AWS CloudFormation. With IaC, the team can define and manage their environment configurations in code, allowing them to provision and configure infrastructure resources automatically. For example, they can define the desired state of their infrastructure, including servers, databases, and networking components, using declarative code. This ensures that each environment is provisioned consistently and eliminates manual configuration errors.

8. **Continuous Monitoring and Improvement**

    Consider a scenario where a team is managing a CI/CD pipeline for a cloud-based SaaS application. They use monitoring tools like Prometheus and Grafana to track key metrics such as build times, deployment frequency, and error rates. By continuously monitoring these metrics and gathering feedback from developers, the team can identify bottlenecks and areas for improvement in their pipeline. For example, they may discover that certain stages of the pipeline are taking longer than expected or that certain tests are failing frequently. By iteratively optimizing their pipeline based on this feedback, the team can improve its efficiency and deliver updates more quickly and reliably.

9. **Foster a Collaborative Culture**

    Imagine a software development team working on a project with cross-functional teams, including developers, QA engineers, and operations specialists. To foster collaboration and alignment, the team adopts Agile methodologies like Scrum or Kanban. They hold regular stand-up meetings, sprint planning sessions, and retrospective meetings to encourage open communication and feedback sharing. Additionally, they use collaboration tools like Slack or Microsoft Teams to facilitate real-time communication and document sharing. By fostering a collaborative culture, the team can leverage each other's strengths and expertise to deliver high-quality software more effectively.

10. **Prioritize Security**

    Suppose a team is developing a web application that handles sensitive user data, such as personal information and payment details. To ensure the security of the application, they integrate security checks and scans into their CI/CD pipeline. For example, they use static code analysis tools like SonarQube to identify potential security vulnerabilities in the codebase. They also perform dependency checks to identify any outdated or vulnerable libraries used by the application. By prioritizing security in their pipeline, the team can identify and mitigate security risks early in the development process, reducing the likelihood of security breaches and protecting user data.

Benefits of CI/CD in Cloud-Native DevOps

The pipeline incorporates various toolsets and frameworks designed to assist developers, testers, operations teams, and other project participants in delivering software to end-users. It offers teams additional flexibility to adapt quickly and enhances the overall effectiveness of the software delivery process. While setting up the pipeline may demand time and involve a significant learning curve, the advantages surpass the invested time, expenses, and effort.

Enhanced Efficiency

Advantage: To improve productivity within a CI/CD pipeline, automation plays a crucial role. Especially in scenarios where the review process spans various environments like development, testing, and production, involving multiple commands across diverse domains, automation becomes essential for streamlining these processes.

By automating tasks such as code compilation, testing, deployment, and monitoring, teams can significantly reduce manual effort, minimize errors, and accelerate the delivery of software updates. This enhanced efficiency allows teams to focus more on innovation and value-added activities rather than repetitive, time-consuming tasks, ultimately leading to increased productivity and faster time-to-market for their applications.

Reduced Defect Risk

Advantage: Detecting and addressing defects early in the development process is crucial for ensuring the overall quality of software applications. When defects are identified late in the development cycle or worse, after the software has been released to production, the consequences can be significant. Not only does it require additional time and resources to fix these defects, but it can also lead to user dissatisfaction, a negative impact on the brand's reputation, and potential financial losses.

A CI/CD pipeline addresses this challenge by facilitating more frequent and automated testing of code changes throughout the development process. As developers commit code to the version control system, automated build and testing processes are triggered, allowing for rapid feedback on the quality of the code. By running unit tests, integration tests, and other automated checks as part of the CI process, potential defects can be identified early on, often before they have a chance to propagate further downstream in the development cycle.

Moreover, the continuous deployment aspect of a CI/CD pipeline enables rapid deployment of code changes to production-like environments, where additional testing and validation can occur. This allows teams to catch defects in a realistic environment and address them before they impact end-users.

By embracing a CI/CD approach, organizations can significantly reduce the time and effort required to detect and address defects in their software. This not only leads to higher software quality but also enables faster delivery of features and enhancements to users. Ultimately, by mitigating risks in real-time through continuous testing and deployment, CI/CD pipelines help organizations deliver more reliable and robust software solutions while minimizing the costs and impacts associated with defects.

Accelerated Product Delivery

Advantage: A seamless CI/CD workflow enables multiple daily releases, automating the building, testing, and delivery of features with minimal manual intervention. Tools like Docker, Kubernetes, and Travis CI contribute to achieving this, leading to faster responses to market shifts, security challenges, consumer needs, and financial pressures.

Effective Log Generation

Advantage: Observability is crucial for DevOps, and logging information plays a vital role in this aspect. A CI/CD pipeline generates extensive logging data at every stage of the software development process, aiding in tracking system performance and studying program behavior.

Quick Rollback Capability

Advantage: A distinctive benefit of a CI/CD pipeline is the ability to swiftly and easily rollback code changes in case of issues in the production environment after a release. This ensures rapid deployment of the most recent successful build to avoid disruptions.

Improved Planning

Advantage: A CI/CD pipeline facilitates organizational adaptability to changing economic conditions by maintaining an organized surplus of items and fostering continuous communication with clients.

Efficient Testing and Monitoring

Advantage: Automated testing and continuous monitoring are integral to a CI/CD pipeline, ensuring that test cases are automated, repeated cycles are minimized, and applications perform optimally. It provides the capability to run test suites on each product assembly without client intervention, emphasizing quality delivery.

Cost-Effectiveness

Advantage: The CI/CD pipeline, likened to an assembly unit's delivery pipeline, takes a cost-effective approach to software delivery. With automated testing at each stage, issues can be fixed early, leading to improved code quality and a substantial enhancement in overall Return on Investment (ROI).

Integration of Version Control

Whether you're working on a big or small project with a team or all by yourself, it's crucial to choose the right tools to create great software. These tools help automate things and make your work easier. It doesn't matter if you're a freelancer doing your own thing, part of a team spread out in different places, or part of a small web agency – having a solid system for releasing your work and a version control system is super important. It keeps everything organized and makes sure things run smoothly.

After talking about the distinctions between continuous integration, continuous delivery, and continuous deployment, let's link them together: having a version control system is important for a continuous deployment tool. The great thing is, you can easily connect DeployBot with your Git repositories, whether they're hosted on GitHub, Bitbucket, GitLab, or your server. This makes the whole process straightforward and seamless. Now, let's delve into how version control operates.

Version Control Overview

Whether you're engaged in website development, coding small scripts, or overseeing extensive software projects, having a version control system is invaluable. Also referred to as revision control or source control, it keeps a record of and manages changes to files and folders. Importantly, it enables you to trace the history of modifications and revert to a previous version if necessary. In collaborative environments, it is essential to resolve editing conflicts among multiple developers working on the same project.

Without delving too deeply into Git, one notable feature is branches. The system adeptly handles different versions of files on separate branches, facilitating collaboration. Creating development branches allows team members to work on new features without jeopardizing the stability of the main version. Once tested and reviewed, merging changes into the master branch is a straightforward process.

By utilizing hosting platforms like GitHub, Bitbucket, or GitLab, projects, along with their entire history, are securely backed up online. In team environments, a VCS is not just a luxury but a necessity, eliminating the inconveniences of shared folders and the risk of accidental overwrites. Team members can collaborate on any file, and the changes can be merged into a common version later.

The most important thing is to keep your code organized and safe. Every change you make to the code should be securely stored in a special system called Version Control.

There are a few tools out there, and Git is one of the most popular ones.

1. Concurrent Versions System (CVS)
2. Distributed workflow
3. Make sure the code stays safe from mistakes or bad intentions

Characteristic of Git

- It's good at handling changes in the code without making things slow.
- Everyone working on the code has their copy of the history.

- When people make changes, they can prove it's really them.
- The history of changes is like a chain, so if you try to change something, it shows.

CI/CD Build Tool Implementation

The next thing needed for CI/CD is a Build Tool. This tool manages the application's source code and automatically creates the desired software. The specific steps and the tools used for building software depend on the technology stack chosen. For example, here are the steps for building a Java application.

1. Generate .java files from the configuration
2. Source code compilation from .java to .bytecode
3. Test code to bytecode compilation
4. Run unit tests
5. Bundle .class files into a JAR archive
6. If required, save the JAR in an Artifact Repository Manager
7. If necessary, label the code appropriately in the Version Control System

To set up the sequence of actions in our example, various build tools can be utilized, such as Ant, the cross-platform XML-based predecessor to all Java build tools, and Maven, a widely used declarative XML-based tool leaning toward convention over configuration.

Cloud-Agnostic in CI/CD Pipeline

In the realm of cloud-based CI/CD setups, we can distinguish between two main types:

Public Managed Cloud CI/CD Suites: These solutions come pre-packaged with a ready-to-use CI/CD pipeline. Users are spared the intricacies of configuring or managing any software or infrastructure. Examples of such platforms include GitLab SaaS and Azure Pipelines.

On-Prem Cloud CI/CD Installations: Alternatively, users have the option to install CI/CD software on cloud server instances, such as those offered by AWS EC2 or Azure Virtual Machines. While this approach eliminates the need to manage host infrastructure, users are still responsible for tasks like installation, configuration, and ongoing management of the CI/CD software.

Irrespective of the cloud type CI/CD has the following advantages:

Easy Setup: The setup process is expedited and simplified, especially with fully managed CI/CD suites that eliminate the need to prepare host servers.

Reliability: Cloud-based servers typically experience less downtime compared to on-premises infrastructure, enhancing the overall reliability of a cloud-based CI/CD platform.

Scalability: Scaling up the CI/CD pipeline, especially when expanding to build additional applications, is more straightforward in the cloud. This involves deploying additional infrastructure, a task that proves more challenging on-premises due to the acquisition and configuration of physical infrastructure.

Deployment: Running the CI/CD suite and hosting applications in the same cloud environment streamlines the deployment of new application releases. Unlike on-premises suites, there's no need to upload the application to the cloud before deployment, resulting in time savings and efficiency.

CI/CD Pipeline Using Jenkins

I'll show you how to make a simple CI/CD pipeline using Jenkins. But before we start, it's important to check that Jenkins is set up right with all the dependencies. Also, it helps if you have a basic idea of how Jenkins works. For our example, we're using Jenkins on a Mac environment. So, let's get started and go through the steps together. Grab the installers or step.

If you aim to start using Jenkins, check the Installing Jenkins section for instructions on how to install Jenkins on the platform of your choice.

Step 1

Sign into Jenkins and select "New Item"

CHAPTER 4   CI/CD PIPELINE IN CLOUD-NATIVE DEVOPS

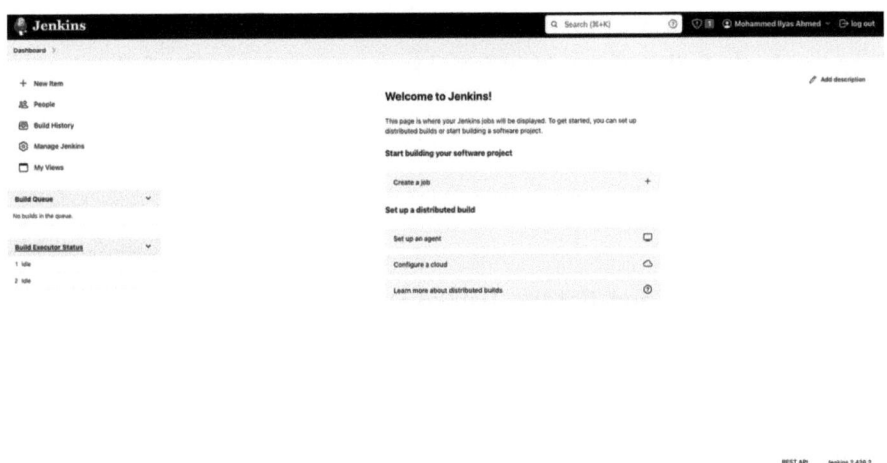

Step 2

Choose the "Pipeline" option from the menu, give a name to the pipeline, and click "Ok."

Step 3

Go to the pipeline configuration screen for setting up the pipeline. Here, you can set build triggers and customize different options. The essential aspect is the "Pipeline Definition" section, where you can define the stages of the pipeline. It's important to mention that Pipeline supports both declarative and scripted syntaxes and uses the following sample script.

```
pipeline {
    agent any
    stages {
        stage('Cloud-Native DevOps: Building Scalable and
        Reliable Applications') {
            steps {
                echo 'Cloud-Native DevOps: Building Scalable
                and Reliable Applications'
            }
        }
    }
}
```

Once the script is configured select "Apply" and "Save."

CHAPTER 4 CI/CD PIPELINE IN CLOUD-NATIVE DEVOPS

Step 4

To execute the pipeline, select "Build Now." This will lead to the execution of the pipeline stages, and you'll see the outcome in the "Stage View" section. We have configured only one stage in this instance, as shown here.

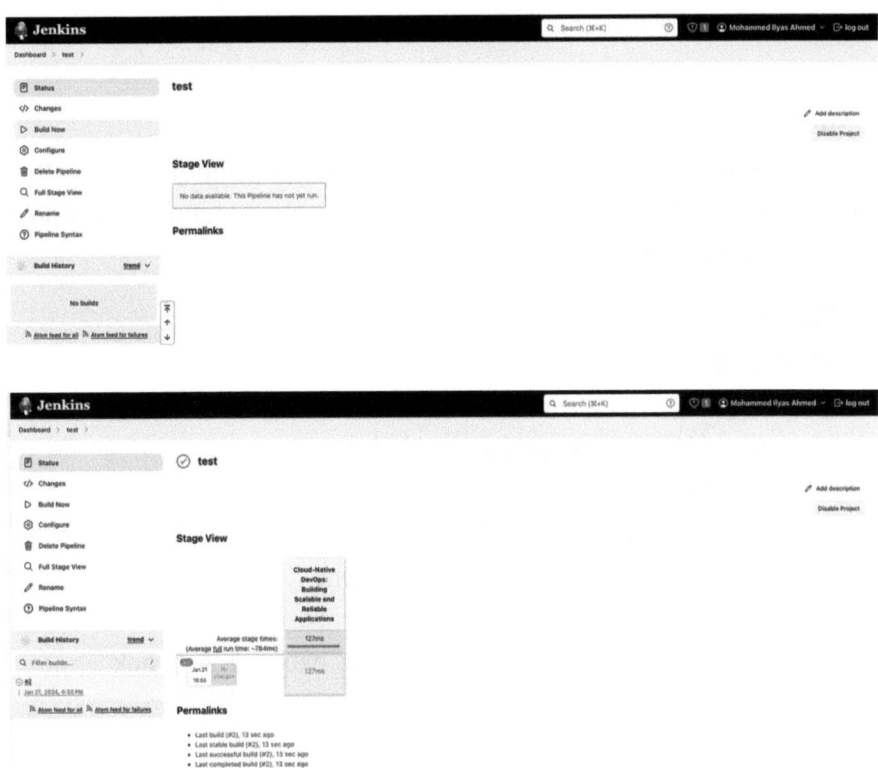

We can ensure that the pipeline ran successfully by examining the console output detailing the build process.

CHAPTER 4   CI/CD PIPELINE IN CLOUD-NATIVE DEVOPS

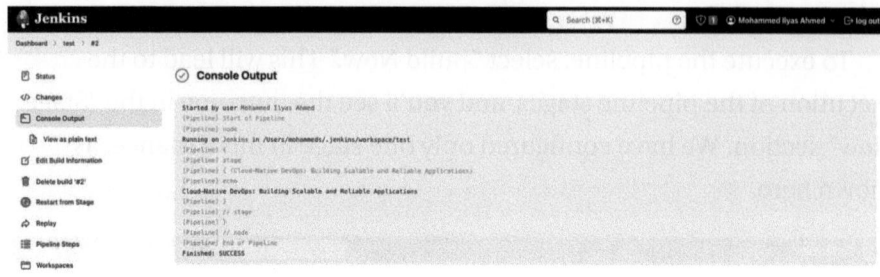

Step 5

Let's enhance the pipeline by incorporating two additional stages. To do this, select the "Configure" option and modify the pipeline definition as per the following code block.

```
pipeline {
    agent any
    stages {
        stage('First execution #1') {
            steps {
                echo ' Cloud-Native DevOps: Building Scalable
                and Reliable Applications '
                sleep 10
                echo 'This is the First execution block'
            }
        }
        stage('Second execution #2') {
            steps {
                echo 'This is the second execution block'
            }
        }
    }
}
```

CHAPTER 4 CI/CD PIPELINE IN CLOUD-NATIVE DEVOPS

After saving the changes, trigger the build by selecting "Build Now" to run the updated pipeline. When it finishes successfully, check the console output.

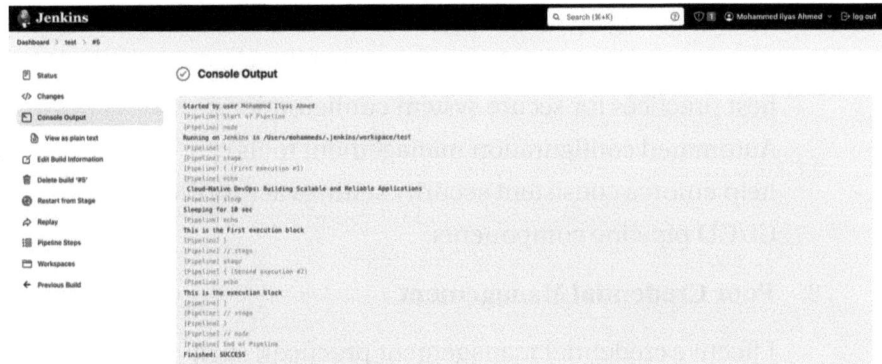

Security in CI/CD

Typically, the key stages of a CI/CD pipeline don't prioritize security. Development teams often build, test, and deploy applications without ensuring security at each step of the CI/CD process. However, neglecting to include security in the CI/CD process exposes you to various risks. Your application might inherently lack security, or you might end up spending time fixing security issues later in the software development life cycle (SDLC). Security should be seamlessly woven into the software delivery workflow, not treated as a separate process.

A growing trend in DevOps that tackles this issue and streamlines the detection and resolution of security issues is DevSecOps. This approach integrates security into the core of DevOps, fostering collaboration among developers, engineers, and security teams. Integrating security into the CI/CD pipeline typically involves including protective measures and security checks at each stage of the pipeline.

CHAPTER 4 CI/CD PIPELINE IN CLOUD-NATIVE DEVOPS

Threats in CI/CD

1. **Misconfiguration**

   Part of managing misconfiguration involves regularly auditing configurations and following best practices for secure system configurations. Automated configuration management tools can help enforce consistent security settings across the CI/CD pipeline components.

2. **Poor Credential Management**

   Effective credential management practices, such as regularly rotating credentials and securely storing secrets, can be automated using credential management tools and solutions. Additionally, implementing role-based access controls (RBAC) can automate access permissions based on predefined roles.

3. **Exploit of Dependency**

   Automated dependency scanning tools can help identify vulnerabilities in code dependencies, and integration with the CI/CD pipeline can automatically trigger alerts or remediation actions. Continuous monitoring of dependency repositories can also help detect and block suspicious or malicious packages.

4. **Poisoned Pipeline Execution (PPE)**

   Implementing automated code review processes as part of the CI/CD pipeline can help detect and prevent malicious code injections. Automated pipeline validation checks can also ensure that pipeline configurations adhere to security policies and standards.

5. **Poor Identity and Access Management (IAM)**

    IAM solutions with automated provisioning and de-provisioning capabilities can streamline user access management across the CI/CD pipeline. Additionally, integrating IAM solutions with identity governance tools can automate identity life-cycle management and access reviews.

6. **Third-Party Service Consumption**

    Automated third-party risk assessment tools can help evaluate the security posture of third-party services accessing the CI/CD pipeline. Integration with identity and access management solutions can automate access controls and permissions for third-party services.

7. **Weak Artifact Validation**

    Automated artifact validation tools can verify the integrity and authenticity of artifacts before they are deployed in the CI/CD pipeline. Integration with artifact repositories and CI/CD platforms can automate artifact scanning and validation processes.

8. **Lack of Adequate Visibility and Logging**

    Automated logging and monitoring solutions can capture and analyze logs from various CI/CD pipeline components in real-time. Integration with security information and event management (SIEM) systems can automate threat detection and response workflows based on predefined security policies.

9. **Weak Pipeline-Based Access Controls (PBAC)**

   Automation of access control policies and permissions management can ensure consistent enforcement of access controls across the CI/CD pipeline. Role-based access control (RBAC) solutions can automate access provisioning and authorization based on predefined roles and responsibilities.

10. **Lack of Effective Flow Control Mechanism**

    Implementing automated approval workflows and gatekeeping mechanisms can enforce flow control in the CI/CD pipeline. Integration with version control systems and issue-tracking tools can automate code review and approval processes based on predefined criteria.

Automated Tools for Securing CI/CD Pipeline

Static Application Security Testing (SAST)

Static Application Security Testing (SAST) is a way of testing that looks at the actual source code and binaries of your software to find potential security problems. It's like a white-box test because it needs access to your source code, aiming to make your application more secure.

Usually, you use special SAST software that scans and analyzes your code. After the scan is done, you get a detailed report showing the security issues in your application and the specific lines of code that need fixing. Using SAST on your project helps make your application less vulnerable. However, there are some downsides to consider. Let's explore the pros and cons of SAST. Although SAST tools have a reputation for generating numerous alerts for minor software flaws and unexploitable defects,

CHAPTER 4   CI/CD PIPELINE IN CLOUD-NATIVE DEVOPS

as well as for identifying only specific types of bugs, they remain vital in any secure development life cycle. Integration into the development environment helps prevent developers from making critical security errors, guiding them to avoid similar mistakes in the future.

To incorporate automated code checking into the development cycle, it's essential to consider how well a SAST tool integrates with the company's existing development environments. Most tools support major web languages like Java and .Net, and they should seamlessly plug into common integrated development environments (IDEs).

While modern application security testing tools are becoming more comprehensive, they still require developers and security professionals to identify false positives. Striking a balance between the depth of testing and the need to avoid excessive false positives is crucial, especially for companies following Agile or DevOps models. The efficiency of static analysis tools in daily development may be impacted by the time it takes to run and the effort required to weed out false positives.

Limitations

1. Unable to identify issues during runtime
2. Not effective in monitoring problems related to user input
3. Faces challenges with libraries and frameworks commonly used in modern applications
4. Needs access to the source code

Dynamic Application Security Testing (DAST)

DAST, also known as Black Box Testing, involves scanning the security of an application while it is actively running. DAST tools conduct automated scans, mimicking different attacks to identify vulnerabilities and areas for enhancement.

CHAPTER 4 CI/CD PIPELINE IN CLOUD-NATIVE DEVOPS

The decision to prioritize static or dynamic analysis tools depends on the context of your organization. Static analysis tools provide developers with feedback and education simultaneously, while dynamic analysis tools offer a quick win for security teams by promptly identifying exploitable vulnerabilities.

In most scenarios, it is advisable to utilize both types of tools. Static and dynamic analysis tools integrate into different stages of the development process. Run static tools as frequently as practical, providing feedback directly to developers. This approach enables managers and the security team to monitor the progress of developers in resolving issues. On the other hand, dynamic analysis tools (DAST) should be employed less frequently and typically by dedicated security and quality assurance professionals. Even in Agile and DevOps development approaches, DAST can be beneficial. Dynamic scanning is applied after obtaining a runtime version of the software, often conducted by QA teams. In a Scrum team, a designated QA team within each sprint may handle dynamic scanning, distinct from the developers.

Using dynamic analysis to identify assets is a crucial step. Before implementing a DAST process, ensure you are aware of the applications running on your network. Integrating network scanning into the DAST process helps security teams discover unknown and rogue applications, enhancing visibility. Understanding the status of software security involves determining the number of web applications in operation, addressing a common issue where companies may lack awareness of all their running applications. This awareness is vital to prevent vulnerabilities in undiscovered websites from leading to potential compromises in the future.

Limitations

1. Demands a functional application for testing
2. Requires specialized testing infrastructure and customizations

3. Typically conducted in the later stages of the software development cycle, often due to performance issues

4. Does not encompass all code paths

Interactive Application Security Testing (IAST)

IAST tools combine the best of SAST and DAST approaches, overcoming their limitations with a new approach known as interactive application security testing (IAST), or "glass-box." They work dynamically while the application is running, scanning the code like SAST, and are especially useful during the quality testing stage alongside functional testing.

Limitations

1. Tools are typically proprietary, leading to a reliance on support from specific suppliers.

2. Unlike SAST, IAST does not examine each line of code.

3. There is limited support for various languages and technologies.

Securing a CI/CD Pipeline: Recommended Approaches

1. **Threat Modeling**

    In the CI/CD process within a DevSecOps cycle, threat modeling plays a crucial role. It involves identifying potential threats, security issues, and vulnerabilities, and then devising techniques or countermeasures to prevent, address, and mitigate them. The threat modeling process typically consists of six steps.

- Identifying assets and dependencies
- Implementing security controls
- Identifying threats
- Analyzing attack surface and attack vectors
- Establishing security goals
- Validating and mitigating threats

2. **Network Security**

    Securing your network is as crucial as fortifying the security of your CI/CD pipeline. If your network lacks security or harbors any risks, all the efforts invested in CI/CD security will be rendered ineffective. Network security encompasses a range of aspects such as firewall protection, network isolation, VPN, email security, Data Loss Prevention (DLP), sandboxing, Intrusion Detection System (IDS), Intrusion Prevention System (IPS), and more.

3. **Secure Authentication**

    Authentication is the process of confirming the identity of a user, device, or application. Similar to an intruder attempting to exploit the entrance to your home, a weak authentication process can be easily circumvented by malicious attackers. Common attack methods include brute force attacks, dictionary attacks, password spraying, and credential stuffing, all favored by attackers.

Access control is a security approach that determines who is granted access and to what extent. Despite being integral, Broken Access Control and Authentication Failure are often overlooked, as indicated by their inclusion in the OWASP Top 10 list. Through access control, one can manage access privileges for users, processes, and applications. Granting elevated privileges to unnecessary resources creates a significant vulnerability, allowing attackers to compromise all data and systems by bypassing the authentication of a low-level user/API with high access privileges.

Methods like multi-factor authentication (MFA), stringent credential policies, approval-based access privileges, need-to-know restrictions, and application vulnerability scanning significantly contribute to maintaining robust security.

4. **Logging**

    Logging is a vital practice that involves maintaining records of events, issues, access, and other activities in your system. This not only aids in the retrospective process but also enables the analysis of logs to pinpoint the cause of any issue and promptly seek resolution. In the event of security breaches, log analysis allows the security team to identify and understand all user, authentication, and access control activities.

5. **Auditing**

   Security auditing, when conducted, can yield advantages as it allows security engineers to examine and reflect on all security-related issues and events. This includes analyzing the root causes, understanding how the issues were mitigated, and determining the necessary steps to prevent similar incidents in the future.

6. **Monitoring**

   A component of observability, monitoring plays a crucial role in upholding the security of your CI/CD pipeline. Critical areas for monitoring encompass system resources, network traffic, application health, individual components/tools, and application delivery status.

7. **Remediation**

   In the event of a security breach in your CI/CD pipeline, have a set plan. Maintain Security and Incident Response SOPs (Standard Operating Procedures) for a swift and organized response. Prioritize actions such as temporarily revoking admin-level access, continuous log tracing, using IDS, and virtually isolating systems for analysis. Integrate remediation actions into SOPs for future prevention and safeguarding systems.

8. **Observability**

   Observability involves utilizing metrics to assess the system's health and analyze the root causes of issues, whereas monitoring captures and presents data in a visualized format. Essentially, monitoring reveals what is wrong with a system, while observability goes further to explain why something is wrong.

Summary

This chapter focuses on "CI/CD Pipeline in Cloud-Native DevOps" which is distinctly focused on elucidating the fundamental principles governing Continuous Integration (CI) and Continuous Delivery/Deployment (CD) within the context of cloud-native applications. It delves into the intricacies of the various stages encompassed by the CI/CD pipeline, offering readers a thorough comprehension of the core concepts essential for efficient software delivery. Notably, the chapter places a significant emphasis on the integration of version control, particularly leveraging Git and platforms like GitHub. It explores collaborative strategies such as branching, pull requests, and code review processes, underscoring their importance in the software development life cycle.

A key highlight of this chapter is the dedicated attention to incorporating cloud agnostics in the CI/CD pipeline. This involves a nuanced exploration of Cloud-Native architecture, microservices, and container orchestration technologies, facilitating adaptability across diverse cloud environments. Importantly, the chapter addresses the critical aspect of security in the CI/CD pipeline, providing insights into vulnerability scanning, code analysis, compliance checks, secrets management, and robust authentication and authorization measures. The chapter's distinctive focus on the remediation of security threats underscores its commitment to equipping practitioners with the knowledge and practices needed to build secure and resilient CI/CD pipelines in the dynamic landscape of Cloud-Native DevOps.

CHAPTER 5

Open-Source Tools for Cloud-Native DevOps

"Open-Source Tools: The jesters of Cloud-Native DevOps!"

In this chapter on we delve into the essential components that streamline and enhance the software development life cycle in cloud-native environments. The chapter begins with an exploration of the foundational principles of Cloud-Native DevOps, emphasizing the critical role of automation in achieving efficiency and scalability. The spotlight then turns to specific open-source tools that have gained prominence in this domain. Argo, a powerful workflow management tool, takes center stage, demonstrating its capabilities in streamlining complex processes. Kubeflow Pipelines is introduced as a dedicated solution for enhancing data flow in machine learning workflows, providing insights into its features and integration capabilities. Additionally, the chapter explores other orchestration tools, comparing their strengths and use cases to help readers make informed decisions based on their specific needs.

Building upon the tool-specific discussions, the chapter transitions into broader considerations for Cloud-Native DevOps tooling. Best practices are highlighted to guide readers in the selection and implementation of these tools, ensuring scalability and flexibility within their DevOps practices. The narrative unfolds with a focus on addressing challenges commonly faced in Cloud-Native DevOps tooling, providing strategies and solutions to overcome obstacles. Real-world case studies exemplify successful implementations, offering practical insights into the application of these tools in various scenarios. As the chapter concludes, it takes a forward-looking approach by examining emerging trends in Cloud-Native DevOps tools, offering predictions on the future evolution of DevOps practices in cloud-native environments. The importance of continuous adaptation and improvement in tooling practices is emphasized, paving the way for readers to stay ahead in the dynamic landscape of Cloud-Native DevOps.

In this chapter, we will be encompassing the following topics:

- Overview of Open-Source Tools in Cloud Native
- Argo Streamlining Workflows
- Kubeflow Pipelines
- Future Trends in Cloud-Native DevOps Tools

Overview of Open-Source Tools in Cloud Native

By now, you're likely familiar with the term "cloud native." When the term is mentioned, does your mind immediately associate it with "Kubernetes" as if it's the superstar of the cloud realm? You're not alone in this perception! While Kubernetes rightfully holds the spotlight, it's essential to recognize that in the expansive cloud-native domain, additional players are contributing to the ensemble – it's not a one-person show! Let's take a moment to acknowledge the other projects harmonizing within the CNCF landscape, collectively creating a symphony of technological brilliance in the cloud-native space!

CHAPTER 5   OPEN-SOURCE TOOLS FOR CLOUD-NATIVE DEVOPS

The cloud-native landscape comprises a variety of tools, services, and platforms shaping the present cloud-native ecosystem. The current list includes numerous well-known DevOps tools, categorized according to their functionality and their position within the cloud-native stack layers. Instead of listing every individual tool, the following sections will delve into each category, offering insights into some of the most widely used tools in each.

1. **Observability and Analysis**

   These tools focus on providing insights into the performance, health, and behavior of applications and infrastructure within a cloud-native environment. They collect, store, and analyze various types of data, such as metrics, logs, and traces, to help developers and operators understand system behavior and diagnose issues.

   - **Kubernetes**

     Kubernetes is a container orchestration platform that automates the deployment, scaling, and management of containerized applications. It allows developers to abstract away the underlying infrastructure and focus on building and running applications. For example, a company running a microservices architecture can use Kubernetes to deploy and scale their services across multiple cloud environments, ensuring high availability and resilience.

- **Jaeger**

    Imagine a large ecommerce platform consisting of multiple microservices handling various functions like authentication, product catalog, payment processing, and order fulfillment. With Jaeger, developers can instrument each microservice to capture tracing data as requests flow through the system. For example, when a user places an order, Jaeger traces the request from the frontend service through the authentication service, product catalog service, payment service, and finally to the order fulfillment service. Developers can use Jaeger's web-based interface to visualize these traces, identifying any bottlenecks or latency issues along the way. For instance, they might discover that the payment service is experiencing high response times, leading to delayed order processing. By pinpointing the root cause of the issue, developers can then optimize the payment service to improve overall system performance and enhance user experience.

- **Prometheus**

    Prometheus is a monitoring and alerting tool designed for cloud-native environments. It collects time-series data metrics from monitored targets, stores them locally, and enables querying, visualization, and alerting based on this data. For instance, a DevOps team can use Prometheus to monitor the CPU and memory usage of their application containers, set up alerts for abnormal behavior, and troubleshoot performance issues.

CHAPTER 5 OPEN-SOURCE TOOLS FOR CLOUD-NATIVE DEVOPS

2. **Continuous Integration and Continuous Delivery (CI/CD)**

   Continuous Integration and Continuous Delivery (CI/CD) is a software development practice that involves frequently integrating code changes into a shared repository and automatically deploying those changes to production environments. For example, in a CI/CD pipeline, whenever a developer pushes code changes to a repository, automated tests are triggered to ensure the integrity of the codebase. Once the tests pass, the changes are automatically deployed to staging or production environments, enabling rapid and reliable software delivery.

   - **Argo**

     Argo is a set of tools for running and managing continuous integration and continuous delivery (CI/CD) pipelines on Kubernetes. It allows developers to define complex workflows as code, automate the deployment of applications, and manage the entire software delivery process. For example, a development team can use Argo to automate the testing, building, and deployment of their applications to different environments, such as staging and production.

   - **Keptn**

     Keptn is an open-source control plane for continuous delivery and automated operations. It helps developers automate tasks like deploying, testing, and scaling applications. For instance, Keptn can be used to automatically trigger performance tests whenever a new version of an application is deployed. Moreover, it supports various use cases including blue-green deployments, canary releases, and auto-remediation of issues in production environments. Its flexibility and extensibility make it a powerful tool for modern DevOps practices, ensuring smooth and efficient software delivery pipelines.

- **OpenGitOps**

    OpenGitOps is a methodology that leverages GitOps principles and open-source tools to manage infrastructure and application deployments. It emphasizes using Git repositories as the single source of truth for declarative infrastructure and application definitions. For example, with OpenGitOps, Kubernetes manifests, Terraform configurations, and application code are all stored in Git repositories, enabling version control, collaboration, and automated workflows. Tools like Argo CD and Flux are commonly used in OpenGitOps workflows to automate the synchronization of Git repositories with the desired state of the infrastructure and applications running in Kubernetes clusters. This approach promotes transparency, repeatability, and scalability in managing cloud-native environments.

3. **Policy and Governance**

    Policy and governance in software development refer to establishing rules, standards, and procedures to ensure compliance, security, and efficiency throughout the development life cycle. For instance, an organization might implement access control policies to regulate who can access certain resources or enforce coding standards to maintain code quality. Additionally, governance frameworks like ITIL or COBIT provide guidelines for managing IT processes and ensuring alignment with business objectives. These policies and frameworks help mitigate risks, promote transparency, and facilitate smoother collaboration within development teams.

- **Open Policy Agent (OPA)**

    OPA is a policy engine that helps organizations enforce policy-as-code across the cloud-native stack. It provides a unified language and framework for defining and enforcing policies related to security, compliance, and governance. For instance, a company can use OPA to define and enforce access control policies for their Kubernetes clusters, ensuring that only authorized users and applications can access sensitive resources.

4. **Service Mesh**

    A service mesh is a dedicated infrastructure layer that facilitates communication, observability, and security between services in a microservices architecture. It abstracts communication complexities away from individual services and provides a centralized control plane for managing service-to-service communication within a distributed system.

- **Envoy**

  Envoy is a high-performance, open-source proxy designed for cloud-native applications. It is often used as a data plane proxy in service mesh architectures like Istio and Kuma. Envoy handles traffic routing, load balancing, and observability for microservices, improving reliability and security. For example, a company deploying microservices can use Envoy to implement traffic management policies, secure communication between services, and collect telemetry data for analysis.

- **Linkerd**

  Linkerd is a service mesh solution that provides secure, reliable communication between services in a cloud-native environment. It includes a control plane for configuration management and a data plane proxy for handling traffic. Linkerd helps developers implement features like mutual TLS encryption, traffic splitting, and distributed tracing. For example, a team building a distributed application can use Linkerd to ensure that services communicate securely and reliably, even as the application scales.

5. **Package Management**

   Package management refers to the process of installing, upgrading, configuring, and removing software packages on a computer system. It involves tools and systems for managing dependencies, versioning, and distribution of software components.

CHAPTER 5   OPEN-SOURCE TOOLS FOR CLOUD-NATIVE DEVOPS

- **Helm**

    Helm is a package manager for Kubernetes that simplifies the process of deploying, managing, and upgrading applications. It uses charts, which are packages of pre-configured Kubernetes resources, to define the structure of an application. Helm allows developers to share and reuse application configurations, making it easier to deploy complex applications. For example, a company can use Helm to deploy a WordPress website with a MySQL database, including all the necessary configurations and dependencies.

6. **Edge Computing**

    Edge computing is a distributed computing paradigm that brings computation and data storage closer to the location where it is needed, that is, the "edge" of the network. Instead of relying solely on centralized data centers, edge computing utilizes resources deployed at or near the source of data generation, such as IoT devices, sensors, or edge servers.

    - **KubeEdge**

        KubeEdge extends Kubernetes capabilities to edge computing environments, allowing organizations to manage containerized workloads at the edge. It addresses the unique challenges of edge nodes, such as limited resources and intermittent connectivity, by providing edge computing features like local data processing and device management. For example, a company deploying IoT devices can use KubeEdge to run machine learning models locally, process sensor data in real-time, and synchronize data with the cloud.

- **OpenYurt**

    OpenYurt is an open-source project that extends the capabilities of Kubernetes to the edge computing environment. It enables the seamless management of Kubernetes clusters across edge devices, allowing for consistent deployment and orchestration of containerized workloads. OpenYurt provides features such as node management, application life-cycle management, and edge-specific optimizations, making it ideal for deploying edge computing applications. For example, it allows Kubernetes clusters to be deployed on IoT devices, edge servers, or remote locations, enabling organizations to leverage Kubernetes' scalability and flexibility at the edge of the network. Its integration with cloud-native tools and technologies makes it a powerful solution for edge computing scenarios.

7. **Storage Orchestration**

    Storage orchestration refers to the automated management and provisioning of storage resources in a computing environment. It involves coordinating storage resources, such as disks, volumes, and file systems, to meet the demands of applications and services efficiently. Storage orchestration aims to optimize storage utilization, improve performance, ensure data availability, and simplify management tasks through automation.

- **Rook**

    Rook is a storage orchestrator for Kubernetes that automates the deployment and management of cloud-native storage solutions. It supports various storage types, including file, block, and object storage, and provides features like replication, snapshotting, and encryption. For example, a company can use Rook to deploy a distributed file system for storing application data, ensuring high availability and durability.

8. **Distributed Databases**

    Distributed databases are systems that store data across multiple nodes or servers, allowing for horizontal scalability, fault tolerance, and high availability. These databases distribute data processing and storage tasks across multiple nodes in a network, rather than relying on a single centralized server.

    - **TiKV**

        TiKV is a distributed key-value store designed for cloud-native environments. It provides horizontal scalability, strong consistency, and low-latency access to data, making it suitable for high-throughput and low-latency applications. For example, a company building a real-time analytics platform can use TiKV to store and retrieve large volumes of data quickly and efficiently, enabling fast data processing and analysis.

- **SchemaHero**

    SchemaHero is an open-source tool designed to simplify database schema management within Kubernetes environments. It allows developers and operators to define, version, and automate the deployment of database schemas using Kubernetes-native resources. For instance, with SchemaHero, database schemas can be expressed declaratively as Custom Resource Definitions (CRDs) and managed alongside other Kubernetes resources in Git repositories. This enables automated schema changes, seamless integration with CI/CD pipelines, and consistent database schema deployments across different environments. SchemaHero supports various databases such as PostgreSQL, MySQL, and CockroachDB, making it a valuable tool for DevOps teams embracing Kubernetes for database management.

Argo Streamlining Workflows

Argo Workflows serves as an open-source, container-native workflow engine designed to orchestrate CI/CD tasks on Kubernetes. It operates as a Kubernetes Custom Resource Definition (CRD), allowing contributors to develop custom API objects, thereby expanding Kubernetes capabilities in a compliant fashion.

Executing workflows on Kubernetes offers the advantages of leveraging its diverse features, including application scaling, canary deployments, and application healing. Kubernetes provides built-in functionalities like jobs, deployments, and services that facilitate the deployment and management of containerized applications by cloud engineers. Additionally, you can enhance its capabilities through custom resources and controllers.

Nevertheless, managing workflows on Kubernetes without a dedicated workflow engine, such as Argo Workflows, can become challenging and may pose scalability issues. Utilizing Argo Workflows to oversee and execute workflows on Kubernetes offers numerous benefits.

Getting Started with Argo

Argo Workflows work with a K8s operator – a Kubernetes-native application – that is deployed in your K8s cluster. This application extends the native behavior of your cluster by watching Etcd, the central datastore associated with a cluster, for Argo-specific manifests – called Custom Resource Definitions – that define the workflow process to be carried out.

The order of processes being carried out can be controlled in several ways. For example, steps within the larger workflow can depend on other steps in the workflow, which means that any dependencies of a given step will have been completed before a given step is carried out, or steps can be made to run sequentially, or if the steps are running independently of each other, they can be made to run in parallel to speed up the execution of the larger workflow. Argo Workflows is implemented using Kubernetes custom resource definitions (CRDs), making it easy to create and manage your workflows using your existing knowledge of managing Kubernetes resources. For instance, you can use the kubectl client to get all workflows, create workflows, and so on. You can also define a workflow and its dependencies using the YAML format, which is easy to follow.

Running your workflows on Kubernetes means taking advantage of its various features and benefits, including scaling of applications, canary deployments, application healing, and much more. While Kubernetes has plenty of baked-in functionalities (such as jobs, deployments, and services) that allow cloud engineers to deploy and manage containerized applications easily, you can also extend its functionality using custom resources and custom controllers.

Concepts of Argo CD

Application

Within the Argo framework, an application refers to a collection of Kubernetes resources collaboratively deployed to manage your workload. Argo stores comprehensive details of these applications within your cluster as instances of an embedded Custom Resource Definition (CRD).

Target State

In contrast, the target state signifies the version of the state as declared by your Git repository. When alterations occur in the repository, Argo initiates actions to transition the live state into alignment with the target state.

Argo Controller

The Argo Application Controller constitutes the element installed in your cluster, adopting the Kubernetes controller pattern to oversee your applications. Its role involves monitoring the state of your applications and conducting comparisons with their corresponding repositories.

Sync

The Sync process involves implementing the changes identified during a Refresh. Each Sync operation progressively aligns the cluster with the target state, ensuring the synchronization of the application with the declared state in the repository.

CHAPTER 5   OPEN-SOURCE TOOLS FOR CLOUD-NATIVE DEVOPS

Live State

The live state represents the current condition of your application within the cluster, encompassing aspects like the quantity of created Pods and the specific image they currently run.

Refresh

Refresh takes place when Argo retrieves the target state from your repository. While it scrutinizes the changes against the live state, it refrains from immediately applying them during this stage.

Implementation of Argo Workflows Using Custom Kubernetes Resources

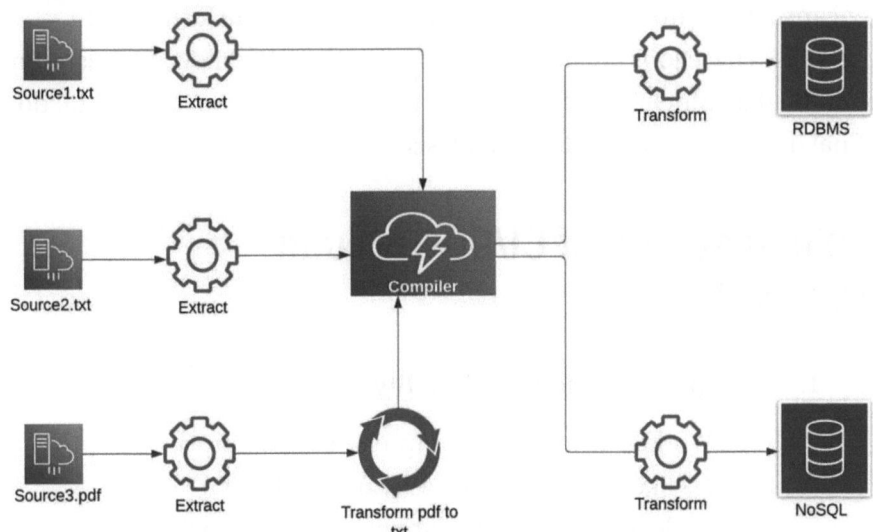

Figure 5-1. Custom kubernetes using Argo workflow

In the given data pipeline scenario, there are three distinct data sources, each generating different types of data. The first two sources produce text files, while the third source generates data in PDF format. The primary objective is to analyze the data obtained from these sources. However, there is a challenge since the compiler, which is responsible for combining and processing the data, can only handle text input.

To address this limitation, an additional step is introduced between the PDF data source and the compiler. This intermediary step involves a process that transforms the PDF data into a text (TXT) format, ensuring compatibility with the compiler.

Following the extraction and transformation steps, the data is aggregated. Subsequently, two supplementary processes are integrated into the workflow to further transform the aggregated text data. These additional processes convert the text data into SQL and NoSQL formats. This is essential because the systems chosen for data analysis operate specifically with these formats.

In the context of an Argo Workflow, the entire sequence of operations is encapsulated into three distinct jobs: "Extract," "Transform," and "Compile." These jobs are defined within the Argo Workflow, orchestrating the entire data pipeline and ensuring a seamless flow from data extraction to final data formats suitable for analysis.

Implementation of CI/CD Through Argo Workflows

1. **Enterprise-Grade Functionality**

   Argo Workflows includes comprehensive enterprise features like Role-Based Access Control (RBAC) and Single Sign-On (SSO), enhancing security and facilitating proper access management within your workflow environment.

2. **Resilience Against Failures**

   Argo Workflows is adept at handling container crashes and failures, ensuring the robustness of your workflows even in the face of unexpected issues.

3. **Scalability Options**

   If your workflow demands scalability, Argo Workflows offers autoscaling capabilities. It excels in efficiently managing numerous workflows simultaneously, accommodating varying workloads seamlessly.

Integration of Argo CD and Kubernetes

1. Begin by visiting GitHub and establishing a fresh repository for your application. Subsequently, clone this repository to your local machine, preparing to commit your Kubernetes manifests.

   ```
   $ git clone https://github.com/<username>/<repo>.git
   ```

2. Generate a YAML file named "deployment.yaml" in the repository you've established.

   ```
   apiVersion: apps/v1
   kind: Deployment
   metadata:
     name: nginx-deployment
     namespace: my-namespace
     labels:
       app.kubernetes.io/name: nginx-app
   ```

```yaml
spec:
  replicas: 3
  selector:
    matchLabels:
      app.kubernetes.io/name: nginx-app
  template:
    metadata:
      labels:
        app.kubernetes.io/name: nginx-app
    spec:
      containers:
      - name: nginx-container
        image: nginx:alpine
        ports:
          - name: http
            containerPort: 80
```

The provided YAML code defines a Kubernetes Deployment for running multiple replicas of a Nginx container. Let's break down the key components:

apiVersion: Specifies the API version for the Kubernetes resource, in this case, a Deployment under the "apps/v1" API version.

metadata: Contains metadata about the Deployment.

kind: Indicates the type of Kubernetes resource, which is a Deployment.

name: Sets the name of the Deployment to "nginx-deployment."

CHAPTER 5   OPEN-SOURCE TOOLS FOR CLOUD-NATIVE DEVOPS

namespace: Specifies the namespace as "my-namespace."

labels: Assigns labels to the Deployment for identification, with the label "app.kubernetes.io/name: nginx-app."

spec: Describes the desired state of the Deployment.

replicas: Specifies the desired number of replicas, set to 3 in this case.

selector: Defines a label selector to match with Pods controlled by this Deployment.

template: Describes the Pod template.

metadata: Specifies labels for Pods created from this template.

spec: Defines the specification of the Pod.

containers: Specifies the containers within the Pod.

name: Sets the name of the container to "nginx-container."

image: Specifies the Docker image to use, in this case, "nginx:alpine."

ports: Configures the container ports, exposing port 80 for HTTP traffic.

In summary, this YAML defines a Deployment named "nginx-deployment" that manages three replicas of an Nginx container, each running in the "argo-demo" namespace. The container uses the "nginx:alpine" image and exposes port 80 for incoming HTTP traffic.

197

3. Create a YAML file named "service.yaml" to configure a load-balanced service for exposing the deployment.

   ```
   apiVersion: v1
   kind: Service
   metadata:
     name: nginx-deployment
     namespace: my-namespace
   spec:
     type: ClusterIP
     selector:
       app.kubernetes.io/name: nginx-app
     ports:
       - protocol: TCP
         port: 8080
         targetPort: http
   ```

4. Include the manifest in the application namespace.

   ```
   apiVersion: v1
   kind: Namespace
   metadata:
     name: my-namespace
   ```

5. Commit your changes and push them to git.

   ```
   $ git add
   $ git commit -m "Initialized repository with Kubernetes YAML files"
   $ git push origin master
   ```

6. Start deploying your application by installing Argo.

CHAPTER 5   OPEN-SOURCE TOOLS FOR CLOUD-NATIVE DEVOPS

7. Get the latest Argo CLI from GitHub and proceed with the following steps.

   ```
   $ wget https://github.com/argoproj/argo-workflows/releases/download/v3.5.4/argo-linux-amd64.gz
   ```

8. Once the preceding tasks are completed, the subsequent action involves modifying the file permissions to enable its execution as a program. This adjustment facilitates the direct execution of Argo commands from the command line, providing you with the necessary functionality.

   ```
   $ chmod +x argocd-linux-amd64
   ```

9. The next step is to transfer this file from the current directory to the /usr/local/bin directory. This enables you to run the "argo" command seamlessly from any location within the terminal.

   ```
   $ mv argocd-linux-amd64 /usr/local/bin/argocd
   ```

10. To confirm the successful installation of Argo Workflows, execute the following command.

    ```
    $ argo version
    argo: v3.5.4
          BuildDate: 2024-01-14T06:08:41Z
    ```

11. The command-line interface (CLI) is also available in Homebrew's package list. Utilize the brew install command to install argocd on your system.

    ```
    $ brew install argocd
    ```

12. Proceed to install Argo within your Kubernetes cluster. This installation will incorporate the Argo CD API, controller, and Custom Resource Definitions (CRDs).

    ```
    $ kubectl create namespace argocd
    ```

13. Employ Kubectl to apply the YAML manifest of Argo CD to your cluster. Before application, you have the option to examine the manifest to identify the resources that will be generated.

    ```
    $ kubectl apply -n argocd -f <path to manifest install.yml>
    ```

Note Argo's components may take a few seconds to be fully operational in your cluster. Monitor the progress by using Kubectl to list deployments in the argocd namespace.

---

14. Retrieve information about Deployments in the "argocd" namespace of your Kubernetes cluster. It lists the Deployments along with details such as the number of replicas, the number of pods running, and the desired state. This command helps you monitor the status and progress of deployments managed by Argo CD within the specified namespace.

    ```
    $ kubectl get deployments -n argocd
    ```

15. Set up a port-forwarding connection in your Kubernetes environment. It forwards local port 8080 to the remote port 443 of the service named "argocd-server" in the "argocd" namespace. After running

this command, you can access the Argo CD UI locally by opening a web browser and navigating to https://localhost:8080. This is a common approach to access services running in a Kubernetes cluster from your local machine during development or troubleshooting.

```
$ kubectl port-forward svc/argocd-server -n argocd 8080:443
```

- Before signing in, it's necessary to acquire the password for the default admin user, which is automatically generated during the Argo installation process.

  ```
  $ argocd admin initial-password -n argocd
  ```

- To access the Argo CLI, execute the following command.

  ```
  $ argocd login localhost:8080
  ```

Kubeflow Pipelines

Remember the last quarter when we practically turned our office into a night owl's paradise trying to launch that recommendation model, and, well, missed the deadline? Good times, right? But fear not! Now we have Kubeflow on our side – the superhero for data nerds like us. It's like the ultimate team player, making data engineering, data science, and business analysis feel like one big happy family. Building, deploying, and monitoring an ML model has never been this much fun. Bonus: No need to learn a new language or sacrifice our old code – Kubeflow's got it covered, making us look good and saving the day.

In the world of Machine Learning, it's like teaching computers to learn and improve by themselves, without telling them exactly how. Machine Learning is everywhere, made up of different parts. When we create models, we sometimes forget about the technical side needed for both training and using them. That's where Kubeflow comes in.

Machine learning engineers often struggle with keeping these systems in good shape. It's tough to handle everything from how the apps work to what kind of resources they need. For example, the part where we teach the computer (training) needs a lot of resources, but when it's making decisions (inference), it needs to be quick and not use up too much. So, we need special tools and plans to handle all this. The usual solutions that work for other apps just don't quite fit machine learning.

This is where Kubeflow comes in. It's like a toolset that aims to make it easy for businesses to use machine learning, not just when they're making the apps but throughout the whole life of those apps.

Kubeflow Overview

Kubeflow, an open-source platform constructed on Kubernetes, strives to streamline the creation and deployment of machine learning systems. Officially labeled as the ML toolkit for Kubernetes, Kubeflow encompasses diverse components catering to different stages of the machine learning development process. These elements encompass environments for notebook development, hyperparameter tuning, feature management, model serving, and, notably, machine learning pipelines.

Problem Identification

The initial step, as the name implies, entails identifying the problem that the ML system aims to solve. Discuss model tradeoffs and consider how outputs from the model will be utilized.

Source, Prepare, and Analyze Data

Define the ground truth for the model. Validate data quality and label the data.

Model Exploration

Start by establishing a baseline performance for your tasks. Begin with a simple model using the initial data pipeline and explore various orthogonal ideas through experiments. Find and modify state-of-the-art models, attempting to set up a benchmark on your dataset. Kubeflow Notebooks are designed for quick experimentation without the hassle of managing scaling.

Model Refinement

Perform model-specific optimizations, such as finding the right set of hyperparameters. Consider targeted data collection or debugging models, potentially requiring iterations on previous steps. Katib facilitates hyperparameter tuning and neural architecture search.

Training the Model

Train the machine learning model for a more extended period, preparing it for production. Leveraging training operators in Kubeflow, supporting a variety of frameworks. Evaluate the model on the test distribution to understand differences between train and test set distributions.

Deploy the Model

Deploy the model, involving serving it over a REST API, maintaining model versions, and handling tasks like model rollbacks, canary deployments, batch prediction, and scaling. Utilize KServe or Kubeflow pipelines for orchestrating various ways of serving models, including TensorFlow Extended, TorchServe, TensorRT, and more.

Maintenance

Beyond the "Deploy" step, ongoing tasks include monitoring live data and model prediction distributions. Monitor for data and concept drifts, using the data to determine whether retraining is necessary or specific changes are required. Incorporate TensorBoard through Kubeflow for effective monitoring in this crucial stage of the ML workflow.

CHAPTER 5 OPEN-SOURCE TOOLS FOR CLOUD-NATIVE DEVOPS

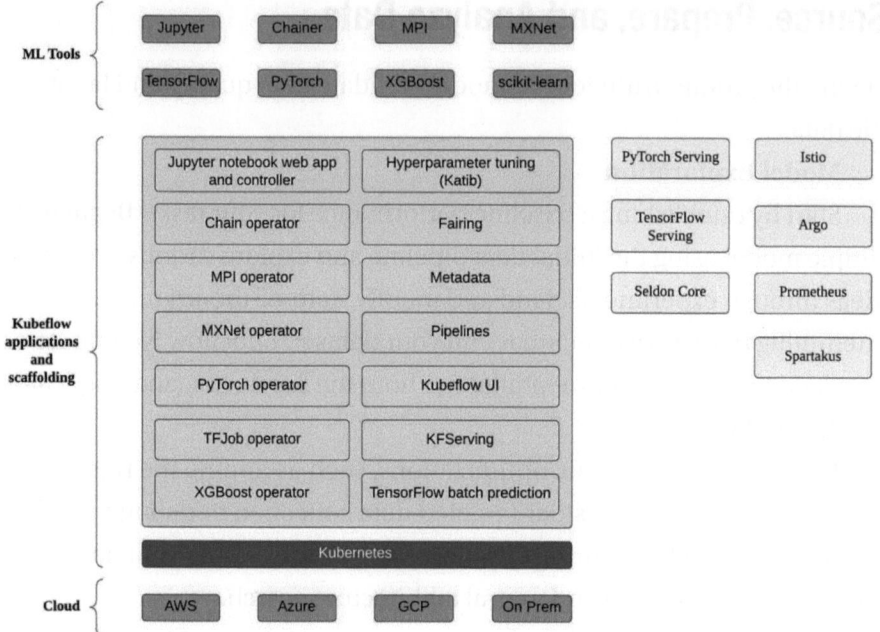

Figure 5-2. *Kubeflow principle*

- **Katib**

    It is utilized to implement Automated Machine Learning, offering a web UI for interaction and incorporating Neural Architecture Search (NAS) to enhance predictive accuracy and model performance.

- **ML Frameworks**

    This encompasses a variety of frameworks, including Chainer (deprecated), MPI, MXNet, PyTorch, and TensorFlow, providing flexibility in machine learning approaches.

CHAPTER 5   OPEN-SOURCE TOOLS FOR CLOUD-NATIVE DEVOPS

- **Feature Store (Feast)**

  It ensures feature sharing and reuse, maintains point-in-time correctness, upholds data quality and validation, and serves features at scale.

- **Pipelines**

  A solution for end-to-end orchestration, simplifying experimentations and enhancing reusability.

- **Metadata**

  It aids in organizing workflows by tracking and managing information about executions, models, datasets, and other artifacts.

- **Tools for Serving**

  Two model serving systems, KFServing and Seldon Core, facilitate multi-framework model serving. Learn more about serving tools here.

- **Jupyter Notebooks**

  Collaborative platforms that support team-based model development.

- **Central Dashboard**

  A user interface for managing Kubeflow pipelines and interacting with various components.

- **Fairing**

  Allows remote execution of training jobs, embedding them in Notebooks or local Python code, and deploying prediction endpoints.

CHAPTER 5   OPEN-SOURCE TOOLS FOR CLOUD-NATIVE DEVOPS

Kubeflow Principles

Kubeflow functions according to fundamental principles that shape its approach to simplifying machine learning workflows.

1. **Composability:** Composability refers to the flexibility of selecting the most suitable components for a project. Often, individuals entering the field of machine learning focus primarily on the final model, overlooking the multifaceted nature of the model-building process. Constructing a model involves various stages, each composed of distinct building blocks that demand thoughtful selection. Whether specific requirements dictate the workflow or different parts of a project necessitate varying versions of TensorFlow, Kubeflow empowers users to extend Kubernetes' capabilities. It enables the execution of independent and configurable steps, integrating machine learning frameworks and libraries seamlessly.

2. **Portability:** Portability signifies the ability to execute all facets of a machine learning project within any environment where Kubeflow is operational. By managing platform-specific details, Kubeflow allows developers to concentrate solely on their models. Write the code once, and Kubeflow takes care of the abstraction, facilitating deployment on local systems or in the cloud.

3. **Scalability:** Scalability entails providing projects with access to additional resources when needed and releasing them when not in use. Environments may differ in computing resources, encompassing

CPUs, GPUs, and TPUs, and there might be a necessity to scale across teams and experiments. Kubeflow capitalizes on Kubernetes' capabilities, optimizing available resources and facilitating scalability with minimal manual intervention.

Kubeflow Pipelines

In Kubeflow, pipelines consist of distinct components, each representing an individual step within the overall workflow. These components are executed in isolated Docker containers, allowing them to have independent sets of dependencies, thereby ensuring modularity and flexibility.

For each component developed, a dedicated Docker image is created. This image accepts specific inputs, executes a defined operation, and exposes designated outputs. Additionally, a separate Python script, named "pipeline.py," is crafted to convert these Docker images into pipeline components and construct the entire pipeline using these components.

The pipeline involves the creation of four distinct components:

1. **Preprocess-data**

    This component loads the Boston Housing dataset from sklearn.datasets and divides it into training and test sets.

2. **Train-model**

    Dedicated to training a model for predicting the median value of homes in Boston, leveraging the Boston Housing dataset.

3. **Test-model**

   This component computes and outputs the mean squared error of the trained model on the test dataset.

4. **Deploy-model**

   Although not the primary focus of this article, this component signals its intention to deploy the model. In a practical setting, this could serve as a generic component for deploying various models to Quality Assurance or Production environments.

By encapsulating each step in a separate Docker container and orchestrating them through a well-defined Python script, Kubeflow ensures modularity, allowing for seamless integration and customization of machine learning workflows. Several other servers have to be taken under the Kubeflow model to avoid security posture and that we see the emergence of IaC tools that are based on the language models. These language models can be used for the consistency and saves iteration time to guide the Kubeflow pipeline for debugging, auditing, and compliance requirements.

Kubeflow in Cloud Native Applications

Kubeflow, embraced as an open-source initiative within the Cloud Native Computing Foundation (CNCF), assumes a crucial role in simplifying, scaling, and enhancing the portability of machine learning (ML) on Kubernetes. Let's explore practical scenarios to showcase how Kubeflow positively impacts various facets of the machine learning life cycle:

CHAPTER 5   OPEN-SOURCE TOOLS FOR CLOUD-NATIVE DEVOPS

1. **Streamlining ML Workflows**

   Scenario: A data science team seeks to streamline the complete ML workflow, encompassing tasks from data preprocessing to model training and deployment.

   Kubeflow's Contribution: Kubeflow empowers teams to construct and manage end-to-end ML pipelines. Leveraging components such as Jupyter Notebooks and Argo, it facilitates seamless collaboration, experimentation, and workflow automation.

2. **Enabling Scalable Model Training**

   Scenario: An organization requires a scalable solution for training ML models across diverse datasets.

   Kubeflow's Contribution: Kubeflow's integration with Kubernetes provides a solution for scalable and distributed model training. Harnessing the orchestration capabilities of Kubernetes, Kubeflow efficiently allocates resources for training large models across clusters.

3. **Simplifying Model Deployment and Serving**

   Scenario: Post-model training, the need arises to deploy models for real-time predictions or inferences.

   Kubeflow's Contribution: Components like KFServing within Kubeflow simplify the deployment and serving of ML models. This ensures a consistent and scalable approach to serving models across various environments.

4. **Facilitating Hyperparameter Tuning and Optimization**

    Scenario: Optimizing hyperparameters is critical for enhancing model performance.

    Kubeflow's Contribution: Katib, an integral part of Kubeflow, streamlines automated hyperparameter tuning. It empowers users to define search spaces, algorithms, and objectives, automating the quest for optimal hyperparameters.

5. **Promoting Collaboration Across Teams**

    Scenario: Data engineering, data science, and business analyst teams seek a unified platform for seamless collaboration.

    Kubeflow's Contribution: Kubeflow serves as a collaborative hub, bringing diverse teams together. Through features like shared Jupyter Notebooks and a central dashboard, it fosters collaboration and knowledge exchange among team members.

6. **Supporting Multiple ML Frameworks**

    Scenario: Development teams work with various ML frameworks such as TensorFlow, PyTorch, and others.

    Kubeflow's Contribution: Kubeflow's support for multiple ML frameworks ensures flexibility. It accommodates the preferences and expertise of different teams, allowing them to work with the frameworks they are most comfortable using.

7. **Ensuring Reproducibility and Versioning**

    Scenario: Ensuring the reproducibility of ML experiments and tracking model versions is crucial for quality control.

    Kubeflow's Contribution: Kubeflow's metadata tracking system aids in organizing and versioning ML workflows. It captures crucial information about executions, models, datasets, and artifacts, ensuring transparency and reproducibility.

Future Trends in Cloud-Native DevOps Tools

Over the years, successful implementation of DevOps tools has been shown to enhance new project intake efficiency to a greater extent. This approach has become the favored project management strategy for complex software development projects, widely recognized for its transformative potential in the industry.

Adopting DevOps involves embracing open communication, and transparency, improving customer experience, enhancing quality, and meeting project deadlines. These benefits enable organizations to leverage DevOps for more seamless, continuous communication, collaboration, and integration between development (Dev) and IT operations (Ops) teams. The ceaseless transformation, emerging trends, and best practices within the DevOps space make it an exciting area to watch both now and in the future. In this blog, let's explore the latest DevOps trends shaping the future.

CHAPTER 5   OPEN-SOURCE TOOLS FOR CLOUD-NATIVE DEVOPS

DataOps

DataOps is emerging as a critical trend in cloud-native DevOps, focusing on streamlining and automating data integration, management, and analytics processes. DataOps tools automate data pipelines, enable self-service access to data, and promote collaboration between data engineers, data scientists, and other stakeholders. These tools facilitate faster and more reliable delivery of data-driven insights, enhancing decision-making and driving innovation in cloud-native environments.

AIOps (Artificial Intelligence for IT Operations)

AIOps leverages artificial intelligence and machine learning techniques to automate and optimize IT operations processes, including monitoring, incident management, and performance analysis. In cloud-native DevOps, AIOps tools provide proactive insights into infrastructure and application health, detect anomalies and potential issues, and recommend remediation actions. By leveraging AI-driven automation, organizations can improve system reliability, reduce downtime, and enhance the overall efficiency of cloud-native deployments.

Hyperautomation

Hyperautomation refers to the integration of advanced automation technologies, such as robotic process automation (RPA), AI, and machine learning, to automate complex end-to-end business processes. In cloud-native DevOps, hyperautomation tools orchestrate and automate the entire software delivery life cycle, from code development and testing to deployment and monitoring. These tools enable organizations to achieve greater agility, scalability, and efficiency by eliminating manual tasks, reducing human errors, and accelerating time-to-market for cloud-native applications.

Adoption of Cloud-Native Technologies

Cloud-native technologies such as microservices, containerization, and serverless computing are continuously gaining traction within DevOps environments. These technologies offer improved scalability, faster deployment and iteration, and greater flexibility and agility. The adoption of cloud-native technologies is expected to continue as organizations aim to improve operational efficiency. Kubernetes and similar orchestration platforms will play a crucial role in this process, fostering a consistent, cloud-based environment for managing containerized infrastructure and applications. This increased adoption of cloud and development is leading to the new trend of "Multi Cloud."

Infrastructure as Code (IaC) Management

Infrastructure as Code (IaC) involves managing infrastructure using the same tools and processes as code. Multi-cloud infrastructure management refers to the use of multiple cloud computing platforms within a single organization. Multi-cloud support for IaC allows organizations to automate the provisioning and management of infrastructure across multiple cloud platforms. This practice enables greater consistency and standardization, reduces complexity, and facilitates workload migration.

Artificial Intelligence (AI) Evolution

Automation and AI are continuously evolving and expected to play a significant role in advancing DevOps. These technologies streamline repetitive tasks, boost productivity, and reduce human errors. Predictive analytics and incident management are areas where AI is making a difference, analyzing historical performance data and log data to predict outcomes and identify issues before they occur. Integrating automation and AI in DevOps enhances process efficiency and application reliability. However, organizations need to carefully consider their impact and align them with business goals and values.

Security and Compliance

Security and compliance are critical considerations, and organizations are expected to prioritize integrating best practices into their processes and tools. Cloud security, application security, and compliance with regulations and standards are crucial areas that will continue to be of utmost importance. This focus on security and compliance will lead to an increased role for DevSecOps specialists in DevOps teams.

Collaboration Between DevOps Teams

DevOps aims to enable efficient collaboration between development and operations teams. Continuous Integration and Delivery (CI/CD), incident management, and capacity planning are crucial areas where collaboration between these teams is expected to be vital in the coming years. Success in DevOps relies heavily on robust collaboration between development and operations teams.

Fresh Dimension in Quantum Computing

In its early phases, quantum computing presents substantial possibilities for DevOps and cloud-native structures. The capability to execute intricate calculations at unparalleled speeds has the potential to transform different facets of software development and implementation. For instance, quantum computing can significantly diminish the time needed for data-intensive activities such as testing and debugging or enhance the efficiency of resource distribution in cloud settings.

Adapting to Change

Agility stands as a fundamental element within a thriving cloud-native DevOps. The essence lies in the capacity to promptly address shifts in the market, evolving customer demands, and technological progress. Achieving agility extends beyond technological solutions; it requires organizational readiness to welcome change and adjust processes accordingly. This entails a willingness to experiment, glean insights from setbacks, and consistently enhance operations.

Artificial Intelligence for IT Operations (AIOps)

AIOps, short for Artificial Intelligence for IT Operations, utilizes machine learning and data science to automate and improve IT operations. Its applications include automating routine tasks, real-time issue identification and response, and predictive analytics for forecasting future problems. The integration of AIOps into DevOps practices has the potential to significantly enhance efficiency and response times. By automating mundane tasks, DevOps teams gain more time to address complex issues. Additionally, real-time issue identification and response contribute to minimizing downtime and enhancing the overall end-user experience.

ChatOps

ChatOps is a collaborative model that merges conversation and work into a unified platform. This model streamlines communication, automates routine tasks, and enhances transparency. In the realm of DevOps, ChatOps facilitates the automation of deployment, system monitoring, and incident response within a chat conversation context. This approach streamlines workflows, improves communication, and accelerates operational speed and efficiency.

GitOps

GitOps represents a method for implementing Continuous Deployment for cloud-native applications, utilizing Git as a singular source of truth for declarative infrastructure and applications. GitOps enables the management of infrastructure and deployment of new features and updates by making changes to a Git repository. This approach offers various advantages, including heightened productivity, improved audit trails, and more stable and reliable deployments. As businesses increasingly adopt cloud-native technologies, GitOps is poised to become an increasingly prominent trend in the DevOps landscape.

No Operations (NoOps)

NoOps is a concept centered around automating IT operations to the extent that a dedicated team is unnecessary. Operations are not eliminated but rather automated and abstracted, enabling developers to focus on coding rather than managing infrastructure. Implementing NoOps can substantially boost efficiency, empowering developers to work without operational hindrances. However, it necessitates a high level of automation and a cultural shift toward a hands-off approach to operations. The NoOps trend is anticipated to persist as automation technologies continue to advance.

Summary

In this insightful chapter, the book navigates through the crucial elements that optimize the software development life cycle within cloud-native environments. It begins by establishing the foundational principles of Cloud-Native DevOps, underscoring the pivotal role of automation for efficiency and scalability. The focus then shifts to key open-source tools,

CHAPTER 5   OPEN-SOURCE TOOLS FOR CLOUD-NATIVE DEVOPS

with Argo taking the spotlight as a robust workflow management tool adept at streamlining intricate processes. Kubeflow Pipelines is introduced as a specialized solution for enhancing data flow in machine learning workflows, providing a comprehensive exploration of its features and integration capabilities.

Moving beyond individual tools, the chapter widens its scope to encompass broader considerations for Cloud-Native DevOps tooling. Best practices are outlined to assist readers in selecting and implementing tools, ensuring scalability and flexibility in their DevOps practices. The narrative addresses common challenges in Cloud-Native DevOps tooling, offering practical strategies to overcome obstacles. Real-world case studies showcase successful tool implementations, providing valuable insights into their application in diverse scenarios.

As the chapter concludes, it adopts a forward-looking stance by examining emerging trends in Cloud-Native DevOps tools. Predictions on the future evolution of DevOps practices in cloud-native environments are presented, emphasizing the continuous need for adaptation and improvement in tooling practices. The chapter encompasses a comprehensive exploration of open-source tools, highlights the capabilities of Argo and Kubeflow Pipelines, offers best practices for tool selection, addresses challenges, showcases real-world implementations, and provides a glimpse into the future trends of Cloud-Native DevOps.

CHAPTER 6

Scalability and Autoscaling Strategies

"Auto-scaling: Why let your applications take a nap when they could be running marathons"

In this chapter, we will explore the fundamental principles and advanced strategies for achieving scalability, with a focus on autoscaling mechanisms. We will begin by examining the core concepts of scalability, distinguishing between horizontal and vertical scaling approaches, and discussing the challenges posed by stateless and stateful services. Understanding these principles will provide a solid foundation for devising effective scalability strategies.

Autoscaling, a key component of modern cloud-native architectures, enables applications to automatically adjust their resource allocation based on workload demands. We will delve into the nuances of reactive and proactive autoscaling, exploring how triggers, metrics, and dynamic policies drive autoscaling events. Implementation of autoscaling mechanisms involves leveraging container orchestration platforms, cloud provider services, or building custom solutions tailored to specific requirements. We will discuss the practical considerations and best practices for implementing and fine-tuning autoscaling configurations.

Furthermore, we will address the importance of monitoring, metrics collection, and testing in ensuring the effectiveness and reliability of autoscaling policies. Balancing performance requirements with cost considerations and mitigating scalability bottlenecks are essential aspects of optimizing autoscaling strategies.

In this chapter, we will be encompassing the following topics:

- Scaling Principles in Cloud-Native Applications
- Multi-cloud Strategies
- Autoscaling Implementation in AWS
- Future Trends in Scalability and Autoscaling

Scaling Principles in Cloud-Native Applications

Cloud-native architecture is a strategic approach to designing and building systems specifically for cloud environments, like those offered by providers such as Amazon Web Services (AWS), Microsoft Azure, or Google Cloud Platform. This approach acknowledges and leverages the unique capabilities and characteristics of cloud computing, such as on-demand resource allocation, elasticity, and pay-as-you-go pricing models.

In contrast, traditional architectures are typically designed for on-premises or fixed infrastructure setups. These setups often require significant upfront investment in hardware and software, and they are typically configured with a fixed capacity to handle peak loads. Scaling up or down in traditional architectures can be time-consuming and may require manual intervention.

Cloud-native architecture, however, takes advantage of the dynamic nature of cloud environments. Instead of relying on fixed infrastructure, cloud-native systems are designed to be flexible and scalable. Not only cloud-native systems but also cloud-enabled systems leverage native Kubernetes services to scale efficiently, ensuring optimal resource utilization and enhanced performance across diverse workloads. This approach enables organizations to harness the full potential of Kubernetes orchestration, whether they are building from scratch or transitioning existing applications to the cloud. They can automatically adapt to changing workloads by dynamically provisioning and de-provisioning resources as needed. This elasticity enables organizations to optimize resource usage.

Synchronization across cloud regions is often necessary, and not all cloud services offer these capabilities uniformly. This refers to setting up an active configuration across cloud regions. Resilience is a central focus of cloud-native architecture, emphasizing fault tolerance and the ability to withstand failures. Cloud-native systems are typically designed as distributed systems, distributing workloads across various servers or regions. In case of component failure, the system can seamlessly reroute traffic to healthy instances, thereby reducing downtime and maintaining uninterrupted availability.

Overall, cloud-native architecture represents a shift in mindset from traditional, fixed infrastructure approaches to more dynamic, scalable, and cost-effective solutions tailored specifically for the cloud. By embracing cloud-native principles and best practices, organizations can unlock the full potential of cloud computing and drive innovation and growth in the digital age.

Utilizing Automation in Cloud-Native Architecture

Automation serves as a cornerstone in software systems, gaining even greater significance within the realm of cloud-native architecture. The cloud environment presents fertile ground for automation, offering unparalleled opportunities to streamline and optimize system management processes. Despite initial setup costs, the long-term benefits of automation far exceed the investment. Automation not only reduces manual effort but also enhances the resilience and performance of cloud-native systems.

A key advantage of automation lies in its ability to expedite critical processes like system repair, scaling, and deployment. Unlike manual interventions, automated workflows can promptly respond to dynamic changes in workload demands, ensuring optimal resource allocation and system responsiveness. Moreover, automation fosters consistency and repeatability in system operations, mitigating the risk of human error and enhancing overall system reliability.

Cloud-native architecture embodies an iterative approach, where continuous improvement and adaptation are fundamental principles. As systems evolve and requirements change, automation plays a pivotal role in enabling agility and scalability. With deeper insights into system behavior and performance, organizations can identify new opportunities for automation, allowing for ongoing refinement and optimization.

Examples

1. Automated scaling in response to fluctuating user demands, ensuring optimal resource utilization and cost-efficiency.

2. Automated deployment pipelines for deploying new features and updates seamlessly, reducing deployment errors and downtime.

3. Automated monitoring and alerting systems that detect and respond to performance issues in real-time, enhancing system reliability and availability.

4. Automated backup and disaster recovery processes that ensure data integrity and minimize data loss in the event of system failures.

Several Key Areas Within Cloud-Native Architecture Are Ripe for Automation

Infrastructure Provisioning and Management

Infrastructure provisioning and management tools like Google Cloud Deployment Manager or Terraform enable organizations to automate the creation and configuration of cloud infrastructure. For example, Terraform allows developers to define infrastructure as code using a simple declarative language, which can then be executed to provision and manage cloud resources. This automation streamlines the deployment process, facilitating rapid scalability and ensuring consistency across environments.

Monitoring and Remediation

Automated monitoring and logging solutions, such as Google Cloud Monitoring or Prometheus, enable organizations to continuously track system performance and identify potential issues in real-time. For instance, Google Cloud Monitoring provides comprehensive visibility into cloud resources, allowing users to set up custom alerts and notifications for specific metrics. Automated remediation actions, such as autoscaling or resource resizing, further enhance system resilience by automatically adjusting resources to meet changing workload demands.

Continuous Integration/Continuous Delivery (CI/CD)

CI/CD automation tools like Google Cloud Build, Jenkins, and Spinnaker automate the build, testing, and deployment processes, enabling organizations to deliver software updates and enhancements seamlessly. For example, Google Cloud Build automatically builds and tests code changes in a CI pipeline, while Jenkins provides extensive plugin support

CHAPTER 6   SCALABILITY AND AUTOSCALING STRATEGIES

for automating various stages of the software delivery life cycle. Spinnaker, on the other hand, offers advanced deployment strategies and canary analysis for safely rolling out changes to production environments.

Dynamic Scaling

Automated scaling mechanisms, such as Google Cloud Autoscaler or Kubernetes Horizontal Pod Autoscaler, dynamically adjust system resources based on fluctuating workload demands. For instance, Google Cloud Autoscaler automatically adds or removes virtual machine instances based on CPU utilization, ensuring optimal resource utilization and cost-efficiency. By leveraging automation across these critical areas, organizations can realize the full benefits of cloud-native architecture, enabling them to remain agile, resilient, and cost-effective in today's dynamic business environment.

1. **Strategic Management**

    Effectively managing various types of data, including user-specific details like shopping cart contents or employee records, as well as system-wide information such as active job instances or deployed software versions, is crucial for building distributed, cloud-native architectures. Therefore, it becomes imperative to meticulously design systems with a keen eye on how and when to handle this data, aiming to minimize reliance on stateful components whenever feasible.

    One approach to achieving this is by leveraging stateless microservices architecture, where each service manages its own data and communicates with other services via APIs. For instance, the ecommerce platform may use a stateless user service to handle user-specific data and a separate inventory service to manage system-wide inventory information. By decoupling data management from individual services, the architecture becomes more resilient and adaptable to changes. Additionally, adopting cloud-native technologies like serverless computing and managed databases can further enhance data management capabilities. For example, using a serverless function to process user orders or employing a managed database service like Amazon DynamoDB for storing user profiles can reduce the complexity of data management tasks and improve scalability. Overall, by carefully considering how and when to handle different types of data and leveraging cloud-native technologies, organizations can design robust and adaptable architectures that enable seamless scalability, fault tolerance, and efficient resource utilization in dynamic cloud environments.

1. Scalability stateless components facilitate seamless scalability by allowing additional instances to be added as demand increases. Conversely, scaling down involves gracefully terminating instances once their current tasks are completed.

2. Fault tolerance repairing a failed instance of a stateless component is straightforward; it can be gracefully terminated and promptly replaced with a new instance.

3. Rollback capability in the event of a faulty deployment, reverting to a previous version is simplified with stateless components. Terminating them and launching instances of the previous version is a straightforward process.

4. Load balancing stateless components streamline load balancing, as any instance can handle any request. Conversely, load balancing across stateful components is more intricate, as each instance typically holds the user's session state, requiring it to manage all requests from that user.

By prioritizing statelessness in component design, organizations can achieve enhanced scalability, fault tolerance, rollback flexibility, and load-balancing efficiency within their cloud-native architectures. This strategic approach ensures systems are well-equipped to meet the demands of dynamic cloud environments.

2. **Defense in Depth**

    In traditional architecture, a significant reliance is placed on perimeter security, where a fortified network boundary separates trusted internal components from potentially harmful external entities. However, this conventional approach is susceptible to both insider threats and external attacks, like sophisticated phishing attempts. Moreover, with the growing demand for remote and mobile work options, the concept of a rigid network perimeter is becoming increasingly outdated.

On the contrary, cloud-native architectures, originating from Internet-facing services, inherently face external threats head-on. Consequently, they adopt a defense-in-depth strategy, which emphasizes authentication between components and reduces the level of trust even among internal elements. This approach effectively eliminates the binary distinction of "inside" and "outside" within the architecture, recognizing that threats can originate from within the system as well.

Moreover, cloud-native architectures extend this concept beyond simple authentication, incorporating additional measures such as rate limiting and protection against script injections. Each component within the architecture is engineered to protect itself from potential threats posed by other components. This not only bolsters the resilience of the architecture but also simplifies deployment in cloud environments, where the absence of a trusted network infrastructure between services and users is common.

3. **Managed Services**

In the expansive landscape of cloud computing, the array of services available goes well beyond basic infrastructure provisioning. Leading cloud providers offer a wide range of managed services, each providing comprehensive functionalities to ease the complexities of backend software and infrastructure management. While the benefits of these managed services are undeniable, some organizations approach them cautiously, wary of potential vendor lock-in. However, it's crucial to understand that leveraging managed services often leads to significant reductions in time and operational overhead, making them a compelling option for many businesses.

The decision to adopt managed services involves a delicate balance between portability and operational efficiency, taking into account both financial considerations and skill-related factors. Generally, managed services can be categorized into three primary groups:

- These services, exemplified by offerings like Cloud SQL or Cloud Bigtable, present minimal risk and straightforwardly offer the benefits of managed solutions.

- Although not inherently compatible with open-source or lacking direct open-source alternatives, services such as BigQuery are so user-friendly that their operational benefits outweigh potential risks.

- Other services: These are the more challenging cases where migration may prove difficult, and the operational advantages are less apparent. Each scenario requires a thorough assessment, considering factors like the service's strategic significance, the operational overhead associated with self-management, and the effort required for migration.

The potential risks associated with migration seldom outweigh the significant savings in time, effort, and operational risks achieved by having the cloud provider manage the service at scale on behalf of the organization. Therefore, embracing managed services can often lead to enhanced efficiency and agility in cloud environments.

4. **Polyglot Architecting**

   An essential hallmark of a cloud-native system is its perpetual evolution, a characteristic that extends to its architecture. As a cloud-native architect, your role entails an ongoing pursuit of refining, simplifying, and enhancing the system's architecture. This continuous refinement is necessitated by the ever-changing needs of the organization, the evolving landscape of IT systems, and the advancing capabilities of cloud providers.

   While this commitment to ongoing improvement undoubtedly demands consistent investment, the lessons learned from past experiences are crystal clear: stagnant, inflexible IT systems quickly become obsolete, hindering an organization's ability to adapt to emerging threats and opportunities. In contrast, systems that are agile, adaptable, and responsive not only thrive but also pave the way for innovation and growth.

   Therefore, the ethos of continuous architecting is essential for maintaining the vitality and relevance of cloud-native systems. By embracing change and actively shaping the architecture to align with evolving requirements and technological advancements, cloud-native architects ensure that their organizations remain resilient, competitive, and future-ready in an ever-evolving digital landscape.

5. **Embrace Immutable Components for Enhanced Agility**

   Achieving a high level of agility and adaptability in your infrastructure can be facilitated by adopting immutable components. This typically involves configuring servers or virtual machines (VMs) in a manner that prevents modifications after deployment.

   Once an immutable server is deployed, there's no need for subsequent modifications. Instead, the focus shifts to maintaining the deployed server in its original state, avoiding any alterations. In the event of issues, swift and straightforward server replacement ensures uninterrupted application functionality.

   The advantages of employing an immutable infrastructure are manifold:

   1. **Consistency and Reliability:** Immutable components contribute to a stable and dependable infrastructure, simplifying testing procedures.

   2. **Simplified Deployment:** Deploying immutable components is straightforward and predictable.

   3. **Versioned and Automated Deployment:** Each deployment of immutable components is versioned and automated, facilitating environment rollback processes.

4. **Mitigation of Configuration Drifts:** Immutable infrastructure helps prevent configuration drifts, snowflake servers, and errors, thereby enhancing system stability.

5. **Seamless Autoscaling:** Cloud services seamlessly support autoscaling with immutable components.

Mutable servers not only escalate costs but also prolong iteration times, thereby delaying time-to-market. In contrast, immutable infrastructure fosters agile development, enhancing reliability, consistency, and efficiency in deployed environments. With immutable infrastructure, recreating environments within minutes becomes achievable, further streamlining operations and bolstering resilience.

Multi-cloud Strategies

Developing a multi-cloud strategy is increasingly essential to safeguard against system failures and avoid dependency on a single cloud provider. Thus, establishing a robust multi-cloud approach is crucial to introduce redundancy and bolster resilience, enabling the distribution of applications across various cloud platforms. To accomplish this effectively, several key steps should be followed:

- **Evaluate Cloud Providers**

    Assess potential cloud providers based on criteria such as geographical coverage, service offerings, pricing structures, performance metrics, and reliability. By thoroughly understanding organizational requirements and conducting comprehensive evaluations, businesses can identify the optimal mix of cloud providers for their multi-cloud environment.

- **Define Deployment Models and SLAs**

  Establish clear deployment models and define service level agreements (SLAs) to ensure consistent performance and availability across multiple cloud providers. This entails specifying uptime guarantees, response times, data governance policies, and compliance measures to ensure accountability and regulatory adherence. It also involves determining how applications and services will be deployed, managed, and integrated across different cloud platforms.

- **Embrace Cloud-Native Architectures**

  Adopt cloud-native architectures and practices, leveraging technologies like Docker to encapsulate applications and their dependencies for seamless deployment and scalability. Additionally, organizations should utilize container orchestration platforms such as Kubernetes to automate container deployment, scaling, and management within a multi-cloud environment.

- **Implement Modern Integration Approaches**

  Adopt contemporary integration methodologies like API management and event-driven architectures to facilitate seamless communication between diverse cloud services and applications. Standardizing data formats and protocols promotes interoperability and simplifies data exchange across various cloud platforms.

By adhering to these guidelines, organizations can establish a resilient multi-cloud environment that enhances redundancy, improves system reliability, and ensures seamless interoperability across diverse cloud platforms.

Reactive and Preemptive Scaling

In our traditional approach, when we need more computational power, we tend to expand by adding more physical machines to our infrastructure. This scalability is crucial for accommodating a growing user base on our platform, ensuring that our services remain responsive and available even during peak usage periods. By adding more machines, we can distribute the workload effectively and prevent system overloads or failures.

However, managing a large number of machines running continuously presents practical challenges. Firstly, it can be financially taxing to maintain a significant fleet of machines, especially if they are not fully utilized at all times. Secondly, there are sustainability concerns associated with the continuous energy consumption and carbon footprint of running numerous servers.

Moreover, the demand for computing resources fluctuates throughout the day. During peak hours, when user activity is high, we require more computational power to handle the increased workload. Conversely, during off-peak hours, such as late at night or early morning, the demand for resources decreases.

To address these challenges, we need to adopt a more dynamic approach to scaling our infrastructure. Instead of relying solely on adding more machines, we should implement mechanisms to adjust the allocation of computing resources based on real-time demand. This involves dynamically scaling up or down the number of servers or virtual instances in response to changes in user activity.

By dynamically optimizing our resource allocation, we can achieve several benefits. Firstly, we can reduce costs by only utilizing the necessary amount of computing power at any given time, thereby minimizing unnecessary expenses. Secondly, we can maintain optimal performance levels by ensuring that our system resources are aligned with current demand. Finally, we can contribute to sustainability efforts by reducing energy consumption and minimizing our environmental impact.

There are two primary methods for scaling machines to meet changing resource requirements: vertical scaling and horizontal scaling.

Reactive Scaling

Reactive scaling is a strategy employed to dynamically adjust the number of machines or servers in a system based on the changing demands of user traffic. Essentially, it involves continuously monitoring the usage patterns of a service or application and automatically scaling the infrastructure up or down to ensure optimal performance and resource utilization.

In the context provided, the approach involved closely observing the demand for a service, known as Spaces, while simultaneously evaluating the number of machines currently active in the system. This evaluation is typically done by analyzing metrics such as CPU usage, memory usage, network traffic, and other relevant indicators.

By comparing the demand for the service with the available resources, the system can make informed decisions about whether to scale up (add more machines) or scale down (remove or deactivate machines) to efficiently handle the workload. This dynamic adjustment helps maintain a balance between resource availability and demand, ensuring that users experience consistent performance and responsiveness from the application.

In essence, reactive scaling enables systems to adapt in real-time to changes in user activity, optimizing resource allocation and overall system efficiency.

Additionally, most cloud providers bill usage time in hourly increments, while machines provisioned for reactive scaling were often used for less than an hour before being deleted. This led to a significant increase in the number of unique machines provisioned, resulting in higher cloud costs due to billing for full hours even if the machine was only utilized for a fraction of that time. In essence, this billing model led to inefficiencies compared to maintaining a consistent number of machines.

Preemptive Scaling

As our platform progressed, we recognized the need for a more efficient approach to enhance performance while mitigating costs. We aimed to anticipate demand on the platform and ensure that machines were provisioned before users accessed the platform. To achieve this goal, we implemented proactive scaling solutions, enabling us to scale machines preemptively based on insights gleaned from historical user traffic data.

The proactive scaling strategy involved analyzing extensive historical data about user usage patterns. By leveraging advanced algorithms, we forecasted the platform's future resource requirements at various points in time. This predictive information empowered us to scale up or down the number of machines well in advance of user traffic spikes or declines.

Essentially, our proactive scaling approach involves the following.

1. **Data Analysis**

    We meticulously examined historical user traffic data, including usage patterns, peak hours, and seasonal trends, to gain insights into future resource demands.

2. **Algorithm Deployment**

   Utilizing machine learning algorithms and predictive analytics, we developed models to forecast the platform's resource needs accurately.

3. **Preemptive Scaling**

   Based on the predictions generated by our algorithms, we proactively adjusted the number of machines in our infrastructure to ensure optimal performance and cost efficiency.

By adopting proactive scaling measures, we were able to optimize resource allocation, minimize service interruptions, and enhance the overall user experience on our platform. This proactive approach significantly improved our ability to meet fluctuating demand and adapt to changing user requirements effectively.

Cloud Native for Edge Computing

The adoption of cloud-native principles has emerged as a pivotal strategy, revolutionizing how applications are managed and deployed at the network edge. Edge computing brings computational resources closer to data sources, minimizing latency and optimizing bandwidth usage, particularly crucial for real-time processing and low-latency applications.

At its core, cloud-native methodologies in edge computing entail structuring applications as collections of microservices encapsulated within lightweight containers. These containers house the application code, dependencies, and runtime environment, ensuring consistency and portability across diverse edge devices and environments. Leveraging containers facilitates seamless deployment, scaling, and management of edge applications, enabling effortless updates and minimizing downtime.

Moreover, container orchestration platforms like Kubernetes play a pivotal role in automating the deployment, scaling, and orchestration of containerized applications in edge environments. These platforms empower dynamic resource allocation, efficient load balancing, and autonomous recovery mechanisms, ensuring optimal performance and reliability, even in highly distributed edge deployments.

Beyond containerization and orchestration, cloud-native practices such as DevOps, continuous integration/continuous deployment (CI/CD), and infrastructure as code (IaC) are integral components in streamlining the development, testing, and deployment workflows in edge computing. This agile and automated approach fosters rapid iteration, accelerates time-to-market, and enhances operational efficiency for edge applications.

In essence, embracing cloud-native principles in edge computing empowers organizations to harness the scalability, resilience, and agility needed to effectively navigate the complexities of edge deployments. By embracing a cloud-native approach, businesses can fully capitalize on the potential of edge computing to deliver innovative, responsive, and high-performing applications at the network edge.

1. **Optimizing Resource Efficiency in Edge Environments**

   Cloud-native principles prioritize the efficient utilization of computing resources within edge environments. A typical cloud-native architecture harnesses containers, which are lightweight and isolated runtime environments for applications. Containers serve as a technology for packaging and deploying applications, ensuring consistent and reliable deployment across diverse environments by encapsulating the following components into a single package:

The executable code responsible for the application's functionality necessitates dependencies to ensure seamless code execution. Additionally, libraries play a crucial role in providing essential functionalities and supporting code execution. Furthermore, all requisite system tools and configurations are essential components for the application's successful operation. Containers leverage the kernel of the host operating system, reducing virtualization overhead and enabling efficient resource utilization. This characteristic is particularly advantageous in edge computing scenarios where processing power and data storage are limited.

Moreover, container orchestration aids in resource allocation by orchestrating tools to allocate resources based on application requirements. This ensures each container receives the necessary resources without over-provisioning or under-provisioning.

Efficient resource utilization directly correlates with cost savings, especially in scenarios where edge devices operate in remote or resource-constrained locations. By optimizing resource usage, organizations can maximize the value derived from their cloud-native architectures while minimizing operational expenses.

CHAPTER 6   SCALABILITY AND AUTOSCALING STRATEGIES

2. **Enhancing Scalability with Cloud-Native Principles**

Cloud-native principles revolutionize the scalability of systems, enabling them to dynamically adjust and adapt to fluctuating demands. Microservices architecture facilitates seamless scaling of instances in response to workload fluctuations and evolving requirements. Dynamic autoscaling empowers edge systems to automatically adjust their capacity in real-time, aligning with changes in demand. During peak usage periods or sudden spikes in processing needs, the system effortlessly scales out to accommodate the increased workload. Conversely, during periods of low demand or reduced activity, the system scales down to optimize resource utilization and conserve energy.

Several edge computing use cases highlight the significant benefits of dynamic autoscaling:

- In a smart city application, edge devices responsible for traffic monitoring can dynamically scale their microservices to handle increased processing demands during rush hours, ensuring efficient traffic management. Conversely, scaling down during quieter periods helps conserve resources and minimize energy consumption.
- In manufacturing plants leveraging Industrial Internet of Things (IIoT) technology, edge devices monitoring machinery can adjust processing

capabilities based on the production load. Scaling up during peak production times ensures optimal efficiency, while scaling down during downtime reduces operational costs.

- Edge devices deployed in healthcare applications can dynamically scale during emergencies or critical health events, ensuring timely processing of vital data. Scaling down during routine periods helps prolong device battery life and optimize resource allocation.

- For video surveillance systems deployed at the edge, dynamic autoscaling enables the adjustment of processing capabilities during events requiring intensive video analysis, such as large crowds or security alerts. Scaling down during periods of minimal activity conserves resources and reduces operational overhead.

- By leveraging cloud-native principles, edge applications can seamlessly scale both horizontally at the edge and vertically in the cloud. This unified architecture ensures flexibility and resilience across diverse deployment locations and strategies, empowering organizations to effectively meet evolving demands and maximize operational efficiency in edge computing environments.

3. **Enhancing Resilience with High Fault Tolerance**

Cloud-native architectures prioritize fault tolerance, leveraging distributed designs and redundant microservices to ensure seamless operation even in challenging scenarios such as network disruptions or device failures. Fault tolerance is particularly crucial for edge devices.

The distributed nature of cloud-native applications minimizes the impact of potential failures by eliminating single points of failure (SPOFs). In the event of an issue or outage affecting a specific microservice, the remaining services continue to operate autonomously, preserving overall system functionality.

Cloud-native edge computing employs several strategies to maintain high fault tolerance:

- Deployment of duplicate instances of critical components and microservices to mitigate the impact of failures and ensure continuous operation.

- Adoption of resilient communication patterns, such as implementing circuit breakers or retry mechanisms, to handle network disruptions and mitigate cascading failures.

- Establishment of redundant routes for data transmission to circumvent potential network bottlenecks or failures.

Additionally, automated recovery mechanisms play a vital role in enhancing fault tolerance. Orchestration tools like Kubernetes monitor the health and performance of edge applications, automatically detecting anomalies or failures. Upon detection, these tools initiate corrective actions, such as replacing problematic instances with healthy ones, to maintain system integrity and reliability.

By implementing these strategies, cloud-native edge computing environments can achieve high fault tolerance, ensuring uninterrupted operation and resilience in the face of unforeseen challenges and disruptions.

4. **Enhancing Security at the Edge**

   Cloud-native edge computing significantly strengthens security measures within edge environments, particularly crucial as devices often vary in their level of trustworthiness. The cloud-native approach to edge computing enhances security in the following ways:

   Containerized Microservices

   Each microservice operates within its own container, effectively isolating it from other components. This containment limits the potential impact of security incidents, as any vulnerabilities or flaws within one microservice do not affect the integrity of other system parts.

   Isolation Benefits

   The isolated nature of containers makes it challenging for intruders to move laterally from one container to another. This isolation significantly reduces the risk of unauthorized access and prevents the spread of malicious activities across the system.

   Rapid Deployment of Security Patches

   The lightweight nature of containers allows for swift deployment of security patches and updates. This agility ensures that vulnerabilities can be addressed

CHAPTER 6   SCALABILITY AND AUTOSCALING STRATEGIES

promptly, minimizing the window of exposure to potential threats.

Fine-Grained Access Control

The modular design of cloud-native edge computing facilitates fine-grained access control and authentication mechanisms. Each microservice can have its own tailored security policy, reducing the attack surface and limiting the impact of potential breaches.

5. **Efficient Deployment and Updates**

   Cloud-native methodologies streamline the process of deploying and updating applications in dynamic and dispersed edge environments. Continuous integration (CI) and continuous deployment (CD), fundamental concepts in cloud-native development, underpin the rapid deployment and updating of applications:

   Continuous Integration (CI)

   This practice involves integrating code changes into a shared repository on a regular basis. It ensures that new features, bug fixes, or enhancements are continuously tested and validated, reducing the likelihood of integration issues and ensuring the reliability of the application.

   Continuous Deployment (CD)

   CD automates the process of deploying validated code changes into a production environment swiftly and reliably.

CHAPTER 6   SCALABILITY AND AUTOSCALING STRATEGIES

In edge scenarios, where devices often possess diverse configurations, CI becomes indispensable for maintaining consistency and reliability across applications. Conversely, CD enables organizations to release updates promptly and securely to edge devices. Cloud-native edge applications frequently employ rolling updates, a strategy that gradually replaces old instances with new versions. This approach minimizes downtime and ensures uninterrupted operation.

Moreover, over-the-air (OTA) updates play a crucial role in edge scenarios, allowing teams to remotely update and manage software on edge devices. OTA updates are particularly significant in industries such as manufacturing, where edge devices on the factory floor must receive updates without disrupting the production process.

6. **Cost-Efficiency in IT Operations**

Optimizing the utilization of computing resources plays a pivotal role in the economic feasibility of deploying applications within edge environments. Cloud-native edge computing offers a range of strategies to lower IT expenses:

Autoscaling

Autoscaling dynamically adjusts resource allocation based on fluctuating workloads, ensuring efficient resource utilization. Edge devices adapt to varying activity levels, efficiently allocating resources during periods of high demand and minimizing costs during idle times.

Containerization

The lightweight nature of containers reduces overhead, allowing multiple containers to run on a single device without compromising performance. This maximizes resource utilization without incurring costly duplication.

Serverless Computing

Organizations leverage serverless computing, paying only for the actual computing resources consumed during the execution of functions or services. This pay-as-you-go model proves particularly advantageous in edge scenarios characterized by sporadic bursts of computation.

Local Data Processing

Cloud-native edge applications utilize data filtering, aggregation, and compression locally to minimize the volume of data traversing the network. By reducing data transmission, bandwidth expenses are minimized, contributing to overall cost savings.

7. **Enhanced Performance**

   Cloud-native methodologies, when combined with strategic network architecture, significantly enhance connectivity reliability and minimize latency in dynamic edge environments.

   Cloud-native edge computing relies on specialized communication protocols tailored for efficient edge interactions. Two prominent protocols are

- **MQTT (Message Queuing Telemetry Transport):** Designed for constrained devices and low-bandwidth, high-latency, or unreliable networks, MQTT is a lightweight and efficient messaging protocol.

- **CoAP (Constrained Application Protocol):** CoAP facilitates lightweight communication suitable for edge environments, ensuring efficient data exchange while conserving bandwidth and minimizing latency.

Moreover, decentralized processing and edge intelligence play a pivotal role in performance enhancement. Cloud-native edge devices boast computational capabilities for advanced local processing, reducing the need for frequent data transfers and alleviating network congestion.

Dynamic load balancing further contributes to performance optimization by distributing traffic across multiple edge devices or microservice instances, preventing network bottlenecks. For instance, in smart grid scenarios where devices monitor and control energy distribution, load balancing ensures the network's ability to handle demand fluctuations while maintaining optimal performance.

Autoscaling Implementation in AWS

Auto Scaling, an Amazon Web Service, enables instances to automatically adjust their capacity in response to changes in traffic or CPU load. This service monitors all instances configured within the Auto Scaling group, ensuring balanced loads across them. Depending on the configured scaling policies, instances are added or removed to maintain optimal performance.

CHAPTER 6   SCALABILITY AND AUTOSCALING STRATEGIES

When setting up the autoscaling group, parameters such as Desired Capacity, Minimum Capacity, Maximum Capacity, and CPU Utilization are configured. For example, if CPU utilization across all instances exceeds 80%, an additional instance is launched, while if it drops below 20%, an instance may be terminated. These thresholds are customizable based on specific requirements. If any instance fails for any reason, the Auto Scaling group automatically maintains the Desired Capacity by launching a replacement instance. Autoscaling operates on the principle of Horizontal Scaling, where resources are added or removed dynamically based on demand. This service is invaluable as it eliminates the need for manual instance provisioning and monitoring, streamlining the management of resources in dynamic environments.

Autoscaling across different regions in AWS involves deploying resources in multiple AWS regions and configuring autoscaling groups (ASGs) to manage the scaling of those resources based on demand. Here's a general outline of how you can achieve this:

- **Deploy Resources in Multiple Regions:** First, you need to deploy your application resources (e.g., EC2 instances, databases, load balancers) across multiple AWS regions. This ensures that your application can handle traffic from different geographic locations and provides redundancy in case of region-specific failures.

- **Set Up Auto-Scaling Groups (ASGs):** Create autoscaling groups for each resource type (e.g., EC2 instances) in each region where you've deployed resources. ASGs automatically adjust the number of instances in response to changes in demand or health checks.

- **Configure Scaling Policies:** Define scaling policies for your ASGs to specify when and how to scale. For example, you can set up policies to scale based on CPU utilization, network traffic, or other custom metrics. Ensure that you configure these policies appropriately for each region based on its specific traffic patterns and requirements.

- **Cross-Region Load Balancing:** If you're using a load balancer to distribute traffic across regions, configure it to distribute traffic evenly among the regions where you've deployed resources. AWS provides services like Route 53 for DNS-based load balancing or the Elastic Load Balancing service for distributing traffic across multiple regions.

- **Monitoring and Alerting:** Set up monitoring and alerting for your autoscaling groups and resources to track performance metrics and respond to any issues proactively. AWS CloudWatch is a useful tool for monitoring various AWS resources and setting up alarms based on predefined thresholds.

- **Testing and Optimization:** Regularly test and optimize your autoscaling configurations to ensure that they effectively handle traffic fluctuations across different regions. This may involve adjusting scaling policies, instance types, or other configuration parameters based on performance data and feedback.

- **Disaster Recovery and Failover:** Implement a disaster recovery plan that includes failover procedures between regions in case of catastrophic failures or

CHAPTER 6   SCALABILITY AND AUTOSCALING STRATEGIES

downtime in one region. This ensures high availability and resilience for your application across different geographic locations.

By following these steps, you can effectively implement autoscaling across different regions in AWS to ensure optimal performance, high availability, and resilience for your applications.

Benefits of Autoscaling

1. **Dynamic Scaling**

    AWS autoscaling service operates seamlessly, requiring no manual intervention from users. It continuously monitors the incoming traffic to the application and dynamically adjusts the number of resources (such as instances or containers) up or down as needed. This ensures that the application can efficiently handle fluctuations in user demand without experiencing performance degradation or downtime. For example, during peak traffic periods, the autoscaling service automatically adds more resources to ensure optimal performance and responsiveness. Conversely, during periods of low traffic, it scales down resources to minimize costs and avoid over-provisioning.

2. **Pay-As-You-Go Model**

    Autoscaling optimizes resource utilization based on real-time demand, resulting in cost savings for users. With this model, users are billed only for the resources they actually use, rather than paying for fixed or over-provisioned capacity. As a result, organizations can optimize their spending by aligning resource usage with actual demand patterns. This flexibility allows businesses to scale their applications without incurring unnecessary expenses, making it a cost-effective solution for managing varying workloads.

3. **Automatic Performance Optimization**

   In addition to adjusting resource allocation, AWS autoscaling ensures optimal application performance. By continuously monitoring workload metrics and performance indicators, such as response times and latency, the autoscaling service proactively adjusts resource levels to maintain desired performance levels. For instance, if the application experiences an increase in traffic, autoscaling can automatically provision additional resources to handle the load, preventing performance bottlenecks and ensuring a seamless user experience. Conversely, during periods of low demand, resources are scaled down to conserve resources and minimize costs while still maintaining acceptable performance levels. This automatic performance optimization allows organizations to meet the demands of dynamic workloads while ensuring consistent and reliable application performance.

4. **Enhanced Resource Allocation**

   Autoscaling optimizes the utilization of cloud resources by dynamically adjusting resource allocation based on real-time demand.

By aligning resource provisioning with actual usage patterns, it ensures that resources are utilized efficiently, leading to cost savings and promoting environmentally sustainable practices through reduced energy consumption in data centers.

Moreover, autoscaling streamlines the scaling process by automating the adjustment of resources, eliminating the need for manual intervention. This automation reduces the burden on IT teams, allowing them to allocate their time and resources to more strategic initiatives rather than spending it on managing capacity and scaling resources manually.

Steps to Create Autoscaling

1. Log in to the AWS Management Console.

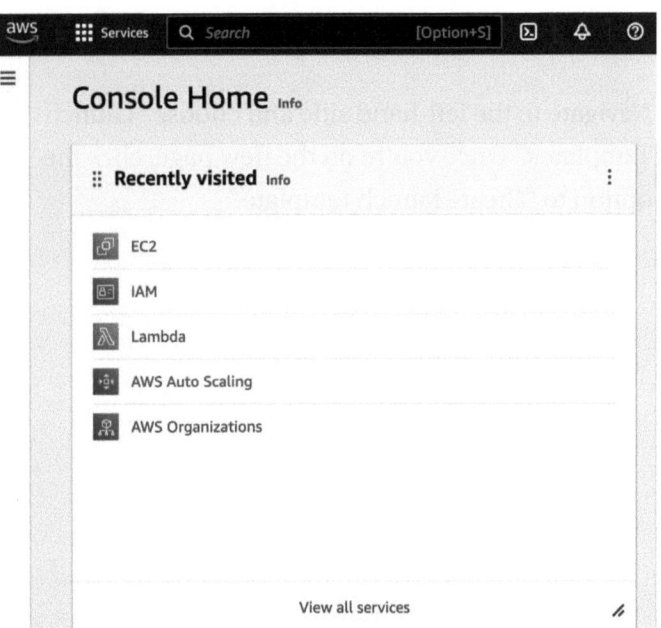

CHAPTER 6   SCALABILITY AND AUTOSCALING STRATEGIES

2. Navigate to the Amazon EC2 console.

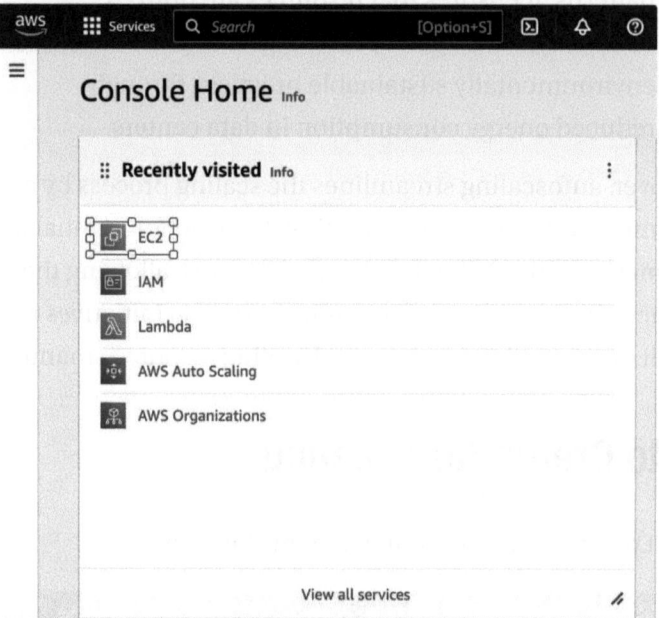

3. Navigate to the left-hand side and choose "Launch Templates." Once you're on the new page, click the option to "Create launch template."

CHAPTER 6 SCALABILITY AND AUTOSCALING STRATEGIES

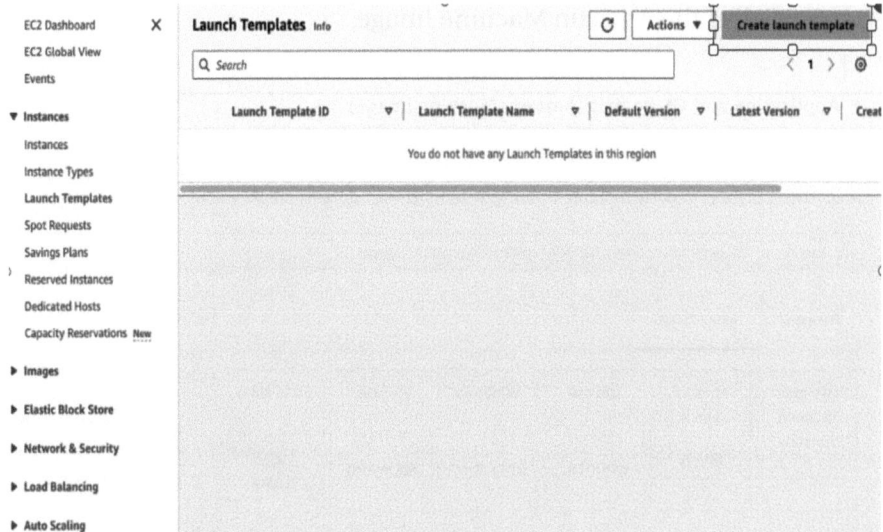

4. Provide the template name as shown in the following screenshot.

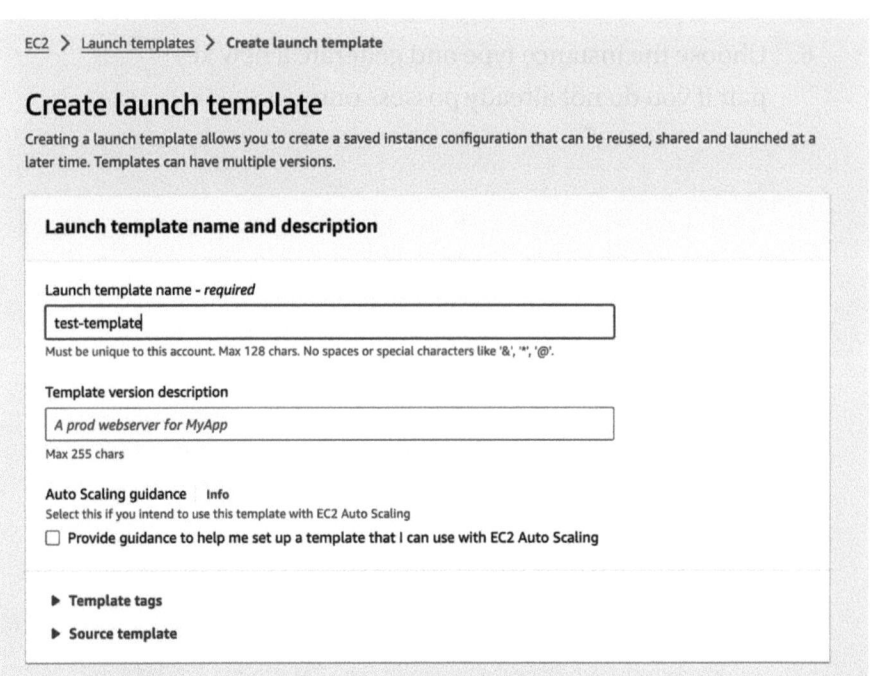

253

CHAPTER 6   SCALABILITY AND AUTOSCALING STRATEGIES

5. Select the Amazon Machine Image.

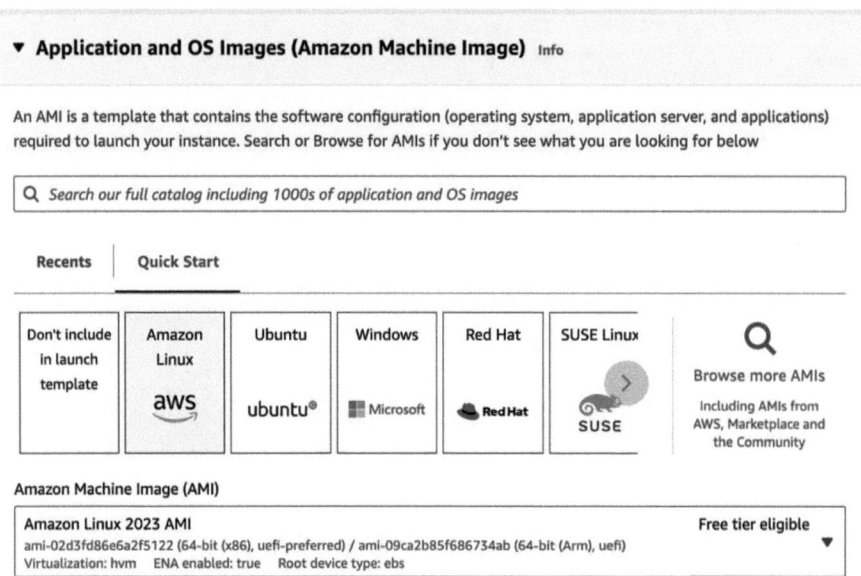

6. Choose the instance type and generate a new key pair if you do not already possess one.

CHAPTER 6   SCALABILITY AND AUTOSCALING STRATEGIES

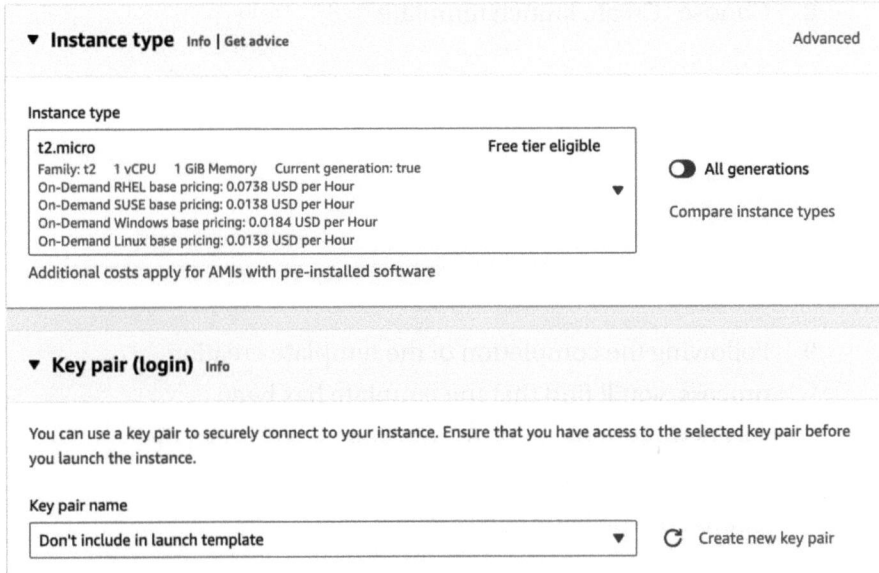

7. Choose the security group and create a new key pair if you do not already possess one.

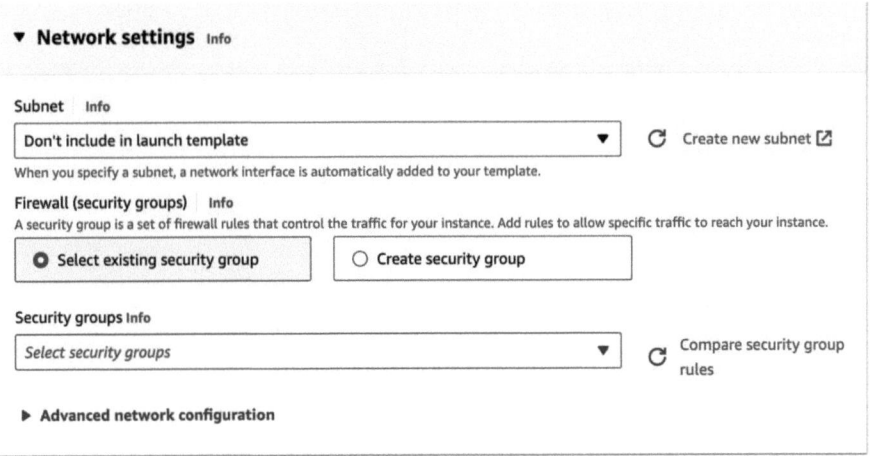

255

CHAPTER 6   SCALABILITY AND AUTOSCALING STRATEGIES

8. Choose "Create launch template."

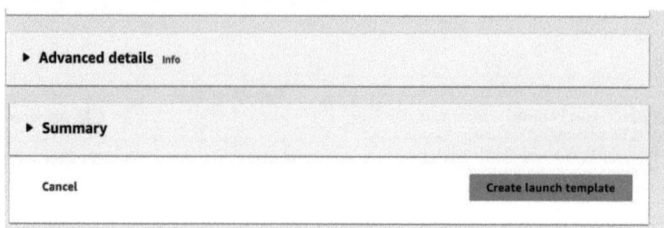

9. Following the completion of the template creation process, you'll find that the template has been successfully generated. To continue, scroll down the page and select the "Auto Scaling Groups" option located on the left-hand side.

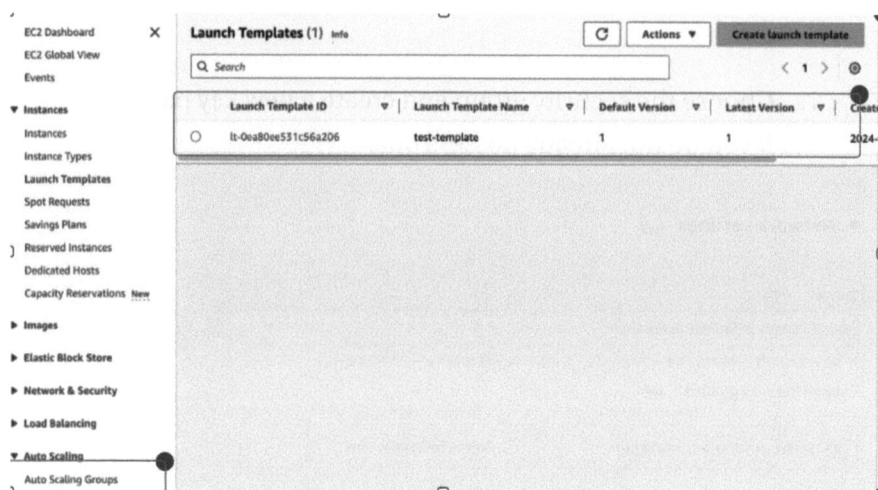

10. Select on the **Create Auto Scaling group**.

CHAPTER 6   SCALABILITY AND AUTOSCALING STRATEGIES

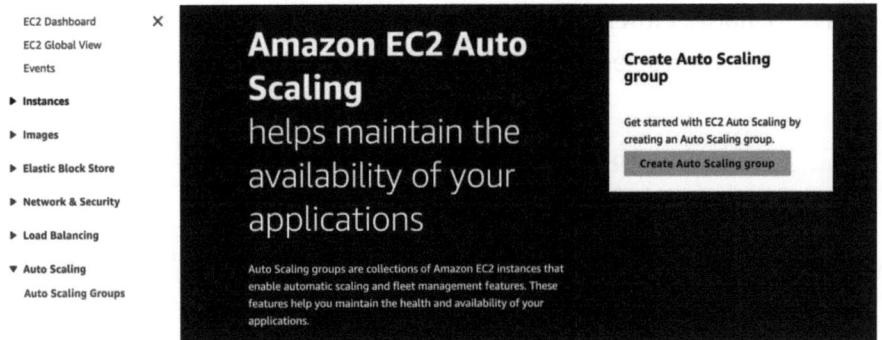

11. Enter the name for the autoscaling group, select the created template "test-template" from the dropdown then select next.

257

CHAPTER 6   SCALABILITY AND AUTOSCALING STRATEGIES

12. Choose either the VPC or stick with the default VPC, and then select the desired Availability Zone.

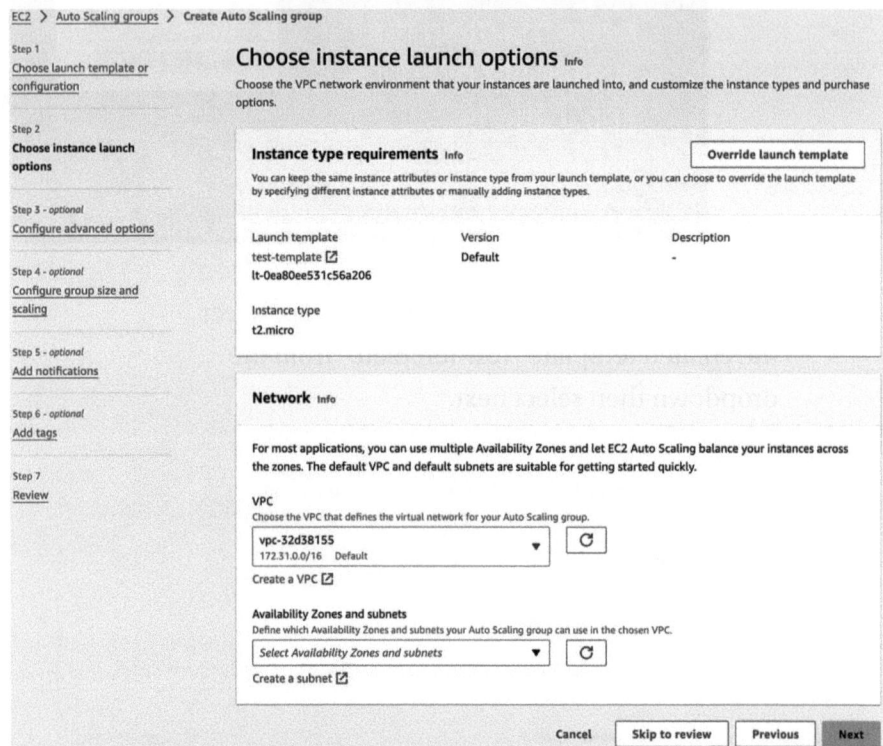

13. Customize the Group size and Scaling policies to suit your specific needs. You have the option to configure the settings as follows: Desired: 3, Minimum: 3, Maximum: 6. Adjust these parameters based on your requirements for optimal scaling behavior.

CHAPTER 6   SCALABILITY AND AUTOSCALING STRATEGIES

14. Select the target scaling policy and then select "Create Auto Scaling Group."

CHAPTER 6   SCALABILITY AND AUTOSCALING STRATEGIES

Scaling Info
You can resize your Auto Scaling group manually or automatically to meet changes in demand.

Scaling limits
Set limits on how much your desired capacity can be increased or decreased.

Min desired capacity	Max desired capacity
3	6
Equal or less than desired capacity	Equal or greater than desired capacity

Automatic scaling - *optional*
Choose whether to use a target tracking policy   Info
You can set up other metric-based scaling policies and scheduled scaling after creating your Auto Scaling group.

○ **No scaling policies**
Your Auto Scaling group will remain at its initial size and will not dynamically resize to meet demand.

● **Target tracking scaling policy**
Choose a CloudWatch metric and target value and let the scaling policy adjust the desired capacity in proportion to the metric's value.

Scaling policy name
Target Tracking Policy

Metric type   Info
Monitored metric that determines if resource utilization is too low or high. If using EC2 metrics, consider enabling detailed monitoring for better scaling performance.

Average CPU utilization ▼

Target value
50

Instance warmup   Info
60   seconds

☐ Disable scale in to create only a scale-out policy

15. As you can see the test-scaling group is created.

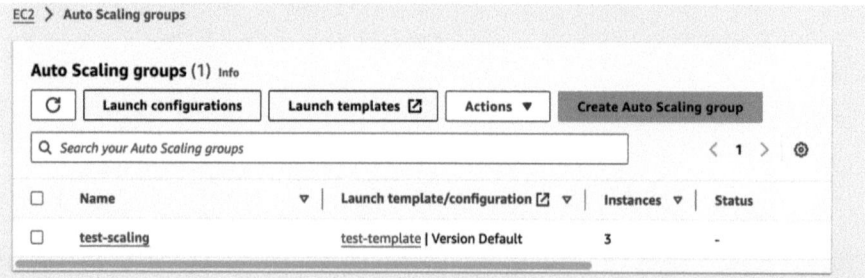

CHAPTER 6   SCALABILITY AND AUTOSCALING STRATEGIES

16. As we set the desired state to 3, you'll notice that there are currently 3 instances running.

☐	i-071c2f10ce43724b4	⊘ Running 🔍 🔍	t2.micro	⊘ 2/2 checks passed	View alarms +
☐	i-03a0ef45fea6f0715	⊘ Running 🔍 🔍	t2.micro	⊘ 2/2 checks passed	View alarms +
☐	i-009038aaf8acbb3c3	⊘ Running 🔍 🔍	t2.micro	⊘ 2/2 checks passed	View alarms +

Future Trends in Scalability and Autoscaling

Machine Learning-Driven Autoscaling

Predictive Autoscaling: By analyzing historical workload patterns and performance metrics, machine learning algorithms can predict future resource demands with greater accuracy. This allows autoscaling systems to proactively adjust resources before demand spikes occur, reducing the risk of under-provisioning or over-provisioning.

Anomaly Detection: Machine learning models can identify anomalies or unusual patterns in application metrics, such as sudden increases in traffic or deviations from expected behavior. Detecting these anomalies early allows autoscaling systems to take corrective actions, such as scaling resources or triggering alerts, to maintain optimal performance and availability.

Serverless Architectures and Event-Driven Scaling

Fine-grained Autoscaling: In serverless architectures, autoscaling operates at a granular level, scaling resources dynamically in response to individual function invocations or events. This fine-grained scalability ensures that resources are allocated precisely where and when they are needed, optimizing resource utilization and minimizing costs.

Dynamic Resource Provisioning: Serverless platforms handle resource provisioning automatically, abstracting away the complexities of infrastructure management. Resources are provisioned dynamically in real-time, allowing applications to scale seamlessly in response to changes in workload without requiring manual intervention.

Edge Computing and Distributed Scaling

Edge-Native Autoscaling: Edge computing environments are characterized by distributed edge nodes located closer to the source of data generation. Autoscaling in these environments requires tailored solutions that can dynamically allocate resources across distributed nodes based on workload demands, taking into account factors such as network latency and device capabilities.

Federated Autoscaling: Federated learning techniques enable collaborative autoscaling across distributed edge nodes while preserving data privacy and security. Edge devices can collectively optimize resource allocation and share insights without compromising sensitive data, allowing for efficient and scalable edge computing solutions.

Hybrid and Multi-cloud Scalability

Interoperable Autoscaling: Hybrid and multi-cloud environments require interoperable autoscaling mechanisms that can seamlessly scale workloads across different cloud providers and on-premises infrastructure. Standardized APIs and protocols facilitate communication and coordination between disparate environments, enabling workload mobility and resource elasticity.

Policy-Based Autoscaling: Organizations define policies governing autoscaling behavior based on business requirements, compliance

CHAPTER 6 SCALABILITY AND AUTOSCALING STRATEGIES

regulations, and cost considerations. These policies dictate how resources are allocated and scaled across hybrid and multi-cloud environments, ensuring optimal performance and cost-efficiency.

Cost-Efficient Autoscaling Strategies

Cost-Efficient Autoscaling Strategies include cost-aware scaling policies that adjust resource allocation based on real-time pricing and usage data, and leveraging spot and preemptible instance utilization to optimize resource costs while maintaining performance and reliability.

Cost-Aware Scaling Policies: Autoscaling strategies incorporate cost optimization algorithms that dynamically adjust resource allocation based on real-time pricing and usage data. By considering factors such as spot instance pricing, on-demand rates, and workload patterns, organizations can optimize resource utilization and minimize infrastructure costs while maintaining service levels.

Spot and Preemptible Instance Utilization: Integrating spot instances and preemptible VMs into autoscaling strategies enables organizations to leverage low-cost resources during periods of low demand. By dynamically provisioning spot instances or preemptible VMs when available, organizations can reduce costs without sacrificing performance or reliability.

Summary

In this chapter, we've delved into the fundamental concepts of scalability and autoscaling mechanisms in cloud-native applications. We began by exploring the basics of scalability, distinguishing between horizontal and vertical scaling methods, and understanding the challenges posed by managing stateless and stateful services. With this foundational understanding, we then delved into the realm of autoscaling, a crucial

CHAPTER 6　SCALABILITY AND AUTOSCALING STRATEGIES

aspect of modern cloud-native architectures. Autoscaling allows applications to dynamically adjust their resource allocation based on fluctuating workload demands. We examined the intricacies of both reactive and proactive autoscaling strategies, including the utilization of triggers, metrics, and dynamic policies to orchestrate scaling events effectively. Implementation considerations were also discussed, covering various approaches such as leveraging container orchestration platforms, cloud provider services, or custom-built solutions tailored to specific requirements. Moreover, we highlighted the significance of monitoring, metrics collection, and rigorous testing in ensuring the reliability and efficiency of autoscaling policies. By striking a balance between performance optimization and cost considerations, organizations can effectively mitigate scalability bottlenecks and optimize their autoscaling strategies. Looking ahead, we discussed emerging trends and future directions in scalability and autoscaling, providing insights into potential advancements such as machine learning-driven autoscaling and the adoption of serverless computing paradigms. Overall, this chapter serves as a comprehensive guide to understanding, implementing, and optimizing scalability and autoscaling strategies in cloud-native environments.

CHAPTER 7

Collaborative Development in the Cloud Native

"Where teamwork makes the dream work... and keeps the servers from getting too lonely!"

This chapter focuses on the symbiotic relationship between collaboration and cloud computing. It delves into key aspects such as improving collaboration between developers and operations teams, optimizing data movement within cloud environments, and implementing specialized processes for supply chain management. By exploring these topics, readers gain insights into maximizing efficiency and effectiveness in cloud-based operations.

    First, we'll see why it's essential for developers and operations teams to work closely, often called DevOps. When they work together well, it helps in making things smoother, faster, and better quality. We'll look at the tools and methods that help them work together effectively, especially in cloud setups.

    Then, we'll talk about making data move around efficiently in the cloud. This is important for organizations that want to use their data effectively. We'll discuss different ways to store, process, and move data in the cloud, showing how it can be done well with real-life examples.

CHAPTER 7   COLLABORATIVE DEVELOPMENT IN THE CLOUD NATIVE

Lastly, we'll discuss using special processes and managing the supply chain in the cloud. We'll show how these can help in integrating data, analyzing it, and making better decisions. When organizations combine these processes with cloud technology, they can see and manage their operations better.

Overall, the chapter highlights that working together in the cloud is not just about using technology; it's also about having a smart strategy. By collaborating, optimizing, and innovating, organizations can make the most out of the cloud and succeed in today's digital world.

In this chapter, we will be encompassing the following topics:

- Enabling Collaboration Between Developers and Operations
- Agile and Scrum Methodology in Cloud Native
- Optimizing Cloud-Based Data Flow
- ETL Processes and Supply Chain Management

Enabling Collaboration Between Developers and Operations

The DevSecOps culture extends beyond simply adopting security tools and procedures; it embodies a mindset that permeates the entire organization. Collaboration and accountability stand as fundamental principles within this culture. Collaboration fosters seamless cooperation among cross-functional teams, while accountability ensures that all individuals assume responsibility for security and reliability throughout the development process.

DevOps Culture

When considering how to encourage cooperation between Development (Dev) and Operations (Ops), I envision a unified team with common goals and tools. The outdated approach of having separate teams for software delivery and infrastructure management is flawed. We should shift the focus toward providing valuable, enjoyable, and seamless customer experiences to boost market share for enterprises. This requires management to structure teams aligned with these objectives and empower them to take ownership. They should design the appropriate tech stack to deliver results effectively and monitor outcomes proactively.

- **Deploy Ambassadors to Every Team**

    To enhance business value, companies must instigate a cultural transformation that amplifies collaboration between development and IT Ops, effectively merging them into one cohesive unit. A proactive approach involves appointing ambassadors from each team to participate in the other's crucial meetings and relay insights back to their respective teams. Regular joint meetings also facilitate this shift. This alteration in team dynamics cultivates a finely tuned operation – developers start considering operational needs, while operations personnel offer assistance in creating deployment scripts. This synchronization empowers the team to confidently deploy new software versions, fostering agility and innovation without compromising software stability and reliability.

    Example: Imagine a company has a software development team and an IT operations team. They appoint one person from each team to attend the other team's meetings. For instance, a developer attends operations meetings, while someone from operations attends development meetings. These ambassadors share insights and concerns from their respective teams, ensuring that both sides understand each other's needs and challenges. As a result, developers learn about the operational requirements for deploying software, while operations personnel gain insights into the development process.

- **Promote Cross-Pollination**

    A fruitful method for fostering collaboration between Development (Dev) and Operations (Ops) is through cross-pollination. In environments where these teams are distinct, encourage members from the Dev team to spend time in Ops, and vice versa, to grasp each other's challenges. Alternatively, consider establishing delivery teams where both development and operations experts collaborate within a unified team structure. This arrangement encourages active pairing to devise solutions that cater to both development and maintenance needs. Additionally, deliberately integrating automation testing for failure scenarios can be instrumental in identifying issues that may otherwise only surface during production.

    Example: Consider a software company where developers spend a week working alongside the operations team, and vice versa. During this time, developers assist with tasks like deploying software updates, while operations staff gain a better understanding of the development process. Additionally, the company forms cross-functional delivery teams comprising both developers and operations experts. These teams work closely together on projects, sharing knowledge and expertise to ensure that applications are both developed and maintained effectively.

- **Eliminate Silos**

  To enhance collaboration between development and IT Ops, it's crucial to blur the boundaries separating them as distinct teams. Instead, transition to a framework of practices that everyone can adopt. By bringing team members together in the same physical space, silos and obstacles can be eliminated, resulting in improved productivity and fostering a culture that prioritizes challenging norms, continuous learning, and, above all, collaboration.

  Example: Picture a company that adopts a new way of working where developers and operations staff sit together in an open workspace rather than in separate departments. By physically bringing everyone together, communication barriers are broken down, and collaboration is encouraged. Team members collaborate on projects from start to finish, leading to increased productivity and a culture of teamwork and innovation.

- **Enhance Learning Methods**

  Improving collaboration between development and operations relies on refining the methods of learning. While discussions in DevOps often center on tools and meetings, these elements can divert attention from the core issues. To truly enhance DevOps, organizations should concentrate on establishing processes that enable rapid learning feedback loops. A valuable starting point is the Plan-Do-Study-Act (PDSA) cycle, initially introduced by W. Edwards Deming, a pioneer in modern quality control. By implementing the PDSA cycle, organizations acquire a powerful mechanism for advancement. This entails planning the DevOps process, implementing it, and then carefully examining the outcomes to extract insights. By posing the question, "What did we learn here?" after each cycle, organizations can progressively refine their processes. This ongoing cycle of improvement, with contributions from various teams, steadily enhances the process with each iteration.

Example: Suppose an organization implements a new learning process inspired by the Plan-Do-Study-Act (PDSA) cycle. In this process, teams plan a new development or operations procedure, implement it, study the results, and then adjust based on what they've learned. For example, after deploying a new software update, the team reviews the process to identify any areas for improvement. By continually learning and adapting, the organization improves its development and operations practices over time.

- **User-Centric Experience Teams**

  Teams specializing in user or digital experience management serve as an effective avenue for Operations and Development to enhance collaboration throughout the application life cycle. This joint effort yields insights not only into performance but also into relevance, usability, and even the expenses associated with service delivery.

Example: Imagine a company forms dedicated teams focused on improving the user experience of its software products. These teams include members from both development and operations backgrounds who collaborate closely throughout the software development life cycle. For example, they work together to identify user needs, test new features, and ensure that software updates are deployed smoothly. By prioritizing the user experience and collaborating effectively, the company delivers high-quality software that meets user expectations.

Agile and Scrum Methodology in Cloud Native

Cloud-native development, when paired with Agile practices, offers a flexible and collaborative approach perfectly suited to the demands of cloud environments. This approach emphasizes iterative development cycles, continuous delivery, and close collaboration among cross-functional teams. Agile's iterative nature complements the dynamic and scalable aspects of cloud-native applications, enabling rapid adjustments and enhancements. Moreover, Agile principles prioritize customer satisfaction and value delivery, ensuring that cloud-native solutions effectively meet evolving user needs. Through automation and continuous improvement, Agile methodologies streamline the delivery of high-quality software optimized for cloud-native architectures and technologies.

- **Collaborate for Intricate Bugs**

  Work together on quickly fixing complex bugs – "But it works on my machine," we all dread hearing. This problem is worsened when teams are dispersed throughout the globe, and the back-and-forth work on bugs costs the developers and, ultimately, the company a lot of time and money. Rather than allowing complex faults or patches to be passed from one person to the next, development and testing teams can use the cloud to interact in real-time and resolve issues more quickly. Remote teams can collaborate utilizing the same online environment, where troubleshooting and issue fixes can happen in real-time, thanks to cloud technologies that enable "VM publishing" and "over-the-shoulder view." Further, having a gold version also allows testers to access a live reproduction of an issue for instant evaluation, as well as provisioning of several environments to protect test teams from being barred from a release.

- **Standard Version for Every Release**

  Create a standardized version for every release by constructing an application that involves numerous intricate tasks beyond just creating virtual machines, such as establishing network connections and configuring firewall policies. Consequently, delivering a complete application, particularly from scratch, can be a challenging and time-intensive endeavor. Cloud technology can aid developers and testers in swiftly and effortlessly provisioning an entire environment or application. By establishing the "gold version" of each release or milestone, developers can revert to the designated version whenever necessary, allowing for multiple copies of any release to be accessible to test engineers and facilitating parallel testing environments.

- **Automate for Hotfix**

    Automate the generation of "hotfix" replicas to align support, development, test, and operations teams – an application's life cycle extends well beyond its initial release. Even after many users have migrated to newer versions, companies must still assist those using older versions of the product. Leveraging cloud technology, test and support teams can significantly streamline this process by replicating previous versions using templates and the "gold" version. This allows teams to reproduce the specific issue reported by the customer, rather than working with the current version, and validate the proposed update with the client.

- **Keeping the Clients Updated with the Latest Updates**

    Finding problems or mistakes early during software creation is important. It's not only cheaper and easier to fix issues and design flaws early on, but it also leads to better results. Using cloud services that allow sharing of new versions with a specific group of clients can offer valuable additional insights and help identify faults or issues at an early stage. Moreover, the ability of the cloud to provide unlimited server access makes experimentation and innovation much easier. Developers don't have to wait as long to create the next version as they would if they were restricted to working on a limited number of physical servers. This means they can iterate more quickly, improving the software more rapidly.

- **Implementation of Agile in Cloud Native**

    Use templates for development and testing to expedite environment setup. These templates contain essential components with clear interfaces, forming the basis of robust applications. By integrating key elements of a software stack, developers can create fresh and innovative products efficiently. Consider crafting comprehensive application stacks as templates to facilitate rapid setup of entire application environments by your development and testing teams, requiring minimal time and effort.

At the core of any cloud technology lies virtualization across all layers. Dev/test templates should seamlessly integrate virtual machines (VMs), networks, storage, installed applications, and security protocols into a unified provisioning entity through the template approach. For even speedier provisioning, development and test teams can establish a repository of pre-made templates containing application components like the application server tier, web tier, and database tier. Then, they can combine these elements as needed to set up the entire application for a specific release. It's crucial to ensure that your library contains the latest versions of these components, incorporating all essential security updates.

Benefits of Agile Methodology

1. **Abundant Testing and Staging Servers:** Embracing cloud-native methodologies means having access to a rich pool of resources for testing and staging environments. Unlike traditional setups that rely on physical servers, cloud-native approaches leverage virtualization or containerization to provide on-demand access to servers. This abundance of resources eliminates delays and ensures that development teams can swiftly initiate or continue work without being hindered by server availability.

2. **Concurrent Development Process:** Cloud-native methodologies enable Agile development to operate concurrently and seamlessly. By leveraging cloud-native infrastructure, teams can rapidly provision resources and platforms, reducing the time spent on setup and configuration. This agility empowers teams to work on different aspects of the project simultaneously, streamlining the development workflow and fostering collaboration. Consequently, development cycles become more efficient and responsive to changing requirements.

3. **Innovation and Experimentation:** Cloud-native approaches foster a culture of innovation and experimentation within Agile teams. The flexibility of cloud-native infrastructure allows teams to quickly spin up development environments to test new ideas or features. This agility encourages

creativity and risk-taking, as teams can experiment freely without worrying about resource limitations. By facilitating rapid iteration and exploration, cloud-native methodologies drive continuous improvement and innovation in products and services.

4. **Enhanced Continuous Integration and Delivery (CI/CD):** Cloud-native practices play a pivotal role in enhancing CI/CD workflows within Agile development. Leveraging cloud-native tools and services, such as container orchestration platforms and serverless computing, teams can automate build, test, and deployment processes. This automation accelerates delivery pipelines, reduces manual intervention, and ensures the reliability of deployments. As a result, teams can deliver value to customers more frequently and consistently, driving business agility and competitiveness.

5. **Expanded Availability of Development Platforms and External Services:** Cloud-native methodologies broaden the availability of development platforms and external services for Agile teams. Cloud-native ecosystems offer a plethora of services, such as managed databases, AI/ML tools, and DevOps solutions, that can be seamlessly integrated into development workflows. By leveraging these services, teams can enhance collaboration, productivity, and innovation, while reducing time-to-market and operational overhead.

6. **Flexibility in Handling Complex Features:** Cloud-native architectures provide Agile teams with the flexibility to handle complex features and evolving requirements. With cloud-native technologies like microservices and serverless computing, teams can decompose applications into smaller, independent components that can be scaled and deployed independently. This modularity and flexibility enable teams to respond quickly to changing demands, deploy updates with confidence, and maintain high levels of performance and resilience. As a result, Agile teams can deliver value to customers more effectively, even in dynamic and unpredictable environments.

Roles in Scrum

In the Scrum framework, the organizational structure is purposefully kept simple, comprising just three distinct team roles: the Product Owner, the Scrum Master, and the Development Team. Each role plays a crucial part in ensuring the successful implementation of the Scrum methodology within a project or organization. Let's delve into each role to understand its significance and responsibilities within the Scrum framework.

- **Scrum Master**

    The Scrum Master, distinct from a conventional project manager, operates as a facilitator and mediator within the team, sharing leadership duties with the Product Owner and Development Team. Responsibilities of the Scrum Master include maintaining the team's focus and motivation while resolving any obstacles hindering their progress. For instance, if a Development Team member faces frequent interruptions from another project, the Scrum Master intervenes to facilitate a resolution. Moreover, the Scrum Master ensures the effective implementation of the Scrum framework and Agile principles. This involves coaching the Product Owner, Development Team, and project stakeholders on Scrum processes, as well as overseeing their proper execution. Additionally, logistical arrangements for activities like sprint review sessions fall under the Scrum master's purview, such as ensuring access to necessary facilities like a meeting room with a projector.

- **Development Team**

    Scrum development teams typically consist of a close-knit group, usually no more than seven members. Traditionally, the Scrum framework prefers these members to be co-located, but the rise of remote work has led to the evolution of distributed Scrum practices. These teams comprise individuals with diverse skill sets, such as front-end developers, back-end developers, and DevOps engineers. Each member brings expertise in coding languages, frameworks, tools, and technologies relevant to the project. It's crucial for the team to be balanced according to the project's needs for optimal efficiency. For instance, if the software system requires a simpler front end but a complex back end, there should be more back-end developers than front-end developers to ensure smooth progress. A successful Scrum development team operates with a "united we stand" mentality, aiding each other toward individual and collective success. They self-organize and collaborate closely to overcome challenges and achieve project objectives.

- **Product Owner**

  The ambassador for the eventual software product, known as the Product Owner (PO), holds the highest authority within the Scrum framework. Their primary responsibility is ensuring the quality of the software produced, representing both internal and external customers, as well as stakeholders like end users. This role demands a profound comprehension of business, customer needs, and market dynamics. To effectively manage the product backlog and organize it into Sprints, the PO must possess this comprehensive understanding. Any proposed changes to the product backlog, its features, or priority order must be advocated to the PO by other team members.

Depending on the project and organization, the Product Owner might also participate in the development team's execution of the product backlog, perhaps as a senior developer. However, more commonly, they oversee the product backlog and delegate tasks to the development team. Additionally, the Product Owner plays a pivotal role in determining when the product reaches its Minimum Viable Product (MVP) status, indicating it's ready for its first working iteration to be shipped.

Artifacts in Scrum

In Agile Scrum software development, the term "artifacts" refers to tangible or intangible entities created throughout the development process, akin to the original Latin meaning of the word, which denotes something crafted or produced. These artifacts serve as essential elements that guide and facilitate the iterative development approach of Scrum. The three primary artifacts in Scrum are the Product Backlog, Sprint Backlog, and Increment.

- **Sprint Backlog**

    The Sprint Backlog represents a distilled subset of items selected from the Product Backlog for implementation during a specific sprint. It reflects the commitment of the Development Team to deliver a cohesive set of features or improvements within the sprint's time frame.

    Unlike the Product Backlog, which outlines the long-term vision, the Sprint Backlog provides a detailed, actionable plan for the current sprint. It is a dynamic document that evolves as the sprint progresses, with tasks being added, modified, or removed based on emerging insights and priorities. The Sprint Backlog serves as a visual aid, enabling the team to track progress, identify bottlenecks, and adapt their approach to ensure successful sprint completion.

- **Product Backlog**

    The Product Backlog serves as the backbone of the Scrum framework, embodying the collective vision and goals of the software product under development. It encompasses a comprehensive list of all features, enhancements, and fixes envisioned for the product, meticulously prioritized based on their perceived value and urgency.

    This backlog is not merely a static document but rather a living artifact that evolves alongside the project. It is continuously refined, updated, and reprioritized by the Product Owner in collaboration with stakeholders and the development team. The Product Backlog ensures alignment between development efforts and the overarching business objectives, guiding the team's focus toward delivering maximum value with each iteration.

- **Increment**

    The Increment represents the tangible outcome of each sprint, comprising the cumulative work completed by the Development Team. It is a functional, usable version of the product that incorporates the latest features, enhancements, and fixes developed during the sprint.

Each increment builds upon the previous ones, gradually shaping the product toward its ultimate vision. The Increment is a testament to the team's iterative and incremental approach, showcasing their continuous progress and commitment to delivering value with each sprint. In summary, these Scrum artifacts work in tandem to facilitate collaboration, transparency, and agility within the development process. They provide the necessary structure and guidance for the team to effectively plan, execute, and deliver high-quality software products in a dynamic and ever-evolving environment.

Optimizing Cloud-Based Data Flow

When discussing cloud optimization, the conversation typically revolves around technical aspects like workload management, resource usage efficiency, and cost-effectiveness. However, as governmental entities increasingly rely on cloud services to fulfill their core mission objectives, the concept of optimization transcends mere technical efficiency and cost

CHAPTER 7　COLLABORATIVE DEVELOPMENT IN THE CLOUD NATIVE

savings. It encompasses deriving maximum value from cloud technologies to advance the organization's mission. Achieving optimal cloud utilization involves more than just optimizing technical parameters; it entails leveraging cloud capabilities to enhance mission delivery, streamline workflows, and contribute to the agency's sustainability initiatives. This multi-faceted approach to optimization necessitates collaboration with a diverse array of stakeholders beyond the traditional IT sphere.

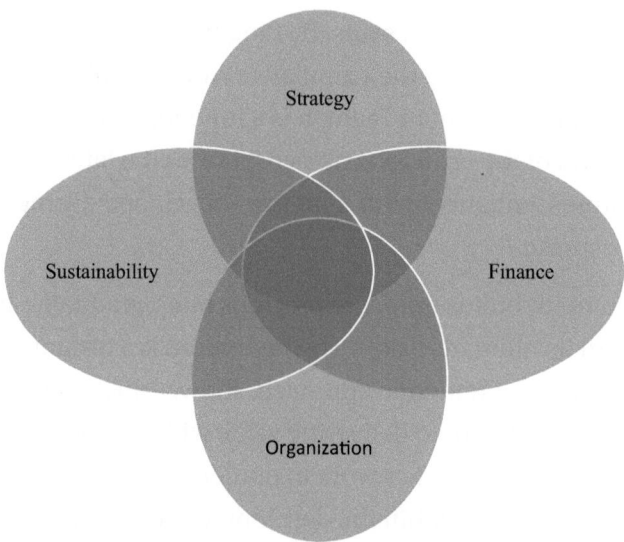

Figure 7-1. *Cloud data flow*

Strategy

Government organizations primarily generate value for their constituents by achieving the strategic objectives outlined in their missions. Therefore, efforts to optimize cloud utilization should be directed toward advancing agencies' mission outcomes and overarching business goals. Beyond facilitating mission execution through the adoption of new applications and workflows, cloud optimization also facilitates the quantification of mission impact by gathering data on mission performance. This data empowers leaders to make informed decisions aimed at enhancing service effectiveness, improving user experiences, and streamlining internal operations.

An IT company migrated its recruitment and hiring application from infrastructure-as-a-service (IaaS) to platform-as-a-service (PaaS) to enhance user experience, automation, and data integrity. This transition to PaaS resulted in reduced system downtime, seamless integration with other hiring applications, a significant reduction in manual intervention, and ultimately led to a decrease in time-to-hire. Additionally, leveraging cloud technology provided the company with enhanced visibility into key metrics for the first time, enabling the measurement of various hiring process milestones such as application submission time, candidate selection duration, background investigation duration, and offer letter issuance time. Traditional IT metrics, including fewer system failures, reduced downtime, and increased automation, provided valuable insights into the user experience for both hiring managers and candidates.

- **Enhanced User Experience:** By transitioning to PaaS, the company could streamline the user interface and optimize the application's performance. This led to a smoother and more intuitive experience for both hiring managers and candidates, resulting in higher user satisfaction.

- **Automation:** Moving to PaaS allowed the company to automate various aspects of the hiring process, such as candidate screening, scheduling interviews, and sending out notifications. This automation not only saved time but also reduced the potential for human error, leading to a more efficient hiring workflow.

- **Data Integrity:** Leveraging PaaS provided better data management capabilities, ensuring the integrity and security of candidate information throughout the hiring process. This helped in maintaining compliance with data protection regulations and mitigating the risk of data breaches.

- **Reduced System Downtime:** PaaS offered better scalability and redundancy compared to IaaS, resulting in reduced system downtime. This ensured that the recruitment application was available and accessible to users at all times, thereby minimizing disruptions to the hiring process.

- Cloud technology provided the company with enhanced visibility into key metrics related to the hiring process. By measuring various milestones such as application submission time, candidate selection duration, and offer letter issuance time, the company gained valuable insights into the efficiency and effectiveness of its recruitment efforts. This data-driven approach allowed for continuous improvement and optimization of the hiring process.

Organization

The evolution of cloud technology into a mission-enabling tool also necessitates a shift in how it integrates with the broader organization. It's crucial for mission leaders to actively participate in decisions regarding cloud investments, just as cloud leaders should be involved in the selection and implementation of cloud-based mission tools. Although adjusting governance structures and organizational cultures to facilitate this level of collaboration may pose challenges, our research underscores its significance in achieving widespread success.

Furthermore, there exists a complex interplay between workforce dynamics and operational strategies. When cloud solutions alter how agencies fulfill their missions, it can prompt changes in workforce composition and operational methodologies. For instance, the widespread adoption of remote work, largely facilitated by cloud technology, has transformed the landscape of modern employment. With approximately half of the US workforce now operating remotely, and forecasts indicating continued growth in cloud-based conferencing technologies, organizations must adapt to heightened cybersecurity demands as employees access data from diverse locations and devices. Consequently, this evolution in security requirements may necessitate the acquisition of new talents with specialized skills.

Therefore, optimizing an organization's approach to cloud integration requires a holistic transformation beyond mere IT-focused migrations. In this comprehensive model, cloud technologies are deeply ingrained in strategic decision-making processes and long-term workforce planning initiatives. Effective execution of a cloud strategy mandates organizational readiness and a robust talent development strategy to meet the evolving needs of the future cloud workforce. Agencies can evaluate their existing organizational structures, delineate the requisite roles and skills for a cloud-centric workforce, and formulate a roadmap for achieving these objectives. Moreover, skill realignment should be complemented by a culture that fosters collaboration and innovation. Cloud optimization presents an opportune moment for agencies to infuse innovation into their operations. By establishing a modernized cloud architecture that serves as a springboard for emerging technologies such as artificial intelligence and machine learning, organizations can drive innovation and advance mission objectives.

Finance

Cost savings is a fundamental aspect of FinOps, but it encompasses more than just reducing expenses. At its core, FinOps aims to enhance mission performance alongside financial efficiency. FinOps contributes to mission improvement through three key mechanisms:

1. Cloud technology facilitates the consolidation of data and operations across various organizational segments, fostering efficiencies. However, this convergence can lead to friction as different cultural norms collide. FinOps plays a crucial role in establishing a common language that allows different organizational units to identify, quantify, and compare mission value. By necessitating value-based decision-making, FinOps encourages leaders to align on uniform terms and definitions for mission value organization-wide. Additionally, embedding FinOps teams in diverse organizational segments promotes the adoption of common terms and practices while preserving each unit's distinct culture.

2. Once a shared understanding of mission value is established, organizations can begin measuring it. FinOps methodologies, such as show-back and charge-back mechanisms, facilitate the definition of common key performance indicators (KPIs) and metrics for mission value. Internal billing for cloud services encourages both service providers and users to assess their contributions in terms of mission value and evaluate the return on investment. Moreover, these practices drive

organizational efficiency by promoting the automation of internal processes, particularly as cloud investments expand.

3. FinOps aids in identifying and addressing common obstacles hindering optimal cloud utilization. Firstly, its continuous nature helps organizations navigate the fast pace of change and frequent decision-making scenarios, such as choosing between lifting and shifting or refactoring applications. Secondly, FinOps sheds light on shadow IT, enabling centralized IT visibility into IT systems deployed by business units independently. This visibility allows organizations to assess whether alternative solutions could better meet their needs. Lastly, FinOps drives the modernization of procurement systems, a critical aspect given the dynamic nature of cloud usage. Several federal agencies are exploring ways to update procurement policies to leverage the cloud's flexibility effectively, such as moving away from static IT budgets set at the beginning of fiscal years.

These concerted efforts enable cloud adoption to not only generate cost savings but also enhance mission effectiveness. For instance, a federal agency streamlined its HR systems by transitioning to the cloud, resulting in reduced administrative burdens, faster processing times, and enhanced flexibility, particularly evident during the pandemic through online employee orientation sessions.

Sustainability

Providing value to communities extends beyond merely offering services; it involves preserving existing value while creating new opportunities. Communities consist of diverse stakeholders with varied needs and interests, and the worth of a government agency transcends its service provision to encompass how those services are delivered. Questions of equity and sustainability arise in this context, and cloud technology offers avenues for government agencies to address them while optimizing benefits for communities.

Moreover, the vast scale of cloud providers enables them to invest significantly in eco-friendly technologies, such as wind, nuclear, and solar power, to support their server infrastructures. Consequently, the technology supply chain of agencies can become substantially more sustainable. Additionally, cloud providers can strategically allocate workloads to minimize overall energy consumption. For instance, the adoption of lower-power chips like ARM processors can yield substantial energy savings for simpler tasks. While individual organizations may not have sufficient workload diversity to justify investing in such processors, cloud service providers explore opportunities to aggregate diverse workloads across multiple IaaS customers, resulting in considerable energy efficiencies.

This transition not only promises billions of dollars in energy cost savings but also stands to mitigate carbon emissions by millions of metric tons. Many cloud providers are also adopting environmental, social, and governance (ESG) metrics to gauge overall sustainability performance, supplementing power consumption data to assess operations' environmental impact comprehensively.

Data Pipeline Architecture Factors

Designing the architecture of your data pipeline requires careful consideration and planning. While this process may demand significant time and effort upfront, it lays the foundation for a system that is straightforward to implement, manage, and scale as your business expands. To avoid potential challenges down the road, here are several factors to keep in mind during the planning stages of your data pipeline architecture.

1. **Cloud Storage Costs Are Not Low**

    In the past, data storage was limited by on-premises servers, which constrained the size of data architecture. However, with the rise of big data, cloud storage has become the norm, offering seemingly affordable solutions. Yet, it's essential to recognize that cloud storage isn't limitless, despite its apparent affordability. When designing your data architecture, prioritize cost-efficiency across all systems, regardless of their pricing structures. Even if you're using inexpensive cloud storage or a budget-friendly data pipeline provider, optimizing these aspects is crucial. This practice not only fosters long-term savings but also becomes vital when transitioning data to more costly platforms.

    Cloud data warehouses like Snowflake and Big Query often have intricate pricing models for both computation and storage, which may catch users off guard. Leverage your data pipeline architecture to transfer data into each system in the most efficient format possible. Store your data in the most space-efficient manner feasible to minimize costs when migrating it to pricier platforms, preventing unexpected expenses.

2. **Focus on Security and Encryption**

    Ensuring the security and encryption of your data infrastructure, including pipelines, is of utmost importance. Pipelines involve the movement of data, making it essential to implement encryption measures at both the source and destination of your data.

Two key aspects of encryption require attention:

   Encryption at Rest: This involves storing data in an encrypted format either at the source or destination systems. While your data pipeline may not directly control this encryption, it must seamlessly integrate with securely encrypted endpoints.

   Encryption in Motion: Data should be encrypted as it traverses through the pipeline. Transport Layer Security (TLS) is a widely used protocol for achieving this encryption during data transmission.

Most tools and platforms used in data management, such as data warehouses, cloud storage solutions, and data pipeline providers, offer built-in encryption mechanisms. It's crucial to assess these mechanisms to ensure they align with your data security requirements and seamlessly integrate. For more complex data architectures, involving a security expert may be necessary to ensure comprehensive protection.

Prioritize Compliance in the Initial Stage

When integrating your data pipeline into a commercial product, ensuring compliance with regulatory standards is paramount. These standards encompass data security and encryption requirements, often extending beyond what might be initially anticipated. Achieving compliance demands dedicated engineering efforts and meticulous planning.

Regulatory laws vary by region, necessitating consideration not only of your current location but also potential future expansions. For instance, in the United States, while there isn't a unified federal law governing consumer data protection, specific states, like California, enforce regulations. Moreover, if your company's growth strategy includes European markets within the next few years, it's imperative to construct pipelines compliant with the General Data Protection Regulation (GDPR) from the outset.

In cases where interpretation of these legal frameworks is unclear, seeking guidance from legal professionals is advisable.

Best Practices in Data Pipeline Architecture

In data pipeline architecture, adhering to industry-standard best practices is crucial for achieving efficiency, reliability, and maintainability. Here are key recommendations:

1. **Establish Clear Data Objectives:** It's imperative to define the objectives of your data pipeline clearly. Ensure alignment with your organization's overarching goals and business strategy to maximize effectiveness.

2. **Integrate Data Quality Checks:** Incorporate data quality checks at different stages of the pipeline to detect and rectify issues early in the data flow. This proactive approach ensures that the data remains accurate and reliable throughout its journey.

3. **Prioritize Security and Privacy:** Implement robust security measures to protect sensitive data. Utilize encryption, enforce strong access controls, and leverage data governance tools to comply with relevant data protection laws and regulations, safeguarding privacy.

4. **Document and Monitor:** Maintain detailed documentation of your data pipeline architecture, including its components and processes. Establish robust monitoring mechanisms to promptly identify and address any issues that arise, ensuring continuous performance optimization.

5. **Conduct Rigorous Testing:** Thoroughly test your data pipeline architecture through various testing methods, including unit testing, integration testing, and end-to-end testing. This comprehensive approach validates reliability and performance, identifying and rectifying potential vulnerabilities.

6. **Foster Collaboration:** Encourage collaboration among data engineers, data scientists, and other stakeholders involved in the data pipeline architecture. By promoting cross-functional teamwork, ensure that the architecture addresses the diverse needs and requirements of your organization effectively.

Consider Future Growth When Planning for Performance and Scalability

Performance and scalability are pivotal factors in data pipeline design. Performance considerations revolve around the pipeline's ability to efficiently process a specified volume of data within a given timeframe. For instance, if the destination system requires processing 100 rows per second, your pipeline must be capable of meeting this requirement.

Scalability, on the other hand, pertains to the pipeline's capacity to accommodate increasing data volumes without compromising service delivery or encountering performance bottlenecks. It's crucial to align your team's expectations with realistic goals and budgetary constraints. Adjustments to goals may be necessary based on feasibility assessments.

An effectively designed architecture will distribute workload across multiple cloud-based servers or clusters, leveraging resources like memory, storage, and CPU efficiently. This distributed approach not only enhances performance but also bolsters resilience against potential failures. Anticipate that the data volume and throughput demand on your pipeline and overall data infrastructure will expand over time. Position your architecture to accommodate future scalability requirements.

Several common approaches to handling scalability include

1. Implementing application containers (e.g., Docker) to manage workloads across server clusters.

2. Adding redundancy by incorporating additional servers to mitigate risks of outages or hardware failures.

3. Continuously balancing incoming request loads across multiple servers.

4. Employing autoscaling mechanisms to dynamically adjust server capacities in response to fluctuating traffic demands.

5. Leveraging automation tools like Amazon Web Services (AWS) CloudFormation, Terraform, and Ansible to streamline the process of adding new servers to your cluster as needed.

CHAPTER 7   COLLABORATIVE DEVELOPMENT IN THE CLOUD NATIVE

ETL Processes and Supply Chain Management

"Cloud-native ETL" refers to the utilization of Extract, Transform, Load (ETL) tools and methodologies that are specifically designed to leverage the capabilities of cloud computing platforms, rather than relying on traditional on-premises infrastructure. This approach offers several advantages over traditional methods.

Firstly, cloud native ETL solutions are typically provided as fully managed services by public cloud providers. This means that the cloud provider handles all aspects of infrastructure management and maintenance, including support requests, software updates, and system monitoring. As a result, organizations utilizing cloud native ETL can offload the burden of managing complex IT infrastructure to the cloud provider, freeing up valuable resources and reducing operational overhead.

Secondly, cloud-native ETL solutions offer enhanced scalability compared to traditional on-premises setups. In the cloud, organizations can easily scale up or down their resources, such as storage or compute power, by provisioning additional server instances or CPUs as needed. This scalability is essential for handling fluctuating workloads and accommodating business growth without the need for costly hardware upgrades or infrastructure redesigns.

Furthermore, cloud services are designed to be accessible from various devices, including smartphones, tablets, and laptops, allowing users to access ETL processes and data remotely. This mobile accessibility enables greater flexibility and efficiency in data management and analysis, as users can access and interact with data from anywhere, at any time.

Overall, adopting cloud-native ETL solutions can significantly streamline data integration and processing workflows, improve scalability and flexibility, and reduce the burden of infrastructure management on

IT teams. By harnessing the power of cloud computing, organizations can unlock new opportunities for innovation and growth in their data-driven initiatives.

Transition from on-prem to ETL

Cloud-native ETL solutions are increasingly becoming a preferred choice for organizations, but understanding why and how organizations transition from on-premises to cloud-based ETL is crucial. Several factors play a role in evaluating cloud-native ETL solutions.

- **Speed**

    The speed of data processing is a critical consideration. While cloud-based ETL solutions can offer impressive speed, they may encounter latency issues, particularly if the cloud servers are located in distant regions. However, if your business operates across multiple locations, some latency may be acceptable.

- **Cybersecurity**

    Both cloud and on-premises ETL solutions can be secured effectively. However, the choice depends on specific security requirements. Many Chief Information Security Officers (CISOs) believe that the cloud is as secure as or even safer than on-premises solutions. Nonetheless, on-premises ETL may be necessary for handling sensitive data subject to strict regulations, such as healthcare or financial information.

- **Reliability**

    Cloud services offer high reliability, with cloud providers responsible for addressing any downtime or service interruptions. This can be a significant advantage, especially for IT support staff who prefer to avoid sudden emergencies. Cloud vendors typically offer Service Level Agreements (SLAs) guaranteeing a certain level of uptime, assuring organizations. For example, AWS Glue, a cloud native ETL solution, ensures a monthly uptime of 99.9%, equivalent to approximately 44 minutes of allowable outages per month.

- **Hybrid Approach**

    Organizations may opt for a hybrid ETL model, combining both on-premises and cloud-based solutions to best meet their specific requirements. In this approach, certain data and processes remain on-premises while others are migrated to the cloud. This hybrid model allows organizations to leverage the benefits of both environments while accommodating their unique needs and constraints.

- **Enhanced Real-Time Monitoring and Collaboration**

    The integration of cloud connectivity into supply chain management offers planners immediate access to live data spanning the entire supply chain network. This empowers decision-makers with up-to-the-minute insights into inventory levels, production progress, order modifications, and notifications of any delays. Through a unified cloud platform, stakeholders across manufacturing and logistics sectors can collaborate seamlessly, ensuring synchronized execution of operations. This real-time visibility and coordination streamline decision-making processes and facilitate agile responses to dynamic market conditions, ultimately optimizing supply chain performance.

- **Transition Management**

  Transitioning from traditional on-premises tools to cloud-based solutions necessitates comprehensive training for planners. It is crucial to effectively communicate the benefits of the new system and provide ongoing support to ensure widespread user adoption throughout the organization. Establishing clear channels for feedback and addressing user concerns promptly can facilitate a smoother transition process.

- **Migration Challenges**

  The integration of data and systems between the cloud platform and internal ERP/IT systems poses significant complexity and demands considerable time and IT resources. Developing a meticulously planned migration roadmap is essential to navigate this process effectively. Additionally, thorough validation of integrations is imperative to ensure seamless connectivity and data synchronization between disparate systems. By proactively addressing migration challenges and adhering to a structured approach, organizations can mitigate risks and optimize the success of their cloud migration initiatives.

- **Enhanced Resilience to Disruptions**

  In the face of natural calamities, cyber threats, and other unforeseen disruptions, conventional on-premises IT infrastructures are vulnerable to significant downtimes and operational interruptions. However, leveraging cloud-based solutions empowers planners with unparalleled resilience. By migrating planning operations to the cloud, organizations ensure that their planners have uninterrupted access to critical plans and data regardless of their physical location. This capability enables seamless continuity of supply chain operations even amidst chaos, ensuring minimal disruptions and maintaining business continuity. Moreover, cloud-based platforms often incorporate robust security measures and data redundancy protocols, further bolstering resilience against potential threats and enhancing overall disaster recovery capabilities. Thus, embracing cloud technology not only safeguards planning operations but also fortifies the organization's resilience in the face of adversity.

Securing Cloud-Integrated Logistics Operations

The cloud-based supply chain presents a multi-faceted landscape with various layers, components, and data sources, posing intricate security challenges. However, these complexities can be effectively managed through a strategic four-step approach:

1. Formulate the Strategy Initiating with a well-defined strategy for the cloud supply chain is paramount. Embracing a shift-left approach, which entails integrating security measures earlier in

the development process, is fundamental. This strategic blueprint doesn't necessitate an extensive document initially but requires outlining the vision, roles, and responsibilities. Continuous iteration and refinement are essential components of this strategic framework.

2. Understand Software Creation Processes Delving into the intricacies of software creation within the organization is crucial. This involves comprehensive documentation and analysis of the software development life cycle, tracking its journey from developers' workstations to the production cloud environment. Understanding these processes lays the foundation for implementing robust security measures effectively.

3. Implement Security Quality Guardrails Incorporating proactive security measures akin to quality controls in traditional manufacturing processes is imperative. Identifying opportune points along the software development pipeline to enforce stringent security checks is essential. Automation plays a pivotal role in supplementing manual code review efforts to ensure scalable and efficient security practices.

4. Consider Certifications Beyond internal security measures, validating the security of applications and cloud infrastructure procured from external providers is crucial. Leveraging certifications such as SOC2 Type II and ISO 27001 aids in assessing the provider's adherence to rigorous security standards and independent verification of their security

CHAPTER 7   COLLABORATIVE DEVELOPMENT IN THE CLOUD NATIVE

controls. These certifications provide insights into the provider's risk evaluation processes, essential for aligning their security practices with organizational standards.

Adopting these strategic steps empowers security leaders to steer their organizations toward robust cloud supply chain security practices. By ingraining security into the development process and leveraging certifications for external validation, organizations can fortify their resilience against evolving cyber threats. With the escalating reliance on cloud infrastructure and native applications, the implementation of a comprehensive cloud supply chain security strategy is imperative to safeguard organizational assets and ensure seamless operations.

Capabilities of Cloud Computing in Supply Chain Management

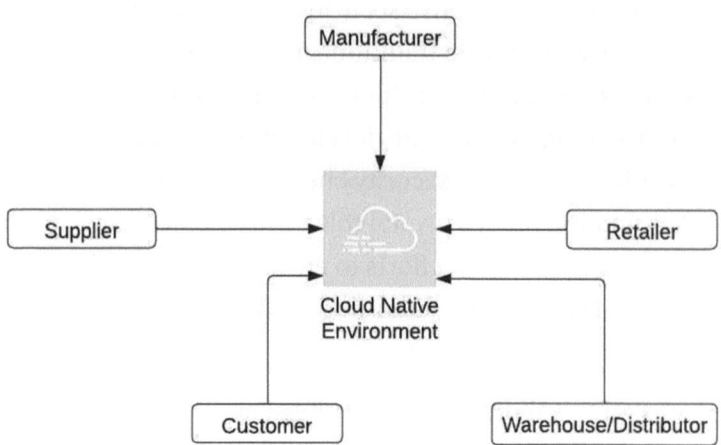

Figure 7-2. *Supply chain management capabilities*

Cloud-native technologies are changing how supply chains work by using cloud computing to make them more innovative and efficient. Let's explore these capabilities further.

1. **Scalability**

    Cloud-native platforms offer the ability to scale computing resources dynamically, enabling organizations to handle fluctuations in demand without incurring significant infrastructure costs. This scalability ensures that businesses can ramp up operations during peak seasons or scale down during periods of low activity, thereby optimizing resource utilization and reducing operational overhead.

2. **Flexibility and Agility**

    Cloud-native architectures, built upon principles such as microservices and containerization, empower organizations to develop and deploy supply chain applications rapidly. This agility enables businesses to respond quickly to market changes, customer preferences, and emerging trends, giving them a competitive edge in the fast-paced global marketplace.

3. **Real-Time Visibility**

    Cloud-native solutions provide real-time visibility into various aspects of the supply chain, including inventory levels, production status, transportation logistics, and customer demand. This visibility enables organizations to make data-driven decisions, anticipate potential disruptions, and proactively address supply chain challenges, ultimately improving operational efficiency and customer satisfaction.

4. **Collaboration and Connectivity**

   Cloud-native platforms facilitate seamless collaboration and connectivity among supply chain partners, enabling secure data exchange and communication across the entire ecosystem. By fostering closer relationships with suppliers, manufacturers, distributors, and customers, organizations can enhance transparency, reduce lead times, and optimize inventory management processes.

5. **Data Analytics and Predictive Insights**

   Cloud-native technologies enable advanced data analytics and predictive modeling capabilities, leveraging machine learning and artificial intelligence algorithms to derive actionable insights from large volumes of supply chain data. By analyzing historical trends, market dynamics, and customer behavior, organizations can optimize inventory levels, identify cost-saving opportunities, and mitigate risks, thereby improving decision-making and strategic planning processes.

6. **Automation and Optimization**

   Cloud-native solutions facilitate the automation of repetitive supply chain tasks, such as order processing, inventory replenishment, and demand forecasting. By automating manual processes and workflows, organizations can reduce errors, increase operational efficiency, and optimize resource allocation, leading to cost savings and productivity gains across the supply chain.

7. **Security and Compliance**

   Cloud-native platforms incorporate robust security features and compliance controls to protect sensitive supply chain data and ensure regulatory compliance. By implementing encryption, access controls, and threat detection mechanisms, organizations can mitigate cybersecurity risks, safeguard against data breaches, and maintain the integrity and confidentiality of supply chain operations.

When developing a cloud-based Supply Chain Management (SCM) application, it is crucial to consider several important factors:

1. **Data Migration:** Plan meticulously for the seamless migration of data from on-premises or existing web-based monolithic systems to the cloud. Assess factors, such as data volume, complexity, and anticipate potential downtime during the migration process to minimize disruptions.

2. **Supplier and Partner Collaboration:** Consider features that promote collaboration with suppliers and partners, fostering transparency and real-time communication within the supply chain ecosystem. This enhances coordination and efficiency across the entire supply chain network.

3. **Cloud Platform Selection:** Selecting the appropriate cloud platform (such as AWS, Azure, or Google Cloud) is essential to align with your company's cloud strategy and meet various criteria like performance, compliance, and budgetary considerations.

4. **Integration Capabilities:** Leverage the capabilities of cloud-specific APIs and services to enhance functionality, enabling innovative solutions to efficiently address supply chain challenges. This facilitates seamless integration with existing software applications, streamlining operations.

5. **Business Continuity:** Develop a comprehensive disaster recovery plan to safeguard supply chain data during unexpected incidents or system failures. Ensure the implementation of data redundancy and backup mechanisms to maintain business continuity and minimize downtime.

6. **Performance Monitoring:** Implement robust performance tracking and reporting mechanisms within the cloud environment to monitor the health and efficiency of supply chain processes. This enables proactive identification of areas for improvement and optimization.

7. **Data Security:** Given the sensitivity of supply chain data stored in external servers, prioritize robust data security measures. Implement encryption, access controls, and compliance with industry regulations to safeguard supply chain data.

8. **User Experience and Training:** Prioritize a user-friendly interface and provide comprehensive training to supply chain professionals to maximize the utilization of the customized cloud solution. Empowering users with proper training ensures efficient utilization of the platform's capabilities.

Summary

In this chapter, the focus was on enabling collaboration between developers and operations teams, a practice commonly referred to as DevOps. It delved into the significance of fostering a cohesive working relationship between these two key groups within an organization, emphasizing the benefits of collaboration in enhancing productivity, accelerating development cycles, and ensuring the delivery of high-quality products and services. By integrating Agile and Scrum methodologies into cloud-native environments, the chapter explored how these adaptive frameworks enable teams to effectively manage projects, respond to changes swiftly, and deliver value to stakeholders in a dynamic and fast-paced cloud environment.

Furthermore, the chapter delved into the optimization of data flow in the cloud, emphasizing the importance of efficient data management practices. It discussed various strategies for storing, processing, and transferring data within cloud environments, highlighting the need for organizations to leverage cloud-native tools and technologies to streamline data operations and enhance scalability and performance. Additionally, the chapter examined the role of Extract, Transform, Load (ETL) processes in supply chain management, illustrating how cloud technology facilitates the seamless integration and analysis of data from disparate sources to drive informed decision-making and operational efficiency.

Overall, the chapter underscored the critical role of collaboration, methodology adaptation, and process optimization in maximizing the benefits of cloud computing for organizational success. By embracing these principles and leveraging cloud-native capabilities, businesses can effectively navigate the complexities of modern IT landscapes, drive innovation, and achieve strategic objectives in an increasingly digital world.

CHAPTER 8

IAM Security in Cloud-Native Environment

"IAM Security in a Cloud-Native Environment: Where we keep our digital clouds cozy and secure, like a fortress in the sky!"

In this upcoming chapter, get ready to plunge into the wild and wacky world of Identity and Access Management (IAM) security in cloud-native DevOps environments. Imagine this: organizations are jumping onto the cloud train faster than a squirrel chasing a nut on a scorching summer day. But amid all this digital chaos, we've got to talk about security.

As we bid farewell to the old-school ways and embrace dynamic and scattered computing setups, managing who gets access to what becomes as challenging as herding a bunch of hyperactive kittens. But fear not! We're here to guide you through building a fortress of security that'll have cyber crooks scratching their heads in confusion.

Throughout this chapter, we'll sprinkle in some practical advice, share real-life examples, and maybe even crack a joke or two to keep things entertaining. Whether you're a tech guru or just starting to dip your toes into the digital waters, we've got your back.

So, grab your life jacket and buckle up! It's time to navigate the choppy waters of IAM security in the cloud-native world. Let's make sure your digital ship sails smoothly and securely through the stormy seas of cyberspace.

CHAPTER 8   IAM SECURITY IN CLOUD-NATIVE ENVIRONMENT

In this chapter, we will be encompassing the following topics:

- IAM Fundamentals in Cloud-Native Environments
- IAM Best Practices for Service Accounts and API Access
- IAM Governance and Policy Management in Cloud-Native

IAM Fundamentals in Cloud-Native Environments

As businesses increasingly migrate to the cloud for its cost savings, ease of use, and efficiency, they also face security challenges inherent in online platforms.

IAM (Identity and Access Management) solutions play a critical role in mitigating risks within native cloud environments. By adopting a zero-trust approach, which treats every visitor and activity as a potential threat, IAM solutions ensure that authentication or authorization is required for every workload.

Foundational Elements of Cloud-Native IAM Infrastructure

1. **Autonomous Components**

    In cloud-native setups, we use a method called microservices, where we split different jobs of an application into smaller, separate services. Each service works on its own, with its own set of instructions and rules to follow. This helps us to be more flexible and faster when we're building

CHAPTER 8   IAM SECURITY IN CLOUD-NATIVE ENVIRONMENT

and running our applications. One cool thing about microservices is that they're really good at growing when we need them to. Instead of making one service bigger when more people are using it, we can just make more copies of it. This is called horizontal scaling. Horizontal scaling, also known as scale-out, is a method of increasing the capacity of a system by adding more instances of the same component in parallel. In the context of microservices architecture, horizontal scaling refers to replicating individual microservices across multiple servers or containers to handle increased workload or user demand.

Microservices architecture decomposes an application into a set of loosely coupled services, each responsible for a specific business function or capability. These services are developed, deployed, and managed independently, enabling greater flexibility and agility in the software development process. Each microservice can be scaled independently based on its resource requirements and workload patterns. With horizontal scaling, instead of increasing the size (vertical scaling) of a single service instance to handle increased load, multiple instances of the same microservice are deployed across different servers or containers. To distribute incoming requests evenly across multiple instances of a microservice, a load balancer is typically employed. The load balancer acts as a traffic router, directing client requests to available service instances based on predefined algorithms such as round-robin or least connections. This ensures efficient utilization of resources and prevents any single instance from being overloaded. Modern cloud platforms and container orchestration systems provide autoscaling capabilities, allowing the infrastructure to automatically provision or deprovision instances of microservices based on predefined metrics such as CPU utilization, memory usage, or request latency. This dynamic scaling ensures that the system can adapt to fluctuating workload demands in real-time, optimizing resource utilization and maintaining performance.

Cloud-native environments, especially ones that use tools like Docker and Kubernetes, make it easy to do this.

Now, in an Identity and Access Management (IAM) system for cloud-native setups, microservices are super important. This system usually has a few different microservices, each doing a specific job related to managing who can access what. For example, there might be a service that checks if a user is who they say they are, another one that hands out access tokens, and another one that deals with managing user profiles. Also, it's a good idea to keep the jobs of managing the IAM system separate from the main parts of the application. This helps keep everything organized and makes it less likely that changing one thing will mess up something else. So, we might have a special service just for managing settings and permissions, like who's allowed to do what.

Use Case Scenario

Consider a large-scale ecommerce platform that operates entirely on cloud infrastructure. This platform handles sensitive user data, including personal information and payment details. Ensuring secure access to various parts of the system is paramount to maintaining trust and compliance with data protection regulations like GDPR or CCPA.

2. **Stateless Elements**

   In cloud-native systems, we use small, independent parts called microservices to build our applications. Each microservice has its own job to do, like handling user logins or managing data. These microservices talk to each other using specific rules, like a shared language, rather than directly sharing information.

   For example, in an Identity and Access Management (IAM) system, we have different microservices for handling things like user authentication, generating tokens, and managing user accounts. Each of these microservices keeps its data separate and communicates with the others through defined rules.

   By keeping data separate and communicating through clear rules, we ensure that our system stays organized and resilient. It means that if one part of the system needs to be replaced or updated, it won't disrupt the others. They can keep running smoothly without losing important information. This approach also streamlines automation processes, a crucial aspect in modern cloud environments. It functions similarly to a well-coordinated team where each member understands their role and communicates seamlessly with others. This organizational structure ensures continuity even when team members change or take temporary breaks, allowing the team to maintain its efficiency and effectiveness.

3. **Uniform Interfaces**

   Microservices can be likened to small teams within an application, each with its own set of tasks and responsibilities. These teams communicate with one another through defined rules known as APIs (Application Programming Interfaces). They often rely on various external services, such as databases or email providers, to accomplish their respective tasks.

   In a cloud-native setup, it's crucial that these microservices treat all services uniformly, without distinguishing between internal and external ones. This uniformity ensures that regardless of the source of support, the microservices adhere to the same communication standards. This flexibility facilitates easier adjustments and updates as needed. For example, if there's a need to switch the database used in an Identity and Access Management (IAM) system, which handles user access, the system should seamlessly adapt without causing disruptions to other parts of the application.

Furthermore, observability plays a vital role in monitoring the performance of the IAM system and promptly identifying any issues. It should integrate seamlessly with tools that offer insights into system operations. Additionally, the IAM system itself should adhere to clear rules and standards, such as standardized protocols like OAuth 2.0 and OpenID Connect. These standards ensure smooth communication with other services and facilitate interoperability within the broader ecosystem.

4. **Consistent Environments**

   When building and deploying cloud-native applications, it's advantageous to break down the process into distinct stages: building, running, and deploying. This workflow can be automated using Continuous Integration/Continuous Deployment (CI/CD) tools. CI/CD allows for the creation of snapshots of the application at each stage of development, facilitating easy deployment and testing.

   Maintaining consistency across different environments, such as testing, staging, and production, is essential. Containers are instrumental in achieving this consistency, as they enable the deployment of the same application image across various environments. Additionally, it's beneficial to share most of the setup information between these environments while keeping some environment-specific details separate. Environment variables are commonly used to store such specific information, like secret codes or settings. These variables can be securely managed and accessed across different environments, even stored in a centralized location like a shared drive if the setup information isn't sensitive.

This approach allows for seamless modifications to the application setup without interrupting its operation. The CI/CD system can manage the majority of setup-related tasks, eliminating the need to incorporate additional features within the application itself. This not only enhances security by reducing the attack surface but also ensures consistency across all environments. Furthermore, employing specialized tools enables tracking of changes made to the setup, facilitating transparency and accountability within the development process.

Fundamental Pillars of IAM

Identity and Access Management serves as a comprehensive structure designed to handle the complexities of managing digital identities, regulating resource access, and enforcing security protocols within an organizational setup. This framework consists of multiple elements and methodologies geared toward these objectives. Among these components, we can discern four fundamental pillars

1. **Active Directory Management (ADMgmt)**

    It is really important for organizations that use Microsoft Active Directory to handle who can access what. It's all about making sure Active Directory is set up securely and works smoothly.

- Making sure Active Directory works well with other systems, like cloud services and special access tools.

- Adding and setting up users and groups in Active Directory, making sure they can only do what they need to.

- Watching what changes are made to Active Directory and keeping a record of them.

- Reporting any important security stuff to follow the rules.

- Making sure only the right people can use Active Directory and what they're allowed to do.

- Adding extra security to protect Active Directory from common problems like weak passwords or sneaky attacks.

ADMgmt tools help organizations handle Active Directory safely and make sure only the right people can access what they need to. They also make it easier to use new security tricks with Active Directory, like giving special access to important accounts.

2. **Access Management (AM)**

   AM tools enable administrators to establish and enforce rules governing user access, whether they are internal employees, external contractors, or privileged users with elevated permissions. While Identity Governance and Administration (IGA) tools may cover some aspects of access management, AM tools typically offer more comprehensive features and finer-grained control.

Key functions of Access Management in IAM security include the following.

- **User Role Management**

  Creating and managing user roles that dictate the actions users are permitted to perform within the system. This centralizes access control and simplifies administration.

- **Authentication Methods**

  Supporting various authentication methods for users to verify their identity, such as passwords, one-time codes, or multi-factor authentication (MFA), using their mobile devices.

- **Job-Based Access Provisioning**

  Granting access to resources based on users' roles or job functions, ensuring they only have access to the resources necessary for their work responsibilities.

- **Multi-factor Authentication (MFA)**

  Adding additional layers of security by requiring users to provide multiple forms of identification, such as a password and a temporary code sent to their mobile device.

- **Temporary and Conditional Access**

  Allowing temporary or conditional access privileges to be granted to users for specific periods or under certain circumstances, enhancing security while accommodating changing business needs.

Access Management safeguards sensitive resources by ensuring that only authorized individuals can access them, without imposing excessive barriers for legitimate users. By aligning access permissions with job roles, it streamlines workflow and minimizes disruptions. Additionally, its flexibility in supporting various authentication methods ensures compatibility with both legacy and modern applications, regardless of their location. A robust Access Management setup enhances overall security posture and contributes to the smooth operation of the organization's IT infrastructure.

3. **Identity Governance and Administration (IGA)**

   Identity Governance and Administration helps security administrators handle user identities and access throughout a company. It gives them a clearer view of who has access to what and lets them set rules to stop any inappropriate access.

   - **Visibility and Control**

     IGA solutions offer a centralized platform for security administrators to gain insight into user identities and their access privileges across various systems and applications. This visibility allows administrators to identify and mitigate potential security risks by setting rules and policies to prevent unauthorized access.

   - **Automated Access Management**

     GA streamlines access request handling through automated workflows, enabling efficient and consistent management of access requests. Automated processes for adding or removing user access to systems and applications reduce the risk of human error and ensure timely provisioning and deprovisioning of access.

- **Integration with Company Systems**

    IGA seamlessly integrates with existing directories and other company systems, facilitating smooth data synchronization and ensuring that access management is aligned with organizational policies and procedures.

- **Access Governance**

    IGA encompasses access governance processes aimed at preventing misuse or fraud by ensuring that individuals have appropriate access rights. This includes implementing segregation of duties (SoD) policies to prevent conflicts of interest and limiting access based on predefined roles and responsibilities.

- **Monitoring and Auditing**

    IGA solutions include tools for monitoring user activity and enforcing compliance with regulatory requirements. Administrators can track user actions, generate audit logs, and conduct periodic reviews to ensure adherence to security policies and regulations.

By enforcing least privilege access principles and automating access management processes, IGA helps mitigate security risks associated with excessive user permissions. It strengthens security posture by ensuring that users only have access to the resources necessary for their roles, reducing the likelihood of unauthorized access and potential security breaches. Additionally, IGA's focus on access governance and auditing enhances accountability and transparency, contributing to overall IAM security effectiveness.

4. **Privileged Access Management (PAM)**

   It is like a set of tools and rules that make sure only the right people can get into really important stuff. These special accounts, called privileged accounts, have extra power to control important systems and data. But because they're so powerful, they're a big target for bad guys trying to break in.

   - Keeping all the important accounts and their secret codes in one safe place.

   - Setting up detailed rules for what each account can do.

   - Making sure only the right people can ask for access and getting special permission if needed.

   - Giving temporary access and changing secret codes automatically to keep things safe.

   - Keeping an eye on who's using these accounts, recording what they do, and checking everything meets the rules.

PAM helps make sure only the right people can get into the most important parts of a company's systems, making it harder for bad guys to get in. It also helps follow the rule of giving people only the power they need to do their job, nothing extra. And by giving out permissions only when needed, it lowers the risk of attacks trying to get more power than they should.

IAM Components

Identity and Access Management (IAM) is a crucial aspect of organizational security, especially in today's digital landscape where data breaches and unauthorized access are significant concerns. Delving deeper into each component of IAM provides a comprehensive understanding of its significance and contribution to ensuring secure access control within organization.

Authentication

- Authentication is the process of verifying the identity of users attempting to access resources.

- IAM systems implement various authentication methods, including passwords, tokens, biometrics, and multi-factor authentication (MFA), to enhance security.

- Multi-factor authentication adds an extra layer of security by requiring users to provide multiple forms of verification before accessing sensitive resources.

Provisioning/Deprovisioning

- Provisioning involves creating, updating, and deleting user accounts based on their roles and status within the organization.

- Deprovisioning ensures that access is promptly revoked for users who leave the organization or no longer require access to certain resources.

- Effective provisioning and deprovisioning processes help organizations maintain security by ensuring that only authorized users have access to resources.

Authorization

- Authorization determines what actions users are allowed to perform and which resources they can access.

- IAM systems enforce role-based access control (RBAC) or attribute-based access control (ABAC) to assign permissions to users based on their roles, responsibilities, and attributes.

- Granular authorization policies ensure that users have the appropriate level of access required to perform their job functions while preventing unauthorized access to sensitive data.

Permissions

- Permissions define the specific actions that users can perform on resources, such as reading, writing, or deleting files.

- IAM systems manage permissions by assigning privileges to users or groups based on predefined access control lists (ACLs) or policies.

- Fine-grained permissions allow organizations to enforce the principle of least privilege, ensuring that users only have access to the resources necessary to fulfill their roles.

Reporting

- Reporting capabilities in IAM systems provide visibility into user activities, access requests, and changes in permissions.

- Auditing user login history, privilege assignments, and access events helps organizations detect and respond to security incidents promptly.

- Regular audit reports aid in compliance efforts by demonstrating adherence to regulatory requirements and security best practices.

Least Privileges Principles

The Principle of Least Privilege, a fundamental aspect of zero-trust security, entails granting individuals access only when necessary to perform their tasks, and for the shortest duration possible. By implementing least privilege access, the likelihood of account compromise is minimized by removing unused or unnecessary accounts and mitigating the potential impact of compromised accounts or insider threats.

While the concept is straightforward, achieving least privilege access within today's intricate and expansive identity environments can pose significant challenges. Nevertheless, striving for least privilege access is imperative for security teams aiming to safeguard their infrastructure and users. According to a 2022 IDSA report, 80% of surveyed firms experienced identity-related breaches in the previous year, with many attributing these breaches to issues such as "inadequately managed privileges," "compromised privileged identity," or "excessive privileges leading to an insider attack." Additionally, least privilege is essential for compliance, as most security-focused regulations mandate access management controls and policies, with least privilege access being a primary guiding principle.

Despite variations in systems and sensitivities, integrating least privilege access best practices into identity security and access control processes can benefit every organization. Here's a starting point for implementation.

Implementation of Least Privileges

1. The initial phase in adopting the principle of least privilege involves identifying the critical systems within your organization. Once these systems are identified, the next step is to determine who has access to them and what level of access they possess, including permissions, roles, and group memberships. Subsequently, the focus shifts to transitioning these access privileges to a time-bound or contextually provisioned model. This approach assumes that users typically do not require continuous access to sensitive resources. Instead, access is granted on a temporary basis or based on specific contextual factors. This transition effectively mitigates the risk of over-provisioning, ensuring that users only have access to resources when necessary. While not all access scenarios may require time-based restrictions, migrating sensitive permissions, applications, and roles to a just-in-time access model guarantees that users will always have the necessary access at the right time. This approach eliminates the need for continuous privileged access, thus minimizing the potential for security breaches due to excessive access privileges.

2. Set clear rules and establish an approval process for accessing sensitive information. Define specific guidelines outlining which individuals or roles are authorized to access important data or resources. Ensure that these rules are consistently followed whenever there is a request for access to sensitive

information, thereby maintaining security and compliance standards. Decide how new people will get access when they start, and how they'll lose access when they leave. Teach everyone about these rules, especially for sensitive access, to keep things fair and easy to understand.

3. The first step to keeping things safe is knowing what's going on. But with lots of different apps and systems to manage, it can be hard to keep track of who has access to what. Security teams need to be able to find this out quickly and easily. To do this, it helps to use tools that automatically collect and organize data about who can access what. So, make sure you have a system that gives you a clear picture of who has access to what, and keep this information in one central place. Once you've got everything organized, it's a good idea to label different roles and permissions so you can easily spot the important ones.

4. When people get access to important stuff, keep a record of who approved it, why they got it, and when. This helps when checking if they still need access and for showing compliance. Make sure this record is easy for IT, Security, and GRC teams to find. Keep this record up to date by automatically updating it when someone gets or loses access.

5. Creating clear rules for who can access what and keeping an updated list of who can access important stuff helps a lot in making sure only the right people have access. But it's also super important to regularly check if everyone still needs access to what they have. Instead of just relying on the list, it's best to

CHAPTER 8   IAM SECURITY IN CLOUD-NATIVE ENVIRONMENT

directly check the apps and accounts to make sure everything is up to date. This way, you can be sure that access hasn't been given out incorrectly and if it has, you can fix it. It's also a good idea to work closely with managers or system administrators to check if everyone has the right level of access. This makes sure everyone only has access to what they need.

6. Checking who has access to what is important to make sure everything follows the rules. It's not just about following the rules, though. Regularly checking access helps to keep things safe by finding and removing access that isn't needed. To make sure only the right people have access, it's important to check often, like every three months for important access. These checks should happen when there are big changes, too. Doing all these checks manually can take a lot of time and money, so it's best to automate them. Set up a schedule for these checks and let your team know so they can help.

7. It's crucial to know how giving someone access or permission might affect security. Sometimes, the effects of giving access might not be obvious right away. For instance, being part of a group could give someone more access than they need, which can be hard to see. Understanding these effects is important when deciding who gets access to what. During regular checks of access, it's important to consider the risks involved, the account that has the access, and how it might affect other things. Make sure the people who decide who gets access understand these security risks so they can make the right choices.

CHAPTER 8   IAM SECURITY IN CLOUD-NATIVE ENVIRONMENT

IAM Best Practices for Service Accounts and API Access

User management is about controlling who can access a computer system or network. It involves creating accounts for users, deciding what they can do, keeping an eye on what they're up to, and managing what parts of the system they can use. But when it comes to cloud-based apps, user management gets more complicated. Cloud-based applications which are allowed to the public network use the Internet to work, which means they can handle a lot of users and adapt to changes easily. But they also bring new challenges for managing users. You need to make it easy for people to sign up, make sure they are who they say they are, decide what they're allowed to do, and make sure they can use other online services too.

Key Components of User Management in Cloud-Native Applications

1. **Authentication and Registration**

    The first step in managing users within a system is the registration process, where individuals provide their information to create an account. This information typically includes details such as a username, email address, and password. When a user signs up, their information is securely stored in the cloud database. To uniquely identify each user, a special code, often referred to as a user ID or account ID, is assigned. This code serves as a unique identifier for the user within the system and helps track their activities and interactions. Once registered, users can log in to the system to access its features and functionalities. Authentication is the process of verifying that the person attempting to log in is indeed the rightful owner of the account. In cloud applications, where access can be granted remotely from anywhere, additional security measures are often employed to ensure the authenticity of the user.

One common method of authentication is through the use of multi-factor authentication (MFA). In MFA, after entering their username and password, the user is prompted to provide an additional form of verification, such as a one-time code sent to their mobile phone via SMS or generated by an authentication app. This extra step adds a layer of security by requiring something the user knows (password) and something they have (their phone).

Implementing robust authentication mechanisms, including MFA, is crucial for ensuring the security of user accounts and protecting sensitive data. By verifying the identity of users during the login process, organizations can prevent unauthorized access and safeguard against potential security breaches. This emphasis on security measures not only enhances the trustworthiness of the system but also instills confidence in users regarding the protection of their personal information and privacy.

2. **Access Control and Authorization**

   Once a user proves who they are, the next step is deciding what they're allowed to do in the system. This is called user authorization. It means setting up rules for different user roles and giving permissions based on these roles. For example, an administrator might have full control over everything, while a regular user might only be able to see and change their own information.

   Access control goes hand in hand with user authorization. It's about making sure that the permissions we've set are followed, so users can only do what they're allowed to. In cloud-based apps, this can be tricky because the system is spread out and can grow quickly. But getting access control right is super important for keeping the app safe and working properly.

3. **Accounts and Settings**

   User accounts and preferences are important for making things just right for each person. An account holds all your info and choices, so the system can work the way you like. In cloud applications, handling user accounts can be tough because the system is spread out. We need to make sure your info stays the same no matter where you access it from. This means we need a strong plan for keeping track of everything.

4. **Security and Account Handling**

    Managing accounts means doing things like changing passwords, turning off or deleting accounts, and keeping user info private. In cloud apps, these tasks can be trickier. For instance, when someone needs a new password, we have to make sure the link to reset it is safe and can only be used once. Safety is super important when dealing with user accounts. We need to keep their info safe from people who shouldn't have it and follow the rules about privacy. In cloud apps, we have to be extra careful, making sure everything from the way you log in to how the system works behind the scenes is secure.

Nowadays, people want to use their favorite apps along with the ones they're using. This might mean logging in with social media, linking up with tools they use for work, or syncing with other online services. Adding these extra apps into a cloud-based system makes things even more complex. We've got to handle special codes and permissions carefully and make sure everything stays safe.

Implementation of User Management in Cloud Native

Implementing user management in a cloud-native environment involves seamlessly integrating user tools and services, ensuring scalability and adaptability to accommodate growing user bases, selecting appropriate user management methods such as cloud-based IAM services or open-source tools, and prioritizing data privacy through encryption, access controls, and transparent data handling practices.

CHAPTER 8   IAM SECURITY IN CLOUD-NATIVE ENVIRONMENT

1. **Connecting User Tools and Services**

   Connecting user tools and services is another important part of setting up user management in cloud-based apps. These tools not only need to work together but also with the rest of the app.

   For example, the system that manages users should work smoothly with the app's front end so people can sign up, log in, and update their profiles easily. It also needs to mesh with the app's backend to store and get user info and make sure only the right people can access things. The user system should work with other systems the app uses. For example, it might need to connect with an email service to send password-help emails or with a payment service to handle transactions.

2. **Creating for Growth and Adaptability**

   As more people use the system and more info gets added, the user system needs to be able to handle the extra load. As the app grows and changes, the user system should be able to adjust to new needs and updates. To handle more users, the system might need to grow horizontally (by adding more copies) or vertically (by making the current copies stronger), or a mix of both. To stay flexible, it should be designed in parts that can be changed or added to without messing up the whole thing.

3. **Choosing the Best Way to Manage Users**

   The key to effectively managing users in cloud-based applications lies in selecting the appropriate method. Various factors influence the selection process, such as the application's functionality, user management requirements, and the available resources and expertise.

One common approach is leveraging cloud-based identity and access management (IAM) services provided by major platforms like Amazon Web Services (AWS), Azure, or Google Cloud. These platforms offer a comprehensive suite of tools for user management tasks such as registration, authentication, authorization, and data management. They support diverse authentication methods and authorization models while prioritizing data privacy and security. Alternatively, another option involves utilizing open-source tools for user management. While these tools offer extensive customization options, they require more time and expertise to implement and maintain.

4. **Making Sure Data Stays Safe and Legal**

   These apps often must follow laws like GDPR, which protect people's info. So, we need to set up the system in a way that follows these rules. This means doing a few things. First, we should only collect the info we need from users, not more. Then, we should keep that info safe by encrypting it when it's moving around or being stored. To implement compliance with regulations like GDPR in cloud applications, several measures must be taken. First, it's crucial to limit the collection of user information to only what is necessary, avoiding the gathering of excessive or irrelevant data. Next, robust encryption protocols should be implemented to ensure the security of user data during transmission and storage. Additionally, transparency with users regarding the use of their information is essential, achieved through clear communication and providing users with control over their data. Access controls should be enforced to restrict access to user information to authorized individuals and services. Finally, maintaining audit trails enables tracking of access to user data, ensuring accountability and compliance with regulatory requirements. By implementing these measures, cloud applications can adhere to data protection laws and safeguard user privacy effectively.

Secure Handling of API Keys

When we create modern cloud-based apps, we put them together using different tools like virtual machines, containers, and services from platforms. These apps need to be kept safe from online dangers. It's important to protect special codes called API keys, which help control access to different parts of the app. Keeping these keys safe from unauthorized use is important for the app's overall security.

1. **Broaden Your Assessment of Application Risks Beyond Software Vulnerabilities**

    In cloud computing, there are more risks than just mistakes in setting up or updating software. Another big problem is keeping secrets safe, like special codes called API keys, passwords that are always the same, and keys for keeping information

CHAPTER 8   IAM SECURITY IN CLOUD-NATIVE ENVIRONMENT

secret. These secrets are often buried inside the instructions and programs that run cloud services. It's really important to make sure that everything is set up correctly so that only the right people can access these secrets.

To do this, it's crucial to regularly check for any potential problems and fix them quickly. Also, we need to make sure that the services we use in the cloud are set up correctly, with the right permissions and connections to keep things safe. It's like making sure all the doors and windows in your house are locked properly to keep out intruders. Overall, protecting secrets like API keys and ensuring that cloud services are set up securely is essential for keeping our data safe from hackers and unauthorized access.

2. **Take a Proactive Approach to Examining Code for Weaknesses During Development**

Enterprise-built applications, including serverless PaaS offerings, must undergo thorough scrutiny to identify both known and unknown vulnerabilities. One prevalent error in cloud-native applications is the utilization of known vulnerable open-source software (OSS) components and frameworks, which constitute approximately 80% of the code in such applications. Furthermore, it is essential to conduct scans on all exposed APIs.

3. **Consider Using a Special Security Tool Called a Cloud-Native Web Application Firewall (WAF)**

   Sometimes, the protection provided by cloud companies isn't as good as what you can get from other companies. You might need to use a different company's WAF or special rules to control how the built-in WAF from your cloud service provider works. Or, the WAF service might be added automatically when you connect to a dynamic security system like SASE. In cloud-based apps, to filter out certain types of traffic, you might need a special kind of WAF that's built into the app or is very small. But for basic protection against denial-of-service attacks, what the cloud company offers should be enough.

4. **Plan for Resilience by Using the Special Features of Cloud Technology**

   Just moving an application from a regular computer to the cloud doesn't automatically make it able to handle lots of users or bounce back from problems. Instead, design apps so they can grow and shrink easily using special tools in the cloud. Also, make sure the app can keep running even if one part of the cloud has trouble by spreading it across different areas.

5. **Protect Web Applications and APIs**

   WAFs are good for guarding the part of an app that users interact with, but they don't cover all the functions exposed in modern cloud-based apps. That's why it's necessary to have extra protection for

CHAPTER 8 IAM SECURITY IN CLOUD-NATIVE ENVIRONMENT

APIs and to stop automated programs (bots) from causing harm. This broader set of protections is what we call web application and API protection.

6. **Don't Think of PaaS Security as Something Completely Different**

    PaaS security isn't a whole new issue or area. It's a growing field that uses a mix of things we've already talked about in this study. PaaS security relies on good identity and access management, setting up infrastructure securely, always checking the security of your cloud setup, keeping an eye on everything happening in your system, and scanning your applications for any security problems.

7. **Make Sure to Have an API Gateway**

    Access to serverless functions should only happen through these gateways or brokers. You can use the one provided by your cloud service or choose a different one from another company. Even if the serverless code is only used inside your organization, having an API gateway or event broker is important for keeping everything secure and under control.

8. **Combine Monitoring for Both Operations and Security**

    You don't need two different tools one for keeping things running smoothly and another for watching out for security issues to keep a close eye on your service at the application level. At the very least, the information should be shared among different teams. Ideally, monitoring how well your application is working and looking out for security problems should be done together, supporting a single team that handles both development and security (DevSecOps). This will be more and more crucial as more managed containers and serverless code are used, and it becomes harder for security teams to directly watch over operating systems.

Least Privilege for Service Accounts

Service accounts are special accounts made for things like computers or programs, not people. They can get into apps, data, and networks to do certain jobs. These accounts work quietly in the background and only act when they're needed by a person, a program, or another service. They have special powers that let them do their tasks and connect to other things on the network.

In lots of companies, these accounts can get into important apps and data that the business needs. One thing to note is that these accounts aren't connected to any specific person, so they can sometimes slip under the radar and not get managed for a while. Lots of companies don't keep track of each special account to say why it's there, who can use it, or what it's connected to.

Difficulties Associated with Service Accounts

- **Operational**

    In many organizations, the management of service accounts presents a significant operational challenge. This challenge stems from what is commonly referred to as "service account sprawl." Essentially, there are too many service accounts scattered across the system, making it difficult for administrators to keep track of them all. This situation is exacerbated by the lack of proper documentation regarding the purpose and usage of each service account. Without clear documentation, it becomes almost impossible to understand why a particular service account was created or who has access to it. This lack of clarity poses risks when it comes to updating or decommissioning service accounts. Administrators must tread carefully because removing or modifying a service account can inadvertently disrupt other services that rely on it, leading to potential business disruptions. Adding to the complexity is the phenomenon where accounts initially designated for human users end up being utilized as service accounts, particularly for tasks involving robotic process automation (RPA). These accounts, though established as "user" accounts, are effectively used for automated tasks within both internal and external applications. Identifying such accounts amid the myriad of user and service accounts poses a significant challenge for organizations.

- **Cybersecurity**

  In cybersecurity, service accounts pose a serious risk because they let attackers get into sensitive data without getting noticed. These accounts let attackers stay hidden while they keep accessing important info and moving around in the company's computer networks and online spaces without anyone realizing. What's more, sometimes these service accounts accidentally have the power to do things to other service accounts, which makes the situation even trickier.

For companies, figuring out who has access to what is already hard enough. But when you add in the possibility that someone could gain access through a service account and then use that to get into even more accounts, it becomes a real headache. It's like trying to solve a puzzle where the pieces keep changing.

- **Risk**

    The risk associated with service accounts lies in the inability to effectively manage their permissions through a common approach such as "model-after." Typically, in managing human-based accounts, administrators may compare the permissions of similar users to determine appropriate access levels, a practice known as "model-after." However, this approach becomes flawed when applied to service accounts.

    Service accounts vary significantly in their roles, functionalities, and the level of access they require. Unlike human-based accounts, which may have some commonalities in terms of access needs based on job roles or departments, service accounts are often created for specific tasks or applications, each with its unique set of permissions. Attempting to apply a "model-after" approach to service accounts can lead to misconfigurations or inadequate access control. Since service accounts do not have a consistent pattern or behavior across the organization, comparing them to others may result in incorrect assessments of their permission requirements. This can leave service accounts either over-privileged, with unnecessary access that increases the risk of security breaches, or under-privileged, lacking the necessary permissions to perform their intended tasks efficiently.

- **Compliance and Regulatory**

    It's crucial to handle service accounts properly to follow the rules about who can access what. Organizations need to show they're following the rules for managing the access of service accounts and the people who can use them. The main idea for managing service accounts is to have strict, automatic systems in place for handling them throughout their life cycle. This is the only way to make sure they meet the rules and regulations. Additionally, it's important to check that what service accounts are allowed to do match up with what they're doing, to make sure they have the least amount of access they need.

Best Practices for Managing Service Accounts

1. **Always Create New Service Accounts**

    When you're making service accounts in the active directory, make sure to only give them the least amount of access they need. Don't give them administrative rights because if someone gets into a service account, they could take over the whole system.

2. **Keep a List of All Service Accounts Updated**

   Having an updated list of all service accounts is important. It helps when you need to make new service accounts or find old ones that aren't being used anymore. It also helps with checking if a service account is still needed.

3. **Assign Limited Access**

   Instead of copying old ones, make new service accounts each time. This is because some old service accounts might have elevated privileges. If you copy an old one, you might end up giving a new service account powers it doesn't need.

4. **Avoid Default Groups with Privileges**

   Putting service accounts in groups with extra powers can be risky. If someone gets into the group, they could get access to all the service accounts' info. And if someone misuses an account, it's hard to tell who did it.

5. **Establish Password Policy**

   Many administrators often neglect to update service account passwords, or they use identical passwords for all accounts. Just like with regular user accounts, it's crucial to establish strict password guidelines for service accounts. These passwords should be robust, lengthy, and complex to enhance security. Utilize tools like Privileged Access Management (PAM) or Password Managers to generate and manage strong passwords, regulate access, and enforce password policies.

CHAPTER 8 IAM SECURITY IN CLOUD-NATIVE ENVIRONMENT

6. **Restricting Access to Sensitive Info**

   Create rules and policies to control who can access sensitive data. Use ACLs to stop service accounts from getting to critical info. Also, use ACLs to block service accounts from changing settings or writing to important files or folders.

7. **Auditing**

   Auditing for all service accounts and things connected to them. Keep an eye on the logs to see who's using the service accounts and what they're doing with them.

8. **Control Where and When They Log In**

   Decide which computer service accounts can use to keep them away from secret info. You can also set them to only log in at certain times. And make sure they don't stay logged in too long.

9. **Remove Unused Accounts**

   Unused service accounts are often targeted by hackers and can let them into your network. Plus, having lots of old accounts makes things messy and harder to manage.

10. **Try to Use Managed Service Accounts**

    These accounts can't be used to log in directly, so they're safer. They also have passwords managed by the system, so nobody needs to remember or change them.

11. **Take Away Extra User Permissions**

    Check and get rid of any rights users don't need. You can do this by setting up a group policy, like one that says "Don't let people access this computer from the network" or "Don't let people log in for batch jobs."

IAM Governance and Policy Management in Cloud Native

Governance

Governance refers to the establishment and enforcement of policies, procedures, and controls to ensure that organizational objectives are met efficiently, ethically, and in compliance with laws and regulations. IAM contributes to governance in several ways:

- **Policy Enforcement:** IAM systems enforce access policies and controls to ensure that only authorized users have access to the appropriate resources. This includes authentication mechanisms like multi-factor authentication (MFA), password policies, and user provisioning/deprovisioning processes.

- **Centralized Control:** IAM solutions provide centralized management of user identities, roles, and access rights across the organization. This centralization enables administrators to define and enforce consistent access policies and streamline access management processes.

- **Auditability and Accountability:** IAM systems generate detailed audit logs and reports of user activities, access requests, and changes to access permissions. These audit trails help organizations track user behavior, monitor compliance with access policies, and demonstrate regulatory compliance during audits.

- **Identity Life-cycle Management:** IAM facilitates the management of user identities throughout their life cycle, from onboarding to offboarding. This includes automating processes for user provisioning, role assignment, access reviews, and deprovisioning to ensure that access rights are granted and revoked in a timely manner based on organizational policies and employee status changes.

Risk Management

Risk management involves identifying, assessing, and mitigating risks that could negatively impact an organization's objectives. IAM plays a crucial role in risk management by addressing security risks associated with identity and access management:

- **Access Control:** IAM systems enforce access controls to prevent unauthorized access to sensitive resources and data. This includes implementing least privilege principles, role-based access control (RBAC), and segregation of duties (SoD) to ensure that users have access only to the resources necessary to perform their job functions.

- **Anomaly Detection:** IAM solutions incorporate features for detecting anomalous user behavior, such as unusual login times, locations, or access patterns. By continuously monitoring user activities and comparing them against baseline behavior, IAM systems can identify potential security threats, such as insider threats or compromised accounts, and trigger alerts for further investigation.

- **Risk-Based Authentication:** IAM systems can implement risk-based authentication mechanisms that dynamically adjust the level of authentication required based on the risk associated with the access request. For example, high-risk activities or access from unfamiliar locations may trigger additional authentication checks, such as MFA, to verify the user's identity and reduce the likelihood of unauthorized access.

Compliance

Compliance refers to adherence to regulatory standards, industry guidelines, and internal policies relevant to an organization's operations. IAM helps organizations achieve compliance by addressing requirements related to identity and access management:

- **Regulatory Compliance:** IAM solutions support compliance with various regulations and standards, such as GDPR, HIPAA, PCI-DSS, SOX, etc., by providing features and controls that align with regulatory requirements. This includes enforcing strong authentication, data encryption, access controls, audit trails, and privacy protections to ensure the security and confidentiality of sensitive information.

- **Access Governance:** IAM systems enable organizations to implement access governance processes, such as access certification and access reviews, to ensure that users' access rights are appropriate and compliant with regulatory requirements. This involves regularly reviewing and validating user access permissions, identifying and remedying access violations or excessive privileges, and documenting access controls for audit purposes.

- **Data Protection:** IAM solutions help protect sensitive data by controlling access to it based on users' roles, responsibilities, and data classification. This includes encrypting data at rest and in transit, implementing access controls to prevent unauthorized access or disclosure, and monitoring data access and usage to detect and respond to security incidents or data breaches.

IAM Standards

1. **Gramm-Leach-Bliley Act (GBLA)**

    GBLA is a federal law that mandates financial institutions to maintain customer information confidentiality and protect it from threats. It includes the Financial Privacy Rule, regulating private financial information collection and disclosure, and the Safeguards Rule, requiring security programs implementation. Moreover,

Pretexting provisions prohibit accessing private information through pretenses. IAM significantly boosts compliance by

- Providing centralized administration for assigning and controlling user access rights
- Enforcing Segregation of Duties (SoD) policies
- Adjusting access rights as job functions change
- Revoking user access upon termination
- Managing access based on job roles and adhering to the principle of "least privilege"
- Performing periodic audits of access rights and privileges

2. **General Data Protection Regulation (GDPR)**

GDPR stands for General Data Protection Regulation. It's a set of rules designed to protect the privacy and personal data of individuals within the European Union (EU). GDPR applies to any organization that collects, processes, or stores personal data of EU residents, regardless of where the organization is located. It aims to give individuals more control over their personal data and requires organizations to implement strong data protection measures, obtain consent for data processing, and promptly notify authorities of data breaches. GDPR also outlines individuals' rights regarding their data, including the right to access, correct, and erase their personal information. Failure to comply with GDPR can result in significant fines and penalties.

GDPR requires organizations to take responsibility for protecting the personal data of EU citizens. This means they must have a system in place to control who can access this data, and Identity and Access Management (IAM) helps make this possible.

IAM also aligns with the GDPR's principle of "privacy by design," which means using strong technology to safeguard data. With IAM, users only get access to the customer data they need for their job. This controlled access reduces the chances of a data breach, lessens the impact if one does happen, and helps avoid expensive GDPR fines.

- **Multi-factor Authentication (MFA):** This adds extra layers of security beyond just passwords. Even if someone steals a password, they'd need additional credentials, making it harder for them to access customer data.

- **Adaptive Authentication:** This analyzes users' access requests and assigns a risk score based on certain factors. If a login seems suspicious, the system may ask for more credentials or even block access altogether. This helps protect customer data and stay compliant with GDPR.

3. **Payment Card Industry Data Standard (PCI-DSS)**

    The Payment Card Industry Data Standard (PCI-DSS) is a set of rules about handling credit and debit card information. It's for businesses that deal with customer credit cards. But it's also important for online stores that take card payments.

One specific rule, called requirement 8.1, talks about identity and access management. It says companies must have rules to make sure they know who's using their systems, especially for employees and administrators.

1. Giving each employee a unique ID for using card data.
2. Controlling what administrators can do with temporary access to financial databases.
3. Using automated systems to manage accounts, like removing old ones.
4. Make sure everyone has strong extra security, like using more than just a password to log in.

4. **Sarbanes-Oxley (SOX)**

It is a law that affects all financial institutions. It focuses on keeping financial reports accurate and making sure companies can provide the right information during audits. One part of SOX, called Section 404, is about making sure data stays safe. Companies have to put security measures in place and keep records of what they're doing to protect financial information.

1. They help manage who can access financial data and control access to it.
2. Companies can set limits on what people can do with sensitive financial info, and give temporary access when needed.

CHAPTER 8   IAM SECURITY IN CLOUD-NATIVE ENVIRONMENT

3. They make sure that no one person has too much power over financial data.

4. IAM systems help bring new employees on board smoothly and remove access when someone leaves.

5. They also keep track of security steps taken and provide proof that the company is following SOX rules.

5. **Health Insurance Portability and Accountability Act (HIPPA)**

It is a law that deals with keeping health data safe. It says that companies must make sure patient information is protected. This applies to all the technology used in healthcare. In 2013, they added something called the HIPAA Omnibus Rule. This made the rules about data protection more up to date. It says that if there's a breach, companies must tell patients about it. They also must control who can access patient data, even if they're outside partners or involved in marketing. The rule also covers how healthcare information is shared electronically.

1. Companies can separate out what different employees can do with the data to keep it safe.

2. IAM systems automatically update who has access to what as people's roles change. They also limit access to patient data as much as possible.

3. When someone leaves a company, IAM systems make sure their access is turned off.

349

4. IAM systems keep track of who's been accessing patient data and make sure it's done securely.

5. They also help partners access data securely without violating patient privacy.

Building Concrete IAM

For individuals in the technology field, overseeing a strong Identity and Access Management system has evolved beyond just protecting resources. It now involves optimizing business processes and fostering innovation. To excel in this realm, professionals need to synchronize IAM plans with business objectives, deploy appropriate identity solutions, and strive for ongoing advancement and creativity. The following is your all-encompassing manual.

1. **Creating the IAM Roadmap to Match Business Goals**

    Creating a roadmap to align Identity and Access Management (IAM) with business goals is essential for strategic success. This roadmap serves as a guide, ensuring that IAM initiatives resonate with the overarching objectives of the organization. Whether it involves modernizing an existing IAM system or implementing a new one, having a clear vision is crucial. Starting with a clear end goal in mind is fundamental; understanding the organization's growth plans, digital transformation objectives, and potential risks provides a solid foundation. Engaging stakeholders, including decision-makers, business unit leaders, and end-users, is vital. Their input helps shape the IAM strategy, ensuring

CHAPTER 8   IAM SECURITY IN CLOUD-NATIVE ENVIRONMENT

that it meets both technical requirements and business expectations. Conducting a thorough risk assessment is also critical. Identifying potential IAM-related risks allows for the design of strategies to mitigate these risks while supporting the organization's broader business goals. By following these steps, organizations can develop IAM initiatives that are closely aligned with their strategic objectives, fostering efficiency, security, and growth.

2. **Integrating Identity Tools**

    Now, let's talk about putting these identity tools into action. When choosing which tools to use, make sure they fit well with how your company operates and can grow as your company grows. Choose wisely. There are lots of different identity tools out there like Single Sign-On (SSO), multi-factor authentication (MFA), and user provisioning tools. Make your decision based on what your business needs and what technology your company already uses.

    Integration is important. It's crucial that these identity tools can easily work together with the other software and systems your company uses, like cloud platforms or other IT tools. This makes things more secure and easier for everyone to use. Test things out before rolling out these tools to everyone, it's a good idea to test them out first. This might mean trying them in a small part of the company to see how they work in practice. It helps to catch any problems early and make sure everything runs smoothly when you do put them in place for everyone.

3. **Moving Forward from Implementing Identity Tools**

   Attention should now turn toward making IAM initiatives operational. This involves several key steps.

   Firstly, knowledge dissemination is essential. Regular training sessions should be conducted to ensure that employees are familiar with the new IAM processes. A team that is well-informed is less likely to overlook security measures, reducing the risk of breaches.

   Secondly, audits play a crucial role in operationalizing IAM. Consistent audits not only ensure compliance with regulations but also reveal any potential vulnerabilities in the system, allowing for timely corrections.

   Lastly, being prepared for unexpected events is vital. Having a structured incident response plan in place is necessary. This plan should include clear protocols for addressing security breaches, outlining immediate mitigation steps and communication strategies to minimize the impact of any incidents.

4. **Progressing IAM Through Maturity and Innovation**

   It is crucial in the ever-evolving landscape of technology and security. This entails staying abreast of the latest developments to ensure the continued relevance and effectiveness of IAM strategies. Regular reviews of IAM approaches are necessary to integrate emerging technologies and methodologies effectively. Furthermore, soliciting feedback from end-users and IT professionals facilitates the identification of practical insights and areas for improvement. In addition, the integration of Artificial Intelligence (AI) and Machine Learning (ML) marks a significant advancement in IAM capabilities. AI and ML technologies offer enhanced threat detection, predictive analytics, and insights into user behavior, enabling IAM programs to operate at a higher level of efficiency and security. Embracing these innovations ensures that IAM remains adaptive and resilient in safeguarding digital assets and supporting business operations effectively.

Summary

In this chapter, we learned about managing who can access what in cloud systems, which is called Identity and Access Management (IAM). It's like making sure only the right people can get into different rooms of your digital house to keep it safe. We found out that IAM is super important for keeping digital stuff secure.

Then, we talked about the best ways to handle service accounts and API access in cloud setups. It's like giving each person their own special key to open certain doors in your house. By doing this right, organizations can make sure only the right stuff gets accessed, stopping bad guys from getting in.

Lastly, we looked into IAM governance and policies in cloud environments. It's like having rules for everyone living in your digital house to follow. By having clear rules and controls, just like house rules, organizations can keep their digital world safe and organized.

Overall, this chapter gave us a good understanding of IAM basics, how to manage service accounts and API access, and why having rules and controls is important in cloud environments. Following these ideas helps keep digital stuff safe and secure.

CHAPTER 9

Threat Analysis for Cloud-Native Deployments

"Threat Analysis for Cloud-Native Deployments: Because in the cloud, even rainbows need protection from the storm!"

Cloud-native deployments have revolutionized the way organizations build, deploy, and scale applications, offering unprecedented agility and cost-effectiveness. However, with these advancements come new security challenges, as traditional approaches to threat mitigation often fall short in the dynamic and distributed nature of cloud-native environments.

In this chapter, we will discuss into the intricacies of threat analysis specifically tailored to cloud-native deployments. We will delve into the unique characteristics of cloud-native architectures, such as containerization, microservices, and orchestration platforms, and uncover the vulnerabilities and attack vectors that adversaries may exploit.

Our exploration will extend beyond mere identification of threats. We will also equip you with strategies and methodologies to assess risk, prioritize mitigation efforts, and fortify your cloud-native infrastructure against potential attacks. Whether you are an IT professional responsible for architecting secure cloud environments, a cybersecurity specialist

CHAPTER 9   THREAT ANALYSIS FOR CLOUD-NATIVE DEPLOYMENTS

tasked with defending against emerging threats, or a business leader seeking to ensure the resilience of your digital operations, this chapter will provide valuable insights and actionable guidance.

By the end of this journey, you will emerge with a comprehensive understanding of the threat landscape surrounding cloud-native deployments and the confidence to implement robust security measures to protect your organization's assets in the ever-evolving digital realm.

In this chapter, we will be encompassing the following topics:

- Understanding Cloud-Native Security Challenges
- Threat Vectors in Microservices Architectures
- Security Testing and Validation
- Security Controls and Countermeasures

Understanding Cloud-Native Security Challenges

Cloud-native security is like building a strong fence around everything you have stored and running in the cloud. It's not just about protecting the buildings (like apps and platforms), but also the valuable things inside (like data). By having this fence, we're keeping out anything bad that could try to sneak in and cause trouble. It's all about making sure everything in the cloud is safe and sound from top to bottom, so you can trust it to work smoothly and keep your information secure.

The 4C's of Cloud-Native Security – Cloud, Cluster, Container, and Code – form the cornerstone of any robust security strategy tailored for cloud environments. These elements, when considered collectively, create a layered defense mechanism, addressing a spectrum of security challenges inherent in cloud computing. While cloud service providers play a role in securing certain aspects of an enterprise cloud-native

CHAPTER 9   THREAT ANALYSIS FOR CLOUD-NATIVE DEPLOYMENTS

architecture, it's crucial for organizations to recognize their own responsibilities within the shared security model of the cloud. As companies develop cloud-native applications, security must be integrated into every stage of the development life cycle. Mere protection of the cloud layer is insufficient; each layer presents its own set of potential vulnerabilities and attack vectors, demanding tailored safeguards to mitigate cyber threats effectively. By understanding the significance of the 4C's, organizations can craft comprehensive security strategies and select appropriate cloud-native security solutions to safeguard their digital assets effectively.

Code

Container

Cluster

Cloud

Figure 9-1. *Cloud-native security 4C's*

Code

Ensuring the safety of the code involves employing standard security practices, such as monitoring where the code is deployed and conducting regular checks to identify any security issues within the programs. Throughout the entire development process, scrutinizing the code can help address numerous security concerns in this domain. Integrating tools that examine the code directly within the development pipeline can identify any security gaps in newly developed code. Additionally, utilizing Static Application Security Testing (SAST) and Dynamic Application Security Testing (DAST) tools can further bolster security measures by scrutinizing the code for vulnerabilities and checking the security of external dependencies used by the code. These tools play a crucial role in identifying and addressing potential security weaknesses, ensuring the robustness of the application against threats and attacks.

Container

In addition to scrutinizing code for vulnerabilities, it's crucial to check for weaknesses and patch security holes in applications and their container images to maintain the safety of your cloud system. Many companies rely on container images from extensive libraries or lists, but not all of these images are guaranteed to be secure. To mitigate risks, it's advisable to utilize container images sourced from reputable and trusted sources, which have been thoroughly vetted and approved by security experts. By leveraging trusted container images, you increase the likelihood of maintaining the security of your containers and reducing the risk of potential breaches or exploits. Furthermore, integrating image and container scanning tools into your development and deployment processes can help identify and address security vulnerabilities, ensuring the integrity and safety of your cloud environment. These tools play a crucial role in proactively identifying and mitigating security risks associated with containerized applications, contributing to overall system security and resilience.

Cluster

When companies create and take care of their cloud-native apps, they have to make sure to keep their Kubernetes clusters safe and control who can use them. Keeping Kubernetes clusters secure is really important because each cluster has lots of little parts called "pods" that talk to each other. If a bad person gets into one pod, they could mess up other parts of the cluster, which could make the whole app unsafe. By setting strong rules for how the pods talk to each other, we can make sure only the right things are happening.

1. **Define Strong Communication Rules:** Establish robust guidelines dictating how pods communicate with each other, ensuring that only authorized interactions occur.

CHAPTER 9   THREAT ANALYSIS FOR CLOUD-NATIVE DEPLOYMENTS

2. **Implement Message Encryption:** Encrypt all messages exchanged between pods to prevent unauthorized access and ensure data confidentiality.

3. **Enforce Authentication Mechanisms:** Implement authentication mechanisms to verify the identity of users or services attempting to access parts of the application, thereby restricting access to sensitive resources to only authenticated entities.

4. **Role-Based Access Control (RBAC):** Employ RBAC policies to restrict access privileges, granting users access only to the parts of the cluster necessary for their specific roles. Additionally, safeguard important credentials and secrets to prevent unauthorized access or misuse.

Cloud

1. In the world of cloud computing, there's a shared responsibility model. This means that while the cloud service providers like Amazon Web Services, Microsoft Azure, or Google Cloud take care of securing the actual infrastructure that runs the cloud, it's up to your company to make sure everything you put in the cloud is secure too.

2. Well, your company is responsible for things like setting up the cloud services properly, making sure you're not using default settings or easy-to-guess passwords, controlling who has access to what, and making sure any automated processes you have in place are doing what they're supposed to do.

It's also about keeping an eye on everything happening in your cloud setup so that if something fishy is going on, you can catch it and deal with it quickly. Essentially, it's your job to keep your stuff safe and sound once it's up in the cloud.

Type of Threats in Cloud Native

1. **Insecure Application Features**

    Unauthorized access to applications often occurs when APIs and old features aren't properly secured. Some of these features are easily accessible to anyone online, which can let them bypass the security and get into parts of the app they shouldn't. To overcome this, organizations need to set up security measures that make sure only the right people can access different parts of the app. This way, unauthorized access is blocked.

2. **Weak Password Protection**

    A lot of times, hackers can get into accounts because they figure out the passwords. This happens a lot when people use the same password for lots of different websites. If there's no extra security like asking for a code from your phone, it's easier for hackers to get in.

    To prevent this, it's important to add extra layers of security for logging in. Different people need different levels of security, so having options like sending a code to your phone can help stop attacks that only need one password.

CHAPTER 9 THREAT ANALYSIS FOR CLOUD-NATIVE DEPLOYMENTS

3. **Improper Setup**

    This happens when developers don't set things up right or forget to change the default settings when they put their apps online. Sometimes, they just leave everything as it is, which makes it easy for hackers to break in and get access to stuff they shouldn't. To avoid this, developers need to make sure they set things up properly before putting their apps online. Changing the default settings and getting rid of any passwords that are already there can help keep things safe.

4. **Limited Oversight**

    When organizations use cloud services from other companies, they don't have as much control over what happens if there's an attack. They have to work with the cloud company to fix things, which can take a long time. To have more control, organizations can choose to use cloud services that they can set up on their own servers if possible. Some cloud companies offer this option, which can help organizations respond faster to attacks.

5. **Confidentiality Risks**

    Since cloud companies have access to the data they store, it's hard for organizations to keep their data safe. Any employee at the cloud company could look at or move an organization's data without them knowing. To deal with this, organizations need to regularly check who's accessing their data, keep an eye on what's happening in their systems, and only give permission to move data to trusted sources.

6. **Detailed Privilege and Key Management**

    Administrators can establish specific roles for cloud users, allowing them to assign permissions that match their needs and expectations precisely. Less experienced users may accidentally delete or store database resources, operations they typically shouldn't perform. This misunderstanding can pose a security threat at the application level.

7. **Vulnerable Interfaces/APIs**

    Cloud infrastructure heavily relies on APIs for automation and seamless integration among various services and resources. Despite being well-documented for ease of use, these APIs can be reverse-engineered by attackers. This exposes a risk wherein attackers can exploit documented API methods to gain unauthorized access or extract data if the APIs lack adequate security.

8. **Malicious Insiders**

    Malicious insiders encompass users with malicious intent who possess privileges to access cloud resources, as well as benign users whose accounts have been compromised by attackers. Preventing insider threats in the cloud presents additional challenges. Cloud-based infrastructure is accessible from the public Internet, making it simpler for attackers to exploit compromised accounts. Security misconfigurations can enable malicious users to escalate privileges across various cloud deployments.

Challenges in Cloud-Native Security

1. **Developers Prefer Not to Focus on Security**

    Security has become increasingly dynamic in today's technology landscape, especially with the advent of cloud computing, which grants developers unprecedented control over infrastructure deployment and management. As a result, companies are faced with the challenge of seamlessly integrating security awareness into the development process.

    Traditionally, there was a distinct separation between roles in software development and network management. This division often led to discussions centered around the balance between what could be achieved technically versus what should be done from a security standpoint. However, with the rise of cloud computing, these conversations tend to be overlooked. Developers, while skilled in creating software solutions, typically lack expertise in security practices. Consequently, security teams are tasked with incorporating effective security measures into developers' workflows without causing disruptions or delays.

    In order to address this gap, there needs to be a shift in the approach to security. Rather than enforcing strict control over development processes, security measures should empower development teams to make informed decisions about security. This means providing developers with the necessary tools, resources, and education to integrate security considerations seamlessly into their work, ensuring that security becomes an intrinsic part of the development life cycle rather than an afterthought.

2. **Deciding What Risks Are Acceptable**

   When it comes to navigating the challenges presented by cloud-native environments, one of the key questions that arises is How do we determine what risks are okay to take?

   In the realm of security, teams are confronted with a myriad of questions as they assess the risks associated with cloud-native deployments.

   - Are containers inherently secure, or do they require additional measures to ensure their safety?

   - Why is it often difficult to detect attacks targeting containers, and what can be done to improve visibility in this regard?

   - What vulnerabilities are inherent in serverless computing frameworks, and how can these be mitigated?

   - Are we confronting a crisis in the software supply chain, and what vulnerabilities does this pose to our IT infrastructure?

   - In instances where default authentication and authorization settings are disabled, how should organizations proceed to ensure the security of their systems?

In this dynamic landscape, DevOps teams strive for agility and rapid deployment, while security teams aim to safeguard business assets without impeding progress. However, it's essential to recognize that this is not a matter of one team versus the other: instead, it's about striking a delicate balance between speed and security. Achieving this balance requires a thorough understanding of the risks that an organization is willing to tolerate. Once these acceptable risks are identified, the focus shifts to implementing measures to mitigate the most critical vulnerabilities effectively. By prioritizing safeguards and aligning them with business objectives, organizations can navigate the complexities of cloud-native security with confidence and resilience.

3. **Keeping Up with Rapidly Changing Technology**

    One of the biggest challenges facing security teams today is the rapid evolution of technology. It seems like every day there's a new development, whether it's Kubernetes for managing containerized applications, the widespread adoption of containerization itself, or the rise of serverless computing. With these innovations constantly emerging, it's difficult for security measures to keep pace.

    In this fast-moving landscape, security teams can often find themselves playing catch-up, struggling to adapt to new technologies and the security implications they bring. The speed at which new frameworks and tools are introduced can leave security practices lagging, creating gaps in defenses that attackers may exploit. To address this issue, security teams must collaborate closely with DevOps teams and other stakeholders right from the beginning of any technological implementation. By integrating security considerations into the development process early on, teams can proactively address potential vulnerabilities and mitigate risks before they escalate.

Furthermore, empowering developers with the right tools and resources is essential. Developers are often focused on delivering features and functionality quickly, and introducing security tasks into their workflow can sometimes slow down the development process. Therefore, providing developers with tools that enable them to make informed security decisions efficiently is key to maintaining both speed and security in the development life cycle. Overall, the key to keeping up with the rapid pace of technological change lies in proactive collaboration, early integration of security measures, and providing developers with the support they need to prioritize security without sacrificing efficiency.

3R's of Cloud-Native Security

The 3R's of security represent an essential framework for ensuring the safety of cloud deployments. This approach revolves around the fundamental principle that the longer attackers have to exploit vulnerabilities, the greater the potential damage they can inflict. Therefore, it's crucial to adopt a proactive stance, embracing change and responding swiftly to threats. Now, let's delve deeper into understanding each of the 3R's.

CHAPTER 9 THREAT ANALYSIS FOR CLOUD-NATIVE DEPLOYMENTS

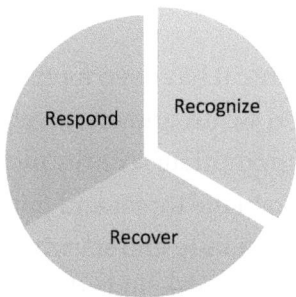

Figure 9-2. *Cloud-native security 3R's*

- **Recognize**

    Identifying threats in a cloud environment requires a proactive approach that combines comprehensive understanding, threat intelligence utilization, and regular security assessments. Organizations must stay informed about emerging attack vectors, known vulnerabilities, and suspicious activity patterns to preemptively address potential risks. By implementing robust monitoring systems and user behavior analytics, they can detect anomalies and unauthorized access attempts in real-time. Additionally, proactive threat hunting activities and collaboration with industry peers enhance the collective ability to identify and mitigate security threats effectively. This multi-faceted approach enables organizations to strengthen their security posture and safeguard their cloud infrastructure against evolving threats.

- **Respond**

    Once a security threat has been identified, the next step is to respond swiftly and effectively. This involves implementing appropriate security measures and protocols to contain the threat and mitigate its impact. Depending on the nature and severity of the threat, response strategies may include deploying security patches and updates, isolating compromised systems, and implementing additional security controls to prevent further exploitation. A rapid and coordinated response is crucial for minimizing the damage caused by security incidents and restoring normal operations as quickly as possible.

    Imagine a scenario where a cloud security team detects unusual activity indicating a potential data breach. Upon identification of this threat, they swiftly initiate their response protocol. First, they deploy security patches and updates to vulnerable systems to prevent further exploitation. Simultaneously, they isolate the compromised systems from the rest of the network to contain the threat's spread. Additionally, they enhance security controls, such as implementing multi-factor authentication or tightening access controls, to fortify their defenses against similar attacks. This rapid and coordinated response aims to minimize the impact of the breach, safeguard sensitive data, and restore normal operations promptly, emphasizing the importance of swift action in mitigating security threats in the cloud environment.

CHAPTER 9   THREAT ANALYSIS FOR CLOUD-NATIVE DEPLOYMENTS

- **Recover**

    In the aftermath of a security incident, the focus shifts to recovery and resilience-building. This involves assessing the extent of the damage, restoring affected systems and data, and implementing measures to prevent similar incidents from occurring in the future. Organizations should conduct thorough post-incident reviews to identify root causes, lessons learned, and areas for improvement. By leveraging insights gained from these reviews, organizations can refine their security practices, strengthen their defenses, and enhance their overall resilience against future security threats.

Security Controls in Cloud Native

Cloud-native security controls encompass various measures aimed at safeguarding cloud-native environments against cyber threats. These controls can be broadly categorized into the following types.

1. **Deterrent Controls**

    Deterrent controls serve as a warning system, alerting users when their actions are potentially harmful. By logging attempted actions in application logs, these controls discourage users from engaging in malicious behavior unintentionally. They help prevent security breaches and data leakage by blocking unauthorized actions.

    ```
    # deterrent control: Captcha verification for suspicious activities
    def captcha_verification(user_action):
    ```

```
    if is_suspicious_activity(user_action):
        require_captcha_verification()

def is_suspicious_activity(user_action):
    # Check if the user action is suspicious
    return user_action == "multiple_failed_login_
    attempts"

def require_captcha_verification():
    # Require captcha verification for suspicious
    activities
    print("Please verify captcha to proceed.")
```

2. **Preventive Controls**

   Preventive controls are proactive measures designed to automate security defenses and thwart cyber-attacks before they occur. These controls may include automated scripts, security software, or policies that reduce the attack surface area and enforce network access control, minimizing the likelihood of successful attacks.

```
# Preventive control: Automated patch management
def automate_patch_management():
    # Automatically apply security patches to prevent
    vulnerabilities
    apply_security_patches()

def apply_security_patches():
    # Apply security patches to vulnerable systems
    print("Applying security patches")
```

3. **Detective Controls**

    Detective controls focus on identifying and monitoring potential security threats and intrusions within cloud-native environments. Intrusion detection systems, software, policies, and procedures are used to monitor applications, servers, open ports, and user behavior for any signs of intrusion or malicious activity. The goal is to detect and respond to security incidents promptly to mitigate their impact.

    ```
    # Detective control: Log monitoring for abnormal
    behavior
    def monitor_logs():
        # Continuously monitor logs for abnormal behavior
        if detect_abnormal_behavior():
            alert_security_team()

    def detect_abnormal_behavior():
        # Check logs for signs of abnormal activity
        return is_abnormal_behavior_detected()

    def alert_security_team():
         Alert the security team about detected abnormal
        behavior
        print("Abnormal behavior detected: Notifying
        security team.")
    ```

4. **Corrective Controls**

    Corrective controls are activated in response to a security breach or incident. These controls aim to remediate the effects of the breach and restore the security posture of the environment. Examples include blocking compromised ports, blacklisting intrusive IP addresses, or halting the execution of malicious programs to prevent further damage.

```
# Corrective control: Data rollback in case of breach
def rollback_data():
    # Roll back data to a previous secure state in case
    of breach
    restore_from_backup()

def restore_from_backup():
    # Restore data from backup to mitigate the impact
    of breach
    print("Restoring data from backup")
```

5. **Workload Controls**

   Workload controls focus on managing and securing containerized workloads within cloud-native environments. This includes managing container images, approved packages, and secure libraries and repositories. Workload controls ensure that data is continuously tracked and controlled, particularly in distributed environments with multiple clients using different versions of workloads.

```
# Workload control: Continuous vulnerability scanning
def vulnerability_scanning():
    # Continuously scan for vulnerabilities in
    container images
    if detect_vulnerabilities():
        update_containers()
```

```
def detect_vulnerabilities():
    # Detect vulnerabilities in container images
    return is_vulnerability_detected()

def update_containers():
    # Update containers with patched versions to
    address vulnerabilities
    print("Updating containers to address
    vulnerabilities")
```

6. **Identity and Access Management (IAM) Controls**

   IAM controls are centered around managing user identities and controlling access to resources within cloud-native environments. These controls prevent unauthorized access and privilege escalation by enforcing access policies and permissions. IAM controls play a crucial role in maintaining the security and integrity of cloud-native environments by ensuring that only authorized users have access to sensitive resources.

```
# IAM control: Role-based access control (RBAC)
def implement_RBAC():
    # Implement role-based access control to manage
    user permissions
    assign_roles()
    enforce_RBAC_policies()

def assign_roles():
    # Assign roles to users based on their
    responsibilities
    print("Assigning roles to users")
```

```
def enforce_RBAC_policies():
    # Enforce RBAC policies to control access
    permissions
    print("Enforcing RBAC policies")
```

Threat Vectors in Microservices Architectures

Threat vectors in microservices architectures within cloud-native environments encompass various avenues through which malicious actors can exploit vulnerabilities to compromise the security of systems. These threat vectors pose significant risks to the confidentiality, integrity, and availability of cloud-native microservices.

Threat Modeling with STRIDE

Before we proceed with the integration process, let's take a moment to review the essence of STRIDE threat modeling. STRIDE is an acronym encompassing six distinct threat categories utilized for assessing potential risks within software systems

- **Spoofing Identity**

    This threat category involves situations where attackers attempt to impersonate legitimate users, systems, or entities within the software system. Examples include forging authentication tokens, manipulating user credentials, or exploiting weaknesses in identity verification mechanisms. By spoofing identity, attackers may gain unauthorized access to sensitive data or resources, leading to potential security breaches and unauthorized actions.

- **Tampering with Data**

    Tampering with data refers to unauthorized alterations or modifications made to data within the software system. Attackers may tamper with data to manipulate system behavior, compromise data integrity, or inject malicious payloads. Common examples include SQL injection attacks, data manipulation attacks, or altering data in transit. Tampering with data can lead to severe consequences, including data corruption, unauthorized access, or the execution of malicious code.

- **Repudiation**

    Repudiation threats involve situations where entities attempt to deny or dispute their actions within the software system. Attackers may engage in repudiation to evade accountability, deny involvement in malicious activities, or dispute the validity of transactions. Examples include falsifying audit logs, deleting transaction records, or manipulating timestamps to conceal malicious actions. Repudiation threats can undermine the integrity of audit trails, hinder forensic investigations, and impede efforts to hold individuals accountable for their actions.

- **Information Disclosure**

    Information disclosure threats involve the unauthorized exposure or leakage of sensitive information within the software system. Attackers may exploit vulnerabilities to access confidential data, such as personally identifiable information (PII), financial records, or proprietary business data. Common attack vectors include insecure data storage, inadequate encryption, or insufficient access controls. Information disclosure can have severe consequences, including privacy breaches, regulatory non-compliance, and reputational damage.

- **Denial of Service**

    Denial of Service (DoS) threats involve attacks aimed at disrupting or degrading the availability of services within the software system. Attackers may overwhelm system resources, exhaust bandwidth, or exploit vulnerabilities to render services inaccessible to legitimate users. Distributed Denial of Service (DDoS) attacks, network flooding, or resource exhaustion attacks are common examples of DoS threats. Denial of Service attacks can result in service downtime, loss of revenue, and damage to the organization's reputation.

- **Elevation of Privilege**

    Elevation of Privilege threats involve unauthorized attempts to gain elevated access rights or permissions within the software system. Attackers may exploit vulnerabilities to escalate their privileges, bypass access controls, or gain administrative privileges. Examples include privilege escalation exploits, backdoor access, or abuse of misconfigured permissions. Elevation of Privilege attacks can lead to unauthorized access to sensitive data, unauthorized system modifications, or compromise of system integrity.

By employing the STRIDE threat modeling framework, software developers and security professionals can systematically identify, assess, and mitigate potential security threats and vulnerabilities within software systems. This proactive approach helps enhance the overall security posture of applications and mitigate risks before they can be exploited by malicious actors.

Security Testing and Validation

Security validation lets companies safely test attacks in their setup and see if they stop them. It's like a test that gives solid proof of whether the security measures are doing their job. By testing security, they can make sure their systems meet all the requirements and truly keep their customers safe. Even if a company has lots of security tools, they won't know if they work until they face a cyber-attack. Some tools might help, but they might not cover all the bases. So, it's crucial to test and validate security measures to make sure they're protecting the company.

Red Teaming in Cloud Native

Red Teaming is an advanced way of testing security that's super smart. Instead of just finding weak spots like regular tests, Red Teaming acts like real bad guys to see how well a company's defenses work. It checks everything like how people work, the rules they follow, and the tech they use to make sure everything's safe.

When companies use a cloud-native setup, they get lots of benefits like being able to change things easily and save money. But it also brings some tricky security problems. Cloud systems are always changing, which makes it hard to keep them safe. Some big issues are hackers getting into data, settings not being set up right, not controlling who can access what, and not knowing exactly what's happening in the cloud.

- **Authentic Simulations**

    Red Team exercises mimic the strategies employed by real threat actors, providing an authentic assessment of an organization's security readiness in a dynamic cloud setting. This enables organizations to pinpoint and rectify vulnerabilities that might be overlooked in traditional security assessments.

- **Comprehensive Assessment**

    Red Teaming surpasses mere technical vulnerabilities by evaluating the effectiveness of people, processes, and technologies. This comprehensive approach ensures a thorough evaluation of an organization's overall security stance in the cloud.

- **Continuous Enhancement**

    Red Teaming isn't a one-off activity; it's an ongoing process. Regular Red Team assessments help organizations stay proactive against emerging threats, adapt to evolving attack tactics, and continually enhance their cloud security measures.

- **Spotting Weaknesses in Cloud Configurations**

    Misconfigurations are a primary cause of cloud security breaches. Red Teaming can pinpoint weaknesses in cloud configurations, ensuring that organizations adhere to best practices for securing their cloud assets.

- **Strengthening Incident Response Abilities**

    Red Teaming exercises often involve simulated incident scenarios, enabling organizations to test and refine their incident response capabilities. This proactive approach assists organizations in minimizing the impact of actual incidents by refining their response protocols.

Implementation Steps

1. **Understanding Cloud Security**

   The corporation collaborated with its cloud service provider (CSP) to thoroughly check its cloud setup. They looked into what security tools the CSP offers and where the organization needs to take care of security themselves.

2. **Making Realistic Threats**

   The Red Team, a group of security experts, worked closely with the organization's own security team to create fake attack situations. They made scenarios that copied how real attackers might try to mess with the organization's cloud stuff, like sending fake emails or trying to break into accounts.

3. **Keeping Skills Sharp**

   The organization knew their Red Team needed to stay sharp, so they gave them extra training. This included learning about cloud security, the latest threats, and practicing with new tools.

4. **Using Tools to Help**

   To test things at a big scale, the organization used special tools to make fake attacks on their cloud setup. This helped them find problems faster and see if their defenses could handle big attacks.

5. **Trying Out the Plans**

   The Red Team put their fake attack plans into action, trying to break into the organization's cloud stuff for real. They tried things like stealing important data or messing up important services.

6. **Testing What to Do in Emergencies**

   While doing fake attacks, the organization also checked how well they could respond if something bad happened. This helped them see if they were ready to handle real emergencies and fix problems quickly.

7. **Finding Problems and Fixing Them**

   After all the tests, the Red Team provided the organization with detailed reports outlining the problems found and how bad they could be. This helped the organization know which problems to fix first to keep their cloud stuff safe.

Best Practices in Cloud-Native Security

1. **Ensure Hygiene and Maintain Visibility**

   Cloud deployments have numerous transient components, including compute instances, containers, data volumes, serverless functions, and managed databases or data stores. It's crucial to maintain an accurate inventory of cloud assets, understanding who deployed them, their functions, and whether they pose any security risks or vulnerabilities.

2. **Use Identity and Access Management (IAM)**

   IAM solutions play a critical role in safeguarding cloud systems since users can access cloud resources from anywhere. IAM offers insight into users' roles and permissions within the cloud environment. You can monitor user activity and set alerts for suspicious behavior. Additionally, most IAM systems offer multi-factor authentication (MFA) and single sign-on (SSO) capabilities.

3. **Protect Credentials to Mitigate Social Engineering**

   To mitigate phishing and other social engineering attacks, employ security measures such as educating users against sharing credentials, implementing email and endpoint protection, setting alerts for login attempts from different locations or multiple IPs, enforcing session timeouts, and mandating regular password changes. Additionally, prioritize the use of multi-factor authentication (MFA).

4. **Keep Services and Cloud Systems Updated**

   Keep in mind that the cloud provider does not shoulder responsibility for workloads. Except for specific managed services like DBaaS, your organization is accountable for patching and updating software such as operating systems, databases, and content management systems. Utilize automated tools to detect vulnerabilities in cloud systems and aim to automate security updates for swift remediation.

CHAPTER 9   THREAT ANALYSIS FOR CLOUD-NATIVE DEPLOYMENTS

Conduct Due Diligence

When utilizing cloud services, software as a service (SaaS), or other development components, conduct security reviews and test resources for security, akin to testing your own systems. While cloud provider software is typically of high quality and secure, the common practice of employing third-party software on the cloud, such as marketplace images, container images, or other third-party services, necessitates caution.

Audit and Improve Configurations

Securing configurations once is insufficient. Cloud environments undergo constant changes, demanding continuous monitoring to verify their safety. With every new compute instance or data volume created, scaled, or replicated, there's potential for misconfiguration that may pose security risks.

Security Controls and Countermeasures

Securing data, apps, and infrastructure in cloud setups is super important. Cloud systems have different parts like the basic setup, the platform where apps run, the apps themselves, and the data they use. Let's talk about how to make each of these parts safe and sound.

1. **Infrastructure Layer**

    Identity and Access Management (IAM): This involves creating and managing user identities, assigning roles, and setting permissions for accessing cloud resources.

    Network Security: Securing the network infrastructure using techniques like firewalls, VPNs, and secure connectivity protocols to protect data in transit.

CHAPTER 9 THREAT ANALYSIS FOR CLOUD-NATIVE DEPLOYMENTS

Encryption: Encrypting data at rest and in transit to prevent unauthorized access. This can be achieved using encryption keys and secure communication protocols.

Logging and Monitoring: Implementing logging and monitoring solutions to track activities, detect anomalies, and respond to security incidents effectively.

2. **Platform Layer**

   Container Security: Ensuring the security of containerized applications by scanning images for vulnerabilities, configuring runtime security policies, and managing access controls.

   Service Mesh: Implementing a service mesh to manage secure communication between microservices, including encryption, authentication, and access control.

   Authentication and Authorization: Implementing strong authentication mechanisms and access controls to ensure that only authorized users and services can access platform resources.

3. **Application Layer**

   Secure Coding Practices: Following secure coding standards and best practices to develop applications that are resilient to common security threats such as injection attacks and cross-site scripting.

Web Application Firewall (WAF): Deploying a WAF to protect web applications from various attacks, including SQL injection, XSS, and CSRF.

API Security: Implementing security measures such as authentication, authorization, and rate limiting to protect APIs from abuse and unauthorized access.

4. **Data Layer**

   Data Encryption: Encrypting sensitive data at rest using encryption algorithms and managing encryption keys securely.

   Access Control: Implementing access controls and data governance policies to restrict access to sensitive data based on user roles and permissions.

   Data Masking/Anonymization: Masking or anonymizing sensitive data in non-production environments to prevent unauthorized access and maintain data privacy.

5. **DevOps and CI/CD Pipeline**

   Security Automation: Integrating security checks and controls into the CI/CD pipeline to automate security testing, vulnerability scanning, and compliance checks.

   Immutable Infrastructure: Adopting immutable infrastructure patterns to minimize security risks by ensuring that infrastructure components are immutable and reproducible.

Continuous Monitoring: Implementing continuous monitoring solutions to detect security vulnerabilities, anomalies, and potential threats in real-time.

Key Management in Cloud Native

Cryptographic or encryption keys management involves overseeing their entire life cycle, from creation to destruction, along with ensuring their secure storage and protection. Key management encompasses various activities.

- **Key Distribution:** Authorized applications, systems, and users should have a mechanism to request and retrieve keys for encryption and decryption purposes.

- **Key Activation:** Keys can be activated either at the time of creation or later, either manually or automatically. If multiple copies of a key are activated, they need to be properly stored and monitored.

- **Key Revocation:** If a key is compromised, it may need to be revoked to prevent further use in encryption or decryption. However, if the key has already been used for encryption, it may need to be retained temporarily for decryption purposes.

- **Key Generation:** Encryption keys are created using a pseudo-random number generator, with each key being meticulously tracked and audited to maintain accountability.

- **Key Rotation:** It's advisable to periodically rotate keys to enhance security. Rotations can occur on a predefined schedule or manually by administrators. When replacing an old key with a new one, the old key must be deactivated and retained for decryption.

- **Key Destruction:** In certain cases, keys may need to be permanently removed, necessitating the deletion of every instance of the key.

- **Key Expiration:** Some encryption keys are created for specific durations, such as one-time encryption keys used for envelope encryption. Expired keys should be retained for decryption until they are no longer needed.

- **Key Storage:** Generated keys must be securely stored and backed up to prevent loss, tampering, or unauthorized access. Additionally, passwords and passphrases used for encryption should also be securely stored.

While it's conceivable to manage these tasks manually, scaling and ensuring CIA (Confidentiality, Integrity, Availability) require automation through a robust key management system. Relying solely on manual methods, such as writing down keys on sticky notes or storing them in text files on laptops, is inadequate, especially in enterprise environments and industries with highly sensitive data. In such contexts, there's often a hierarchical structure of keys encrypting other keys, further emphasizing the need for effective key management practices.

Summary

In this chapter, we explored how to keep cloud-based systems safe. We talked about how these systems have changed the way organizations work, making things quicker and cheaper. But, they also bring new problems with security, as old ways of keeping systems safe don't always work well with the new cloud-based systems.

We looked at the problems that can come up with keeping cloud-based systems safe. We talked about how these systems are set up and how they work. We found out where bad actors might try to attack these systems.

We didn't just talk about the problems, though. We also talked about how to figure out which problems are most serious and how to fix them. Whether you're someone who sets up these systems, someone who protects them from bad guys, or someone who runs a business that uses them, we gave you some good advice on what to do.

We talked about a lot of things in this chapter, like what makes keeping cloud-based systems safe so hard, where bad guys might try to attack, how to check that everything is safe, and what you can do to keep your systems safe.

With all this information, you're in a better position to keep your cloud-based systems safe from bad guys. As we finish up this chapter, we encourage you to keep these ideas in mind and make sure your systems are as safe as they can be.

CHAPTER 10

Future Trends in Cloud Native

"Future Trends in Cloud-Native: Transforming cloud dreams into digital realities!"

In this chapter, we will discuss a journey to explore the cutting-edge developments and emerging paradigms shaping the landscape of Cloud-Native DevOps. As technology continues to evolve rapidly, organizations and practitioners must stay informed about the latest trends and innovations to maintain a competitive edge and effectively leverage the power of the cloud.

Throughout this chapter, we will delve into various areas poised to revolutionize the way we design, deploy, and manage applications in cloud-native environments. From the rise of serverless computing and the advent of edge computing to the integration of artificial intelligence and machine learning into DevOps workflows, we will examine how these advancements are reshaping traditional approaches to software development and operations. Furthermore, we will explore emerging best practices and methodologies that are driving efficiency, scalability, and reliability in cloud-native architectures. Moreover, we will discuss the importance of embracing DevSecOps principles to address security challenges in increasingly complex and dynamic environments. We will also examine the role of observability, compliance automation, and

CHAPTER 10   FUTURE TRENDS IN CLOUD NATIVE

environmental sustainability considerations in driving innovation and fostering a culture of continuous improvement.

By the end of this chapter, readers will gain valuable insights into the trends and technologies shaping the future of Cloud-Native DevOps. Whether you are a seasoned practitioner or new to the world of DevOps, this chapter aims to equip you with the knowledge and understanding needed to navigate the ever-changing landscape of cloud-native development and operations.

In this chapter, we will be encompassing the following topics:

- Serverless Computing and Function as a Service (FaaS)
- AI and Machine Learning Integration Intersection in Cloud Native
- Evolution of Containerization Technologies Beyond Docker and Kubernetes
- The Rise of No-Code/Low-Code Platforms in DevOps Workflows

Serverless Computing and Function as a Service (FaaS)

Serverless computing simplifies the process of deploying and managing applications by outsourcing the management of servers and infrastructure to a cloud service provider. This means that instead of worrying about setting up and maintaining servers, databases, and other components, developers can focus solely on writing and deploying their applications.

Think of it like renting a fully equipped kitchen rather than building one from scratch. You have access to all the tools and equipment you need without the hassle of purchasing and maintaining them yourself. Similarly, with serverless computing, developers have access to the necessary computing resources without the burden of managing the underlying infrastructure.

One of the key benefits of serverless computing is its scalability. Resources automatically scale up or down based on demand, ensuring optimal performance and cost-efficiency. This is akin to having a kitchen that magically expands or contracts depending on the number of guests you're cooking for.

For instance, if you need to set up a database in the cloud, instead of going through the complex process of provisioning servers, configuring databases, and managing infrastructure, you can simply use a serverless database service. With just a few clicks, the database is up and running, adjusting its capacity in real-time to handle fluctuations in workload, all without any intervention from the developer.

In essence, serverless computing simplifies the development and deployment process, allowing developers to focus on building great applications without getting bogged down by the complexities of managing infrastructure.

Benefits of Serverless Computing

- **Cost Optimization**

    Serverless architecture follows a "pay as you go" model, meaning you only pay for the computing resources you use. This eliminates the need for upfront investment in hardware or software licenses, reducing operational costs significantly. With traditional setups, businesses often over-provision resources to handle peak loads, leading to wasted resources and higher costs. In contrast, serverless architectures dynamically scale resources based on demand, ensuring efficient resource utilization and cost optimization.

- **Improved Latency**

    One of the key advantages of cloud-based serverless architectures is their ability to deliver low-latency experiences to users worldwide. Traditional server setups often suffer from latency issues due to the geographical distance between the user and the server. However, with serverless architectures leveraging cloud infrastructure, data can be served from locations closer to the user, reducing latency and improving responsiveness. This is particularly crucial for real-time applications like video streaming, online gaming, or financial transactions, where even minor delays can impact user experience.

- **Easy Deployment**

    Serverless architectures simplify the deployment process, allowing developers to focus on building and updating applications without worrying about infrastructure management. With traditional setups, deploying new features or updates often involves complex configurations and downtime. In contrast, serverless platforms offer seamless deployment mechanisms, enabling developers to upload code modules or functionalities directly to the cloud environment. This streamlined process accelerates time-to-market and enhances agility, enabling businesses to respond quickly to changing market demands.

- **Scalability**

    Scalability is a core feature of serverless architectures, allowing applications to handle varying workloads without manual intervention. Traditional setups often require businesses to provision and manage physical servers or virtual machines, which can be time-consuming and costly. In contrast, serverless platforms automatically scale resources up or down based on demand, ensuring optimal performance and cost-efficiency. This dynamic scaling capability enables businesses to handle spikes in traffic or seasonal fluctuations without over-provisioning resources, leading to better resource utilization and cost savings.

- **Eco-friendly Setup**

    Cloud-based serverless architectures offer environmental benefits compared to traditional data center setups. Traditional data centers consume large amounts of energy to power and cool servers, contributing to carbon emissions and environmental degradation. By leveraging cloud infrastructure, businesses can reduce their carbon footprint by offloading server management to cloud providers who operate energy-efficient data centers. This shift toward eco-friendly practices aligns with corporate sustainability goals and helps mitigate the environmental impact of IT operations.

- **Flexibility in Development**

    Serverless architectures enable developers to focus on writing code and building innovative features without being burdened by server management tasks. In traditional setups, developers often spend significant time and effort on provisioning, configuring, and maintaining servers, diverting resources away from core development activities. With serverless platforms handling infrastructure management, developers can allocate more time to coding, testing, and iterating on new features. This increased flexibility empowers teams to deliver higher-quality software faster, driving innovation and competitive advantage in the marketplace.

Function as a Service (FaaS)

In the past, applications were often built as one big piece, which meant they had to run all at once whenever they were triggered. But as time went on, developers started moving toward a different approach called microservices. Microservices are like building blocks for applications – they're smaller pieces that can be developed and managed independently.

Now, imagine a microservice as a tiny worker who can only do one specific task whenever it's asked. That's essentially what a function is in the context of FaaS (Function as a Service). When you use FaaS, the service provider sets up a server just for that task when it's needed. Once the task is done, the server is shut down until it's needed again. This means resources are only used when they're doing something, and they can be used elsewhere when they're not needed.

FaaS makes things simpler for developers because they only need to focus on writing code for each specific task. But there's a catch – each function should only do one thing, and it should do it well. If a function tries to do too much, like using lots of different tools or calling other functions, it can slow down the whole application and end up costing more in the long run. So, keeping functions small and efficient is key to getting the most out of FaaS.

Benefits of FaaS

- **Simplified Code**

    With FaaS, developers can break down their applications into smaller, independent functions. This makes it easier to manage and update code, as each function can be developed, tested, and deployed separately. Additionally, FaaS platforms allow developers to upload individual functions or their entire application at once, providing flexibility in development. This simplified approach to coding reduces complexity and makes it easier for developers to focus on writing efficient and scalable code.

- **Faster Time to Market**

    FaaS enables developers to quickly develop and deploy applications, reducing time to market. Because functions can be developed and tested independently, developers can iterate on their code more rapidly and make changes quickly. This agility allows businesses to respond to market demands and customer feedback faster, gaining a competitive edge in the market. Additionally, the ability to scale resources automatically means that applications can handle increased demand without any delays in deployment, further speeding up time to market.

- **Costs**

    With Function as a Service (FaaS), you only pay for the computing resources you actually use. Unlike other providers where you have to pay upfront for a certain amount of bandwidth whether you use it all or not,

FaaS allows for more precise billing. This means that if your application doesn't require much computing power or bandwidth at a particular time, you won't be charged for resources you didn't use. This can lead to significant cost savings, especially for businesses with fluctuating workloads.

- **Scalability**

  FaaS platforms automatically adjust the resources allocated to your application based on demand. This means that if your application experiences a sudden increase in traffic or usage, the platform will automatically scale up to handle the load without any intervention from the developer. Conversely, if the demand decreases, the platform will scale down to save resources. This scalability feature ensures that your application can handle varying workloads without any downtime or performance issues, providing a seamless experience for users.

- **Reduced Latency**

  By running applications closer to end-users, FaaS platforms can reduce latency and improve the responsiveness of applications. This is achieved by deploying functions in data centers located geographically closer to the users, minimizing the distance data needs to travel. As a result, requests can be processed more quickly, leading to faster load times and a better overall user experience. Reduced latency is particularly important for real-time applications, such as online gaming or video streaming, where even small delays can be noticeable to users.

Best Practices for FaaS

1. **Keep Libraries to a Minimum**

   When you write code for a function, you might use libraries or external code to perform certain tasks. However, using too many libraries can make your function slower and more complex.

   Example: Let's say you're building a function that calculates the total price of items in a shopping cart. Instead of importing multiple libraries for different calculations, such as currency conversion or tax calculation, you can try to write custom code within the function itself to perform these tasks efficiently.

2. **One Task Per Function**

   Each function in a FaaS architecture should focus on performing a specific task in response to a particular event. This ensures that the code is well-organized, easy to maintain, and executes quickly.

   Example: Suppose you're building a web application where users can upload images. You might have one function to resize images upon upload, another function to compress images for faster loading, and a separate function to send a notification to the user once the image processing is complete. Each function has a clear and distinct purpose, making the application easier to manage and scale.

3. **Avoid Function-to-Function Calls**

   In FaaS, functions are designed to be independent and isolated from each other. While it may be tempting to have one function call another for complex workflows, this can lead to increased costs and reduced efficiency.

   Example: Imagine you're developing a chat application where users can send messages to each other. Instead of having one function handle message sending and then call another function to log the message, it's better to log the message directly within the sending function. This avoids unnecessary function calls and keeps the application's architecture simple and cost-effective.

Key Challenges in Serverless Computing

1. **Depending on One Company**

   Serverless computing relies heavily on services provided by major cloud providers like Amazon Web Services (AWS), Microsoft Azure, or Google Cloud Platform. By choosing serverless, businesses become tied to the ecosystem of a single vendor. This means they're limited to the services and tools offered by that specific provider, making it challenging to switch to another vendor or integrate services from different providers.

CHAPTER 10 FUTURE TRENDS IN CLOUD NATIVE

Example: Suppose a company develops its application using AWS Lambda functions. If they later decide to switch to Azure Functions, they'll need to rewrite and restructure their application to fit the Azure environment, which can be time-consuming and costly. Additionally, if AWS experiences a service outage, all applications relying on Lambda functions could be affected, potentially causing significant disruptions to business operations.

2. **Watching and Fixing Issues**

   Monitoring and debugging serverless functions pose unique challenges due to their ephemeral nature. Unlike traditional servers where metrics and logs are readily available, serverless functions scale dynamically and execute only when triggered, making it difficult to monitor performance and identify issues.

   Example: Let's say a company experiences a slowdown in their application's performance. With traditional servers, they could analyze logs and metrics to pinpoint the cause and make necessary adjustments. However, with serverless functions, detailed insights may be lacking, requiring developers to resort to alternative methods, such as running functions locally or using specialized monitoring tools, to diagnose and troubleshoot issues effectively.

3. **Slow Starts**

   Cold starts refer to the delay in launching a new instance of a serverless function, particularly when it hasn't been invoked recently. This delay can vary in duration, ranging from milliseconds to several seconds, depending on various factors such as the runtime environment and function complexity.

   Example: Imagine a user accesses a mobile application that relies on serverless functions for processing requests. If a function experiences a cold start, the initial delay in response time could frustrate the user and negatively impact their experience. For time-sensitive applications like real-time gaming or financial transactions, minimizing cold start latency is crucial to maintaining user satisfaction and retention.

4. **Testing and Putting Stuff Online**

   Deploying serverless functions differs from traditional application architectures, requiring teams to adjust their testing and deployment strategies accordingly. With serverless, developers deploy individual functions rather than entire applications, which necessitates a shift in testing methodologies and deployment pipelines.

   Example: Suppose a development team is tasked with deploying a new feature for an ecommerce website using serverless functions. Instead of deploying the entire application at once, they need to test and deploy each function individually. This requires setting up automated testing frameworks and continuous integration/continuous deployment (CI/CD) pipelines tailored to the unique characteristics of serverless architectures.

5. **Learning and Skills**

    Serverless represents a paradigm shift in application development, requiring developers to adopt a new mindset and skill set. This includes not only mastering new tools and services offered by cloud providers but also understanding the principles and best practices of serverless architecture.

    Example: A team of developers accustomed to traditional server-based architectures may face a learning curve when transitioning to serverless. They'll need to learn how to design and optimize functions for efficiency and scalability, as well as how to leverage serverless-specific services like AWS Lambda or Azure Functions effectively. Additionally, the scarcity of educational resources and expertise in serverless may require organizations to invest in training programs or hire experienced professionals to bridge the skills gap.

AI and Machine Learning Integration Intersection in Cloud Native

In today's rapidly advancing world of technology, the merging of Artificial Intelligence (AI) and Cloud-Native Applications is a clear sign of innovation. This combination isn't just about using fancy terms; it's a mutually beneficial partnership that boosts the strengths of each, leading to significant progress in different fields.

CHAPTER 10   FUTURE TRENDS IN CLOUD NATIVE

To understand the significance of this teamwork, we need to grasp what AI and cloud-native applications are all about. AI is a game-changer that allows machines to mimic human intelligence, learning, reasoning, and adapting. On the other hand, cloud-native applications are a modern way of developing and running software that takes advantage of the cloud's scalability, flexibility, and resilience.

The collaboration between AI and cloud-native applications is causing a stir in various industries, from healthcare and finance to manufacturing and entertainment. Let's explore further to see the exciting innovations and real-world applications that showcase the power of this partnership.

1. **Revolutionizing Industries**

    AI and cloud-native applications are driving a significant transformation across various industries, including healthcare, finance, manufacturing, and entertainment. This collaboration is reshaping how businesses operate, interact with customers, and deliver services. For instance, predictive maintenance systems powered by AI algorithms deployed on cloud platforms are revolutionizing manufacturing operations by enabling proactive equipment maintenance, reducing downtime, and optimizing resource utilization. Similarly, AI-driven recommendation engines hosted on cloud-native infrastructure are enhancing user experiences on ecommerce platforms by providing personalized product recommendations based on individual preferences and behaviors.

2. **Personalization and Enhanced Customer Engagement**

   The integration of AI and cloud-native applications is revolutionizing customer engagement by enabling hyper-personalized experiences. Through advanced analytics and machine learning algorithms deployed on cloud platforms, businesses can analyze vast amounts of customer data to understand preferences, behaviors, and purchase patterns. This enables them to tailor products, services, and marketing campaigns to meet the unique needs of individual customers, thereby driving increased engagement, customer satisfaction, and loyalty.

3. **Advancements in Healthcare**

   The synergy between AI and cloud-native platforms is driving significant advancements in the healthcare industry. AI algorithms deployed on cloud infrastructure are revolutionizing patient care by enabling early disease detection, personalized treatment plans, and drug discovery. For example, AI-powered diagnostic tools can analyze medical images and patient data to identify patterns indicative of diseases like cancer or identify potential drug candidates for specific conditions. By harnessing the power of cloud computing, healthcare providers can access scalable resources and computational capabilities to analyze vast amounts of medical data rapidly and accurately, ultimately improving patient outcomes and saving lives.

4. **Empowering Autonomous Systems and IoT**

   AI and cloud-native technologies are empowering the development of autonomous systems and Internet of Things (IoT) devices, revolutionizing automation and real-time data processing capabilities. Cloud platforms provide the computational resources and scalability required to deploy AI algorithms for processing data from sensors and devices in real-time. This enables applications such as self-driving cars to make split-second decisions for safe navigation or smart home devices to automate tasks and provide intelligent insights. By leveraging AI and cloud-native infrastructure, businesses can create innovative solutions that enhance efficiency, safety, and convenience in various domains.

5. **Addressing Challenges and Seizing Opportunities**

   While the collaboration between AI and cloud-native applications offers immense potential, it also presents challenges such as security, privacy concerns, and integration complexities. However, these challenges also present opportunities for innovation and the development of novel solutions. For example, advancements in federated learning, where AI models are trained across distributed devices without centralized data collection, address privacy concerns in cloud-native AI systems. Additionally, investments in research and development can lead to the creation of robust security measures, ethical frameworks, and scalable architectures that unlock the full potential of AI and cloud-native technologies. By addressing these challenges head-on, businesses can seize opportunities for growth, differentiation, and competitive advantage in the digital landscape.

Challenges and Considerations Implementing AI in Cloud Native

Artificial Intelligence (AI) and Machine Learning (ML) have revolutionized how businesses operate by enabling them to analyze data and derive insights that lead to smarter decision-making processes. With AI and ML, businesses can now understand customer preferences, predict trends, and personalize experiences, ultimately enhancing customer satisfaction and loyalty. As technology continues to advance, more companies are transitioning to cloud-native application development. Cloud-native apps are built and deployed in cloud environments, providing scalability, flexibility, and resilience. Integrating AI and ML into these cloud-native applications has become increasingly important as businesses seek to leverage the power of data-driven insights to gain a competitive edge. However, integrating AI and ML into cloud-native apps comes with its own set of challenges. These challenges can include ensuring seamless data integration, managing the complexity of model training and deployment, addressing scalability and resource management issues, and navigating security and compliance concerns.

Challenges in Security and Compliance

Security and compliance are paramount when dealing with AI/ML in cloud-native apps, as data breaches or non-compliance can have severe consequences.

Solution: Develop a comprehensive security strategy for your AI/ML cloud-native apps, incorporating encryption and access control mechanisms for data protection. Utilize cloud-native security services like AWS IAM, Azure AD, or Google Cloud IAM for user access management. Implement regular monitoring using security tools like AWS GuardDuty or Azure Security Center to detect potential threats. Ensure compliance with regulations like GDPR or HIPAA through appropriate measures and audits.

Complexity in Deployment and Model Training

Model training and deployment are critical stages in AI/ML development, but they can be complex in a cloud-native environment.

Solution: Implement DevOps practices and utilize containerization to streamline model training and deployment processes. CI/CD pipelines can automate testing, training, and deployment, facilitating easier updates and version control. Tools like TensorFlow Serving and Kubernetes can efficiently manage model deployment, while model monitoring solutions help track performance and identify issues in real-time.

Obstacles in Data Integration

One of the main hurdles in incorporating AI/ML into cloud-native apps is ensuring smooth data integration. AI and ML models need access to large amounts of data, and making this data available across a cloud-native setup can be complex.

Solution: To tackle this challenge, it's crucial to establish a robust data integration strategy. Cloud-native platforms offer various data connectors and services to help ingest, store, and manage data efficiently. Services like AWS Glue, Azure Data Factory, or Google Cloud Dataflow can simplify data collection, transformation, and preparation for AI/ML tasks. Additionally, tools like Kubernetes can manage data pipelines and ensure data availability to your AI/ML models.

CHAPTER 10   FUTURE TRENDS IN CLOUD NATIVE

Scalability Management

AI/ML workloads can be resource-intensive, posing challenges in maintaining scalability and resource management for cloud-native apps.

Solution: Adopt containerization and orchestration techniques to ensure scalability and resource efficiency. Tools like Docker and Kubernetes are ideal for deploying and managing AI/ML workloads, allowing horizontal scaling and dynamic resource management. Autoscaling rules can be set up to adjust resources based on demand, optimize performance, and reducing operational costs.

Best Practices of Integrating AI/ML in Cloud Native

1. **Establish a Clear Strategy:** Before embarking on AI/ML integration, it's crucial to define a clear strategy. This involves identifying the specific objectives you aim to achieve with AI/ML, outlining relevant use cases, and understanding how these initiatives align with broader business goals. A well-defined strategy provides direction and ensures that AI/ML efforts contribute meaningfully to the success of cloud-native applications.

2. **Utilize Managed Services:** Leveraging managed AI/ML services offered by cloud providers can significantly simplify the integration process. These services typically come with pre-built models, APIs, and tools that enable developers to incorporate AI/ML functionalities into their applications with minimal effort. By utilizing managed services,

organizations can accelerate the deployment of AI/ML capabilities and reduce the complexity associated with building and maintaining custom solutions.

3. **Design for Scalability and Flexibility:** Cloud-native architectures should be designed with scalability and flexibility in mind to accommodate the dynamic nature of AI/ML workloads. This involves adopting containerization and orchestration technologies like Kubernetes, which enable automatic scaling of resources based on demand. By designing for scalability, organizations can ensure that their cloud-native applications can efficiently handle fluctuations in AI/ML usage and accommodate future growth.

4. **Implement Effective Data Management and Governance:** Effective data management and governance are essential for the success of AI/ML initiatives in cloud-native environments. Organizations must establish robust practices for data quality assurance, security, and regulatory compliance. This includes implementing data governance frameworks to govern data access and usage, as well as leveraging data lakes and warehouses for centralized data management and analysis.

5. **Continuous Monitoring and Optimization:** Monitoring and optimizing AI/ML models is critical for ensuring their effectiveness and performance. Organizations should implement monitoring and

logging mechanisms to track key metrics such as model accuracy, latency, and resource utilization in real-time. By continuously monitoring AI/ML models, organizations can identify potential issues or inefficiencies and take proactive steps to optimize their performance through iterative improvements and updates.

6. **Ensure Robust Security and Compliance Measures:** Security and compliance are paramount considerations when integrating AI/ML into cloud-native applications. Organizations must implement robust security measures to protect sensitive data and ensure compliance with relevant regulations such as GDPR or HIPAA. This includes implementing encryption, access controls, and authentication mechanisms to safeguard data integrity and prevent unauthorized access.

7. **Foster Collaborative Workflows and Knowledge Sharing:** Collaboration between different teams, including data scientists, developers, and operations teams, is essential for successful AI/ML integration. Organizations should foster a culture of collaboration and knowledge sharing to facilitate seamless integration of AI/ML capabilities into cloud-native applications. By encouraging cross-functional collaboration, organizations can leverage the expertise of diverse teams to drive innovation and achieve better outcomes.

8. **Embrace Iterative Development and Experimentation:** Adopting an iterative approach to AI/ML development allows organizations to experiment with different models and techniques to identify the most effective solutions. By starting with small-scale projects and iterating based on feedback and insights, organizations can refine and optimize AI/ML models over time. This iterative approach enables organizations to adapt to changing requirements and refine their AI/ML strategies based on real-world usage and feedback.

Evolution of Containerization Technologies Beyond Docker and Kubernetes

The growing demand for alternatives to Docker stems from various drawbacks associated with Docker technology. These drawbacks include the following.

- **Complexity:** Docker requires a deep understanding of containerization processes. Users need technical expertise to create Docker files and effectively manage and maintain containers.

- **Security Concerns:** Misconfigurations in Docker containers can expose applications to security vulnerabilities, posing risks to users and their data.

- **Performance Limitations:** Although Docker containers are efficient, they may not be suitable for resource-intensive applications that demand high performance and low latency, as resources are shared with the host system.

- **Limited Support for GUI Applications:** Docker is primarily designed for isolated containers and is more commonly used for console-based applications. However, it may not perform optimally for graphical user interface (GUI) applications.

1. **Buildah**

   Another useful tool in the open-source world is Buildah, which is based on Linux. Buildah is designed to help create containers that follow the OCI standards, making them compatible not only with Docker but also with Kubernetes. It allows users to construct images from scratch or based on existing ones. Buildah offers a more adaptable and secure approach to building container images, suitable for various runtime environments. As a command-line tool.

   - Building tools within the image itself, which results in smaller image sizes, increased security, and easier transportation with fewer resources

   - Creation of user-specific images, allowing for easy organization by the user who created them

   - Building container images with or without Dockerfiles, which are text documents containing commands for assembling an image

   - Creating container images from scratch or using existing ones as a starting point

   - Compatibility with Dockerfiles, enabling a smooth transition from Docker

Reason to Choose Buildah over Docker

Buildah offers more advanced features and capabilities for building containers compared to Docker. While Docker is suitable for basic container building and simple docker files, Buildah provides a cleaner approach and better scripting capabilities.

2. **Podman**

    Podman is a tool that works on Linux and doesn't need a special background process to run. It's free and open-source, and it helps with putting together, making, and spreading containers. Podman uses standards called OCI to make sure everything works smoothly. Like other container tools, Podman also uses OCI standards, so it works just like Docker. Its way of giving commands is very similar to Docker's, which makes it easy for people who already know Docker to use Podman. Plus, you can use Docker commands with Podman, so even if you're new to containers, you can get started with Podman without any trouble.

    - Supports rootless containers without requiring elevated privileges.

    - Highly adaptable to different computing environments and adjustable according to specific needs.

    - The Podman Top command provides comprehensive insights into container processes.

- Simplifies container execution through Systemd files, streamlining the process as simple as writing a file.

Reason to Choose Podman over Docker

Unlike Docker, which relies on a persistent runtime managed by its daemon (Dockerd), Podman operates independently without a daemon. It initiates containers as individual processes and communicates directly with the registry, offering a more lightweight and streamlined approach to container management.

3. **Containerd**

Containerd are a popular alternative to Docker and can be run on both Linux and Windows. As a container runtime, Containerd provides tools that manage the complete container life cycle of its host system, including image transfer, storage, container execution, and supervision to low-level storage of network attachments and beyond.

- Support for pushing and pulling images
- Managing network interfaces by creating, modifying, and deleting them
- Supporting multi-tenancy with CAS storage for global images
- Adherence to OCI Runtime Spec (also known as runC)
- Handling container runtime and life cycle
- Managing network namespaces for containers to connect to existing namespaces

Reason to Choose Containerd over Docker

Compared to Docker, Containerd is a simpler low-level Daemon program with all the essential features to build a container. It is less complex and more flexible in making basic containers.

4. **LXD**

   LXD is another great option if you're looking for an alternative to Docker. It's both a powerful virtual machine manager and a container system. LXD mainly works with Ubuntu images and spreads them across Linux setups. It relies on a strong REST API and can work on a single machine or across a whole group. This makes it useful for both development and production. LXD is light on resources and speeds up the process of containerizing data. It uses special Linux features like control groups and namespaces to manage containers.

   - It can adjust resources like CPU, memory, network speed, disk space, and some parts of the kernel.

   - Supports advanced snapshots, scheduling, and automatic expiration.

   - Makes it easy to set up for multiple users and offers better security.

   - Supports live migration, saving the current state of containers, and passing through hardware like GPUs, USBs, network cards, and more.

   - Offers advanced networking support, including OVN, SR-IOV, and hardware acceleration.

Reason to Choose LXD over Docker

LXD performs better than Docker, particularly in scenarios involving multiple processors. Additionally, LXD has a longer history than Docker and manages larger resource sets more effectively.

5. **OpenVZ**

   OpenVZ is a no-cost, Linux-oriented container virtualization software. It ensures the isolation and security of various Linux containers on a single server. This enhances server performance and prevents applications from interfering with each other. OpenVZ presents a viable alternative to Docker due to its extensive range of beneficial functionalities.

   OpenVZ makes it easy to create virtual versions of operating systems, so containers start up quickly and cost less. You can quickly give out resources to containers using its portal. It's reliable for saving copies of container images, which helps if there are any problems.

   ### Reason to Choose OpenVZ over Docker

   OpenVZ makes it easy to create virtual versions of operating systems, so containers start up quickly and cost less. You can quickly give out resources to containers using its portal. It's reliable for saving copies of container images, which helps if there are any problems.

6. **RunC**

   RunC is a simple and lightweight tool for running containers. It includes all the necessary code from Docker for running containers securely, without needing the entire Docker setup.

   - Supports all security features available in Linux, making it safe to use.
   - Allows live migration through CRIU, a tool developed by Parallels.
   - Can handle complex hardware features like DPDK, and secure enclave.

   Reason to Choose RunC over Docker
   RunC is commonly used in various industries to run containers with Docker, Containers, and CRI-O. It's user-friendly and effective, making containerization easier for everyone.

7. **Minikube**

   Minikube offers an alternative to Docker by creating virtual machines (VMs). It allows you to build images and VMs on your local computer and sets up a simple cluster with just one node. This makes minikube lightweight and easy to use, and it works on Linux, macOS, and Windows systems.

   - It supports both the newest and older versions of Kubernetes.
   - You can use it on macOS, Linux, and Windows.
   - You can set it up as a virtual machine, a container, or directly on your computer.

CHAPTER 10 FUTURE TRENDS IN CLOUD NATIVE

- It's compatible with different container runtimes such as Containerd and Docker.

- It includes a speedy API endpoint for loading images.

Reasons to Choose Minikube over Docker

Docker Desktop's Kubernetes lacks the features found in minikube, k3d, or kind. Docker also faces restrictions in handling cross-platform application activities and other functionalities.

8. **Kubernetes**

   Many developers consider Kubernetes as a dependable substitute for Docker and favor it for various reasons. While Docker serves as a container environment, Kubernetes acts as a platform managing containers from various runtimes. Docker is excellent for modern app development, but it struggles with scalability when handling numerous containers. In contrast, Kubernetes excels in managing many containers from different runtimes.

   - Uses a declarative model, stating how things should be, and K8s makes sure they stay that way, fixing any problems.

   - Automatically change the size of containerized apps and their resources based on needs.

   - Provides storage as needed, adding more when necessary.

   - Automate the process of setting up and updating, with the ability to go back to earlier versions if needed.

Reasons to Choose Kubernetes over Docker

Kubernetes is like a manager for Docker containers, helping to organize and automate how they're set up, resized, and run. It's especially useful for handling more complicated containers that Docker might struggle with.

9. **Rancher**

   Rancher offers a comprehensive solution for teams adopting containers, addressing the operational complexities associated with managing Docker and Kubernetes clusters. One key feature is its support for cross-host networking, which facilitates secure communication by creating a private software-defined network for each environment.

   Additionally, Rancher provides container load balancing, ensuring efficient distribution of container workload across processors. Its distributed DNS-based service discovery feature allows containers to register automatically over the network, enhancing ease of use. Moreover, Rancher monitors host resources and simplifies container deployment directly from Docker Machine, streamlining the development and management process for containerized workloads.

   Reasons to Choose Rancher over Docker

   Docker offers simple container management and creation, while Rancher provides more advanced functionalities. Rancher serves as an extension of

Kubernetes and can even replace Docker Desktop. Unlike Docker, Rancher is open-source and available for free.

The Rise of No-Code/Low-Code Platforms in DevOps Workflows

Low-code and no-code (LCNC) platforms have gained popularity for their ability to empower users to create applications without extensive coding knowledge. These platforms provide an alternative to traditional software development methods by offering intuitive visual interfaces and pre-built components. No code platforms, as the name suggests, eliminate the need for writing any code. Users can build applications entirely through graphical interfaces, selecting from a library of pre-designed elements and functionalities. This approach simplifies the application development process, making it accessible to individuals with limited technical expertise.

On the other hand, low-code platforms offer a middle ground between traditional coding and no code solutions. While they still require some level of coding, it is minimal compared to traditional development methods. Low-code platforms typically provide visual development environments where users can drag-and-drop elements, configure settings, and use pre-built functions to create applications more efficiently.

Both low-code and no-code platforms aim to democratize software development by enabling a broader range of users, including business analysts, citizen developers, and entrepreneurs, to create custom applications tailored to their specific needs. These platforms accelerate the development life cycle, reduce reliance on IT departments, and foster innovation within organizations.

CHAPTER 10   FUTURE TRENDS IN CLOUD NATIVE

Benefits of No Code and Low Code

1. **Making Apps Easier to Build**

   Regular coding can be intimidating for people without much tech know-how. But with low-code and no-code platforms, things are simpler. They use visual tools and easy drag-and-drop features, making it easy for anyone to create apps, even if they're not tech-savvy. This simplicity encourages more people to get involved in app development, letting them turn their ideas into real apps. It's all about fostering innovation and creativity among a wide range of folks.

2. **Cutting Down on Costs**

   Building software from scratch usually means hiring pricey developers with specialized skills. But LCNC platforms aim to lower these costs by cutting down on the need for highly skilled developers and simplifying the development process.

   This means businesses can manage their resources better since they won't need such a big development team. It's especially helpful for startups and small businesses with tight budgets.

3. **Enabling Non-Expert Developers**

   No-code and low-code platforms give people with specific knowledge but little coding experience the power to build applications. These "citizen developers" can contribute to software creation even without advanced coding skills. By involving

CHAPTER 10   FUTURE TRENDS IN CLOUD NATIVE

more people in the development process, these platforms help ensure that technology meets business needs more effectively. This inclusive approach fosters innovation within organizations by bringing diverse viewpoints into the creation of solutions.

4. **Quick Development**

   Building software the traditional way takes a lot of time with coding, fixing errors, and testing. LCNC speeds up this process a lot. With no-code and low-code platforms, users can quickly put together applications using easy interfaces, ready-made parts, and existing building blocks. This fast pace is handy for projects that need to get out there fast or for making prototypes and MVPs.

5. **Faster Prototyping**

   Entrepreneurs and startup companies can swiftly test their ideas, cutting down the time it takes to bring new concepts to market. They can easily create prototypes and minimum viable products (MVPs) in a short time, allowing for faster validation in the market.

6. **Cutting Down Development Expenses**

   Creating software from the ground up usually means hiring expensive specialized developers. However, LCNC platforms can cut down software development costs by needing fewer specialized developers and simplifying the development process. This efficiency allows businesses to use their resources more wisely since they won't need a big development team. This is especially helpful for startups and small businesses with tight budgets.

7. **Centered on Business**

   Many times, developers spend a lot of effort dealing with basic code and infrastructure issues. However, low-code and no-code platforms handle much of this technical stuff, letting developers concentrate on the main business logic and special features of the application. This means developers can use their skills more effectively.

8. **Flexibility and Improving**

   In today's fast-paced business world, being able to adjust swiftly is key. No-code and low-code platforms support a process of making small changes and improvements to applications as you go along. This flexibility is especially useful for projects that need to change often or to address feedback from users efficiently.

9. **Keeping Things Running Smoothly**

   As time goes on, traditional code can get more complicated, making it harder to maintain and update. No-code and low-code platforms usually take care of updates and maintenance automatically, so you don't have to worry about it as much, and it doesn't disrupt your app.
   Top of Form

10. **Promotes Creativity**

    By making development simpler, these platforms inspire creativity and experimentation. Teams can try out new ideas and features without investing too much time and resources, fostering a culture of constant improvement and innovation. The emergence of no-code and low-code platforms marks a significant change in software development, making it more accessible and effective. However, they're not a universal solution. The future of software development will likely involve a mix of traditional coding and these modern methods, allowing developers to choose the best approach for each project. Moving forward, it's crucial to acknowledge that while no-code and low-code platforms offer convenience, they won't replace the traditional coding methods that have driven the tech industry for years. Embracing these platforms alongside traditional approaches will unlock new opportunities and reshape how we create software.

Use of No Code and Low Code

No-code and low-code platforms are tools that help people make software without needing to know a lot about coding. They are used in many different industries and for many different reasons.

- **Making Tools and Automating Things Inside a Company:** Instead of waiting for the IT department, employees can use these platforms to create tools that help them work faster.

- **Quick Solutions for Short-Term Projects:** When a project doesn't last long or has a deadline, these platforms can help get it done quickly.

- **Testing Ideas Quickly:** Startups and companies can use them to make basic versions of their products to see if people like them.

- **Building Websites and Phone Apps:** They can be used to make all kinds of websites and apps, like online stores or customer portals.

- **Seeing Data in Useful Ways:** They help people make charts and graphs that show important information from different sources of data.

- **Making Work Easier:** They can be used to automate tasks like sending emails or moving data around, saving time.

- **Managing Content on Websites:** They help make websites where people can easily change the text and pictures without needing to know how to code.

- **Starting Online Stores:** Businesses can use them to make websites where people can buy things.

- **Keeping Track of Customers:** They can help keep track of information about customers and help with sales.

- **Simple Internet Things:** They can be used to make simple devices that connect to the Internet, like sensors.

- **Making Chatbots and Virtual Helpers:** They can make robots that talk to people and answer questions.

- **Teaching Tools:** Teachers can use them to make websites where students can learn and take quizzes.

- **Organizing Events:** They help make websites where people can sign up for events and buy tickets.

- **Connecting Buyers and Sellers:** They help make websites where people can buy and sell things.

- **Helping with Healthcare:** They can be used to make apps that track patients or help with appointments.

- **Helping Non-Profit Organizations:** They can be used to make websites that help charities and volunteers work together.

- **Showing Ideas to People:** They help make basic versions of apps to show to people who might want to invest in them.

- **Connecting Different Software:** They help connect different programs so they can share information.

Summary

In this chapter, we explored Cloud-Native DevOps, which is all about using the latest technology to develop and manage software in the cloud. We talked about how important it is for companies and people working in this field to keep up with new trends and ideas to make the most out of cloud technology. We looked at some exciting new developments, like serverless computing, edge computing, and using artificial intelligence and machine learning in DevOps. These new ideas are changing the traditional ways we design, put out, and look after software in the cloud.

CHAPTER 10 FUTURE TRENDS IN CLOUD NATIVE

We also talked about new ways to make cloud systems more efficient, scalable, and reliable. We stressed the importance of keeping things secure, especially as cloud systems get more complex. And we touched on how observing, automating compliance, and considering the environment are key to improving and coming up with new ideas. By the end of the chapter, readers should have a better understanding of where Cloud-Native DevOps is heading. Whether you're already experienced or just starting out, we hope this chapter has given you useful insights to help you navigate the world of cloud-native development and operations.

Index

A

Access control lists (ACLs), 321, 341
Access Management (AM), 169, 194, 315–318, 342, 406
Active Directory Management (ADMgmt), 314–315
Agile methodologies
 architectures and technologies, 271–274
 benefits, 275–277
Agility, 6, 29, 215, 230, 301
AI/ML, DevOps, *see* Artificial intelligence (AI)
Amazon ECR, 152
Amazon Web Services (AWS), 18, 136, 220, 246, 331, 398
API keys, 332–336
Application Programming Interfaces (APIs), 7, 50, 105, 125, 224, 262, 312
Argo, 179, 183, 192–195, 209, 217
Argo streamlining workflows
 CI/CD implementation, 194, 195
 controller, 192
 custom kubernetes, 193, 194

integration, 195–198, 200
K8s operator, 191
sync process, 192
target state, 192
Artificial intelligence (AI), 353, 389
 containerization technologies, 410–418
 data integration, 406
 implementation challenges, 405
 innovations and real-world applications, 402–404
 LCNC platforms, 419
 model training/deployment, 406
 practices, 407–409
 scalability management, 407
 security/compliance, 405
Artificial Intelligence for IT Operations (AIOps), 212, 215
Attribute-based access control (ABAC), 321
Automated scaling mechanisms, 224
Autoscaling, 68
 AWS, 246, 247
 benefits, 249, 250
 cost-efficient, 263

INDEX

Autoscaling (*cont.*)
    creation, 251, 253, 254, 256–261
    edge computing/
        distributed, 262
    hybrid and multi-cloud
        environments, 262
    machine learning-driven, 261
    serverless architectures/event-
        driven, 261
Autoscaling groups (ASGs), 247,
    248, 256, 257
AWS Certificate Manager
    (ACM), 105
Azure Functions, 19, 399, 401

B

Black Box Testing, 171

C

ChatOps, 215
Cloud computing, 5, 17–20, 47, 220,
    227, 265, 300–305
Cloud computing services
    cloud types, 26
    hybrid cloud, 26, 27
    IaaS, 28–30
    PaaS, 30–32
    private cloud, 23–25
    public cloud, 20–23
    SaaS, 33, 34
Cloud data flow
    data pipeline, 291, 292

    data pipeline
        architecture, 288–290
    finance, 286
    FinOps, 286, 287
    organization, 284, 285
    performance/scalability,
        292, 293
    prioritize compliance, 290
    strategy, 282, 284
    sustainability, 287, 288
Cloud-native
    architecture, 3
    CI/CD, 17
    CNCF, 15, 16
    containers, 16
    fundamentals, 14
    layers, 37
        application definition/
            development, 42
        orchestration/
            management, 40, 41
        provisioning, 38
        runtime, 37–39
    mainframe computing
        advantages, 5, 6
        architecture, 4
        disadvantages, 6, 7
        monolithic applications, 5
    orchestration tools, 3
Cloud Native Computing
    Foundation (CNCF), 15,
    180, 208
Cloud Native Maturity Model
    (CNMM), 35–37

INDEX

Cloud service provider (CSP), 21, 28, 33, 288, 356, 379
CloudWatch, 248
Collaborative development
    developers/operations, 266
    Devops culture, 267–271
Compliance, 8, 42, 94, 101, 115, 214, 303, 339, 344–345
Concurrent Versions System (CVS), 159
Constrained Application Protocol (CoAP), 246
Containerization tools, 7, 50
Continuous integration and continuous delivery (CI/CD), 2, 17, 87, 183, 214
Continuous integration and continuous deployment (CI/CD) pipelines, 237, 313, 401
    approaches, 173, 175, 176
    automation, 136
    benefits, 155–158
    cloud-agnostics, 161, 162
    cloud technologies, 136
    Jenkins, 162, 163, 165, 166
    practices, 150–155
    principles, 137–141
    security
        DAST, 171, 172
        Devops, 167
        IAST, 173
        SAST, 170, 171
        threats, 168, 169
    stages, 141
        build, 144–146
        deploy, 148, 149
        source, 142–144
        test, 146–148
    version control, 158–160
Cryptographic/encryption keys management, 385
Custom resource definitions (CRDs), 190–192, 200
Cyberattacks, 82, 103, 133

D

Data Loss Prevention (DLP), 174
DataOps, 212
Denial of service (DoS), 16, 121, 334, 376
DevOps, 137
    approaches, 46
    continuous deployment, 50
    continuous development, 49
    continuous feedback, 52
    continuous integration, 49
    continuous monitoring, 53
    continuous operations, 53
    continuous testing, 49, 50
    definition, 47
    flexibility/portability, 47
    infrastructure automation, 51, 52
    principles, 46, 48
    technologies, 46

INDEX

DevSecOps, 87–94, 103, 173, 214, 266, 336, 389
Distributed databases, 189
Distributed Denial of Service (DDoS) attacks, 376
Docker, 7, 39, 70, 111, 145, 157, 208, 293, 310, 390, 407, 410
Docker Hub, 11, 152
Dynamic Application Security Testing (DAST), 87–89, 171–173, 357
Dynamic scaling
    agility and adaptability, 230
    defense in depth, 226, 227
    managed services, 227, 228
    polyglot architecting, 229
    strategic management, 224–226

E

Edge computing, 187, 236–246, 262, 389, 425
Environmental, social, and governance (ESG), 288
Extract, Transform, Load (ETL)
    cloud-integrated logistics operation, 298, 299
    services, 294
    supply chain management, 300–305
    transition, 295–297

F

FinOps, 286, 287
Function as a Service (FaaS)
    benefits, 395, 396
    challenges, 398–400
    practices, 397

G

General Data Protection Regulation (GDPR), 291, 311, 331, 344, 346, 406, 409
GitOps, 184, 216
Glass-box, 173
Google Cloud Functions, 19
Google Cloud Platform (GCP), 19, 22, 107, 220, 398
Governance, 34, 35, 169, 184, 232, 288, 342–343
Gramm-Leach-Bliley Act (GBLA), 345–346

H

HashiCorp Configuration Language (HCL), 106
Health Insurance Portability and Accountability Act (HIPPA), 349
Helm, 70, 187
Horizontal Pod Autoscaler (HPA), 65, 68–70, 72–74, 224

Horizontal Pod Autoscaling (HPA), 68–72
Hotfix, 273
Hyperautomation, 212

I, J

Identity and Access Management (IAM) security
  ADMgmt, 314
  AM, 315–317
  building concrete, 350–353
  compliance, 344
  components, 320, 321
  foundational elements, 308–314
  governance, 342, 354
  IGA, 317–319
  least privilege, implementation, 323–325
  least privilege principles, 322
  PAM, 319
  real-life examples, 307
  risk management, 343
  service accounts/API access
    API keys, 332–335
    cloud-based applications, 326
    difficulties, 336–338
    implementation, 329–331
    key components, 326, 328
    least privilege, 336
    practices, 339, 340, 342
  standards, 345–349

Identity Governance and Administration (IGA), 315, 317–319
Infrastructure-as-a-Service (IaaS), 28–30, 283
Infrastructure as code (IaC), 153, 213, 237
  infrastructure processes, 101, 102
  practices, 114, 115
  scanning, 92
  security strategy, 103
  terraform, 105, 106
  tools, 104, 105, 109–112
  value proposition, 112, 113
Integrated development environments (IDEs), 171
Interactive application security testing (IAST), 87, 89–90, 173
Internet of Things (IoT), 187, 188, 239, 404
Intrusion Detection System (IDS), 174, 176, 322
Intrusion Prevention System (IPS), 174

K

Keptn, 183–184
Key performance indicators (KPIs), 35, 286
KubeEdge, 187–188

INDEX

Kubeflow pipelines
    components, 207, 208
    definition, 202
    machine learning engineers, 202
    ML, 208–211
    principles, 206
    problem identification, 202
    source/prepare/analyze
        data, 203–205
Kubernetes, 3, 45, 79, 181, 407, 417
    definition, 54
    fundamental architecture, 54
    installation, 57
    master node, 55
        autoscaling, 68
        HPA, 68–71
        kube-brench, security, 62, 63
        manual scaling, 66, 67
        scaling, 64–66
        steps, 58, 60, 61
        VPA, 74, 75
        YAML file, 72, 73
    monolithic *vs.* public managed
        kubernetes cluster, 76–78
    worker node, 56, 62

L

Linkerd, 39, 186
Low-code and no-code (LCNC)
    platforms
    benefits, 420–422
    pre-built components, 419
    uses, 423, 425

M

Machine learning (ML), 202–204, 208, 302, 353, 389, 405, 425
Message Queuing Telemetry
    Transport (MQTT), 246
Microservices, 1, 15, 43, 177, 185, 236, 242, 394
Microsoft Azure, 19, 22, 136, 220, 359, 398
Minikube, 70, 74, 416–417
Multi-cloud strategy
    edge computing, 236, 237, 239–246
    platforms, 232, 233
    preemptive scaling, 235, 236
    reactive/proactive scaling, 233, 234
Multi-faceted approach, 282, 367
Multi-factor authentication
    (MFA), 175, 316, 327, 342, 351

N

Non-functional testing, 50, 138
No Operations (NoOps), 216

O

OpenGitOps, 184
Open Policy Agent (OPA), 185
Open-source software (OSS), 333

Open-source tools
    Argo, 217
    kubeflow pipelines, 179, 180
OpenVZ, 415
OpenYurt, 188

P

Package management, 186–187
"Pay as you go" model, 5, 22, 23, 29, 249–250, 391
Payment Card Industry Data Standard (PCI-DSS), 347–348
Physical security, 2
Plan-Do-Study-Act (PDSA), 270
Platform-as-a-service (PaaS), 30–32, 283
Podman, 412, 413
Policy and governance, 184–185
Privileged Access Management (PAM), 319, 340
Privileged accounts, 319
Proactive scaling strategy, 235
Product backlog, 49, 279–281
Prometheus, 15, 39, 41, 66, 154, 182, 223
Public cloud, 20–25, 51, 76, 105, 294
Public Kubernetes Cloud, 77
Pynt, 124–126
    security testing, 127–133
    setup, 126–127

Q

Quantum computing, 214

R

Rancher, 418, 419
Reactive scaling, 234, 235
Red Teaming, 377–379
Resilience, 15, 61, 181, 195, 221–223, 277, 298, 334, 402, 405
Role-based access control (RBAC), 61, 170, 194, 321, 343, 359
Rook, 189
RunC, 413, 416
Runtime Application Self-Protection (RASP), 87, 91–92

S

Sarbanes-Oxley (SOX), 348–349
Scaling principles
    automation, 221, 222
        CI/CD, 223
        dynamic scaling, 224
        infrastructure provisioning/management tools, 223
        monitoring/logging, 223
    synchronization, 221
SchemaHero, 190
Scrum framework
    artifacts, 279, 280
    roles, 277–279
Scrum Master, 277, 278
SecOps, 85

Security information and event management (SIEM) systems, 169
Segregation of duties (SoD), 318, 343, 346
Serverless computing
 advantages, 18
 benefits, 391–393
 cloud service provider, 390
 database service, 391
 definition, 17
 disadvantages, 19
 platforms, 18
Service mesh, 39, 185–186, 383
Shift-left approach, securing API
 making apps, 117
 Pynt, 124, 125
 Pynt security testing, 127, 128, 130–132
 Pynt setup, 126
 risk factors, 118–123
 testing, 123
Shift-left security
 benefits, 99, 100
 compliance checks, 94
 DAST, 88, 89
 Iac scanning, 92
 IAST, 89
 infrastructure scanning, 93
 model, 83
 RASP, 91
 SAST, 88
 SCA, 90
 securing right, 84, 85
 security testing, 94, 95, 97–99
 software development life cycle, 82
 technologies, 87
 third-party component, 86
Single points of failure (SPOFs), 241
Single Sign-On (SSO), 194, 351, 381
Software-as-a-Service (SaaS), 33–34, 116, 154, 382
Software Bills of Materials (SBOMs), 84
Software Composition Analysis (SCA), 90–91
Software development life cycle (SDLC), 48, 97–100, 137, 167
Sprint Backlog, 280
Static Application Security Testing (SAST), 170–171, 357
Static Application System Testing (SAST), 87, 88
Storage orchestration, 188–189
STRIDE threat modeling, 374, 377
Supply chain management (SCM), 265, 266, 294–296, 300–305

T, U

Terraform
 architecture, 108, 109
 definition, 105
 use, 105
 working, 106, 107
TestNG, 50

TestSigma, 50
Threat analysis
    cloud-native deployments, 355, 356
    cloud-native security controls, 369–372, 374
    microservices architectures, threat vectors, 374–377
    practices, 380–382
    security 3R's, 366–369
    security challenges, 356–359, 363–365
    security controls/countermeasures, 382, 384–386
    security validation implementation steps, 379
    Red Teaming, 377, 378
    types of threats, 360–362

Threat modeling, 117, 173–174, 374–377
TiKV, 189
Transport Layer Security (TLS), 104, 290
Twelve-Factor App, 8–13

V

Vault, 63, 104
Vertical Pod Autoscaler (VPA), 65, 74
Vertical Pod Autoscaling (VPA), 68, 74–75
Virtual machines (VMs), 16, 51, 107, 161, 230, 274, 393, 414

W, X, Y, Z

Web Application Firewall (WAF), 334, 384

TestSigma, 50
Threat analysis
 cloud-native deployments,
   358, 356
 cloud-native security controls,
   369–372, 374
 microservices architectures,
   threat aspects,
   374–377
  practices, 380–382
  security DFS, 366–367
  security challenges,
   358–359, 360–367
  security controls/
  countermeasures,
   382, 384–388
  security validation
   Impersonation
   steps, 379
  Red Teaming, 377–378
  types of threats, 360–362

Threat modeling, 117,
 173–174, 374–379
TLM, 189
Transport Layer Security (TLS),
 104, 290
Twelve-Factor App, 8–13

V

Vault, 62, 101
Versioned Pod Autoscaler
 (VPA), 16, 26
Vertical Pod Autoscaling (VPA),
 60, 74–78
Virtual machines (VMs), 16, 51,
 102, 161, 230, 274, 352, 414

W, X, Y, Z

Web Application Firewall (WAF),
 314, 364

MIX
Papier aus verantwortungsvollen Quellen
Paper from responsible sources
FSC® C105338

If you have any concerns about our products,
you can contact us on
ProductSafety@springernature.com

In case Publisher is established outside the EU,
the EU authorized representative is:
**Springer Nature Customer Service Center GmbH
Europaplatz 3, 69115 Heidelberg, Germany**

Printed by Libri Plureos GmbH
in Hamburg, Germany